JOHN CALVIN'S

ON CHURCH AND SOCIETY,

1509-2009

MW01504650

John Calvin's Impact on Church and Society, 1509-2009

Edited by

Martin Ernst Hirzel *&* Martin Sallmann

On behalf of the Federation of Swiss
Protestant Churches

With the cooperation of
Kerstin Groß

WILLIAM B. EERDMANS PUBLISHING COMPANY
GRAND RAPIDS, MICHIGAN / CAMBRIDGE, U.K.

Published in German 2008 by TVZ under the title

1509 — Johannes Calvin — 2009: Sein Wirken und Gesellschaft. Essays zum 500. Geburtstag.

Published in French 2008 by Labor et Fides under the title

Calvin et le Calvinisme: Cinq siècles d'influence sur l'Eglise et la Société, 2008.

This English edition
© 2009 William B. Eerdmans Publishing Company
All rights reserved

Published 2009 by
Wm. B. Eerdmans Publishing Co.
2140 Oak Industrial Drive N.E., Grand Rapids, Michigan 49505 /
P.O. Box 163, Cambridge CB3 9PU U.K.

Printed in the United States of America

14 13 12 11 10 09   7 6 5 4 3 2 1

Library of Congress Cataloging-in-Publication Data

John Calvin's impact on church and society, 1509-2009 /
   edited by Martin Ernst Hirzel & Martin Sallmann.
      p.   cm.
   ISBN 978-0-8028-6474-1 (alk. paper)
   1. Calvin, Jean, 1509-1564 — Influence. 2. Calvinism.
   I. Hirzel, Martin Ernst, 1965-   II. Sallmann, Martin, 1963-

BX9418.J635   2009
284'.2092 — dc22

                    2009006930

www.eerdmans.com

Contents

Preface

What does Calvin have to say to us today? The twelve essays of this volume invite us to consider this question. They do, however, demonstrate in an impressive manner the renewing power of Calvin's biblical theology for the society and church of his time in western Europe and later in North America — without turning a blind eye to the problematic aspects of Calvin's character and work. These essays illustrate, in a variety of ways, Calvin's dictum that "wherever God is recognized, humankind is provided for," thus urging us to consider the close connection between theology and ethical, social, and political responsibility.

Could there be a better occasion for this than the upcoming 500th anniversary of John Calvin's birth in 2009? Although Calvin was from France, his Reformation originated in Geneva, a city closely linked with the Swiss Confederation. Alongside Heinrich Bullinger, it was John Calvin who was responsible for the unification of Protestantism in Switzerland (the Zurich Agreement) and thus for the development of Reformed Protestantism as such. Calvin's influence has been particularly strong with regard to Protestantism around the world, a movement that the Swiss Reformed churches have remained linked to in many ways.

The Federation of Swiss Protestant Churches (FSPC) continues to maintain the great relevance of the work of John Calvin, and has thus taken it upon itself to initiate a number of different events and projects — both national and international — for Calvin Year 2009. This includes the simultaneous publication of this volume of essays in German, French, and English editions.

I am looking forward to a lively exchange on John Calvin's work and its historical influence. This pursuit can indeed serve as a manifold contribution to our present world. It can help to clarify the theological and religious foundations of our churches and societies so that we can learn to understand ourselves better, and to provide new theological and ethical impulses for the future. And a look back at Calvin's work will provide us with an opportunity to strengthen the self-awareness of the Reformed churches of Switzerland as a community and to bring together Reformed churches from around the world. It is my hope that this will lead to the discovery of new ecumenical commonalities as well.

REV. THOMAS WIPF
President of the Council
of the Federation of
Swiss Protestant Churches

Introduction

Few personalities of the sixteenth-century Reformation are as controversial as John Calvin. While some depict him as a dark, totalitarian figure, others emphasize his human, even pastoral traits. While some protest that Calvin ruled Geneva with an iron fist, others praise his organizational talents used in building his church and a more just society. Even his later influence can be judged in different ways. While some believe that Calvin's work paved the way for our modern, democratic society, others view him as having had a repressive, reactionary influence. There has, however, time and again, been a broad agreement, and correctly so, that presenting a nuanced and balanced depiction of Calvin's life and work is extremely difficult.

July 10, 2009, will mark the 500th anniversary of John Calvin's birth in Noyon, France. Jubilees of this sort provide a broad opportunity for an improved understanding of the biography and influence of the personalities being celebrated, both in the context of their own time and throughout later history. Researchers regularly use the occasion of a jubilee to reflect, obtain an overview, and take stock. The individual results of their research are drawn together to present as plausible a view as possible. Jubilees thus often provide impetus for research as an opportunity to make additions and corrections, to prioritize old information anew, and to develop new perspectives. Jubilees are also a welcome occasion to provide a broader scope of a person with a better understanding of the personality in question, to discuss the possible relevance of his or her life and work for the present world, and to contribute to the maintenance and continuation of one's own connected traditions. This diverse approach can give way to a wide range of reflections on the figure, his or her work, and his or her life and times. Each generation needs to engage with such historical figures anew and reassess the appropriateness of the images that they associate with them.

This volume is an attempt at a contribution toward this considerable task. Our aim is to familiarize a broad readership with the history of the Reformation in Geneva as well as Calvin's theology and its reception in the church and in society at large. The authors were asked to submit essays that are comprehensible to the general public and feature the latest research on a topic or area of inquiry. The volume is organized into three loosely connected thematic categories: the Reformation in Geneva and its reception in Europe and North America; the main principles of Calvin's theology; and the major problems connected with Calvinism, including tolerance, democracy, and capitalism, which continue to be disputed to this day. We have indeed collected an exciting range of essays, which reflect the difference among the German, Dutch, French, British, and North American academic cultures. As originally planned, some of the essays did without or with little in the way of documentation and academic trappings. Others developed into small treatises, complete with detailed notes, revealing new and insightful angles on the subject matter. Suggestions for further reading have been compiled as a bibliography for the entire volume.

These twelve essays represent a concerted attempt at providing a concise sketch of Calvin's Reformation in Geneva and its reception in the church and in society at large. If this reveals the complexity of this task and illuminates the fascination and continued relevance of Calvin's life work, the book has indeed achieved its primary goal and has contributed toward the great task at hand.

It remains only for us to express our appreciation where it is due. We would like to thank the Council of the Federation of Swiss Protestant Churches (FSPC) for its cooperation and support for the project, the authors for their essays, and the translators for their constructive collaboration. Special thanks go to Kerstin Groß, assistant for modern church history at the Theological Faculty of the University of Bern, for her research work, and to Reverend Annemarie Bieri, executive assistant at the FSPC, for her administrative support. We would also like to express our appreciation to Professor Elsie Anne McKee of Princeton Theological Seminary for her friendly advice.

MARTIN ERNST HIRZEL &
MARTIN SALLMANN

Abbreviations

CO	*Ioannis Calvini Opera quae supersunt omnia*
COE	*Ioannis Calvini opera exegetica*
COR	*Ioannis Calvini opera omnia. Denuo recognita et adnotatione critica instructa notisque illustrata. Auspiciis praesidii Conventus internationalis studiis calvinianis fovendis*
CSTA	*Calvin-Studienausgabe*
HBBW	Heinrich Bullinger, *Briefwechsel*
Inst.	John Calvin, *Institutes of the Christian Religion*
Migne PL	Jaques-Paul Migne, ed., *Patrologiae Cursus Completus, Serie Latinae*
OS	*Joannis Calvini Opera Selecta*
SC	*Supplementa Calviniana*
VadB	*Die Vadianische Briefsammlung der Stadtbibliothek St. Gallen*
WA	*D. Martin Luthers Werke. Kritische Gesamtausgabe*

Calvin and the Transformation of Geneva

Philip Benedict

Few aspects of John Calvin's life work are more remarkable than the impact he had on transforming Geneva in the sixteenth century. Few are also richer in contemporary echoes. A leading Reformation historian has called Calvin with good reason the great apostle of the sixteenth-century "Reformation of the refugees." The transformations wrought in Geneva in his lifetime resulted largely from his ability to convince that city, in which he always considered himself an outsider, to open its arms wide to foreign immigrants. Geneva was called to be, he declared in his sermons, "a bright lamp to illuminate those who are still far from the Gospel" and "a nest and shelter for his poor faithful, who are like little chicks frightened by birds of prey." The faithful were not to be turned away. "Those who cry out against foreigners, and consider this word an insult, could not show more clearly that they are not worthy to be numbered among the children of God, and no more belong in His Church than do dogs or pigs."[1] This sixteenth-century advocate of asylum for persecuted believers secured the transformation of Geneva in his lifetime not simply through his exceptional eloquence, vehemence of speech, and mastery of the Bible, which overwhelmed all local rivals in debate, but also through the establishment of a system of moral surveillance of unprecedented severity and efficacy, through recourse to the secular authorities to silence those who dissented from him, and through acquiescence in the use of torture against his political enemies.

1. Peter, "Geneva," pp. 29-30, citing CO 51,537, CO 42,70, and CO 53,270.

1

When Calvin arrived in Geneva, it was a city of eight to ten thousand people of nothing more than regional importance. It had not always been quite so insignificant. In the final centuries of the Middle Ages it had emerged as a center for trade moving between Italy and northern Europe. Its trade fairs were important enough for the Medici bankers to establish an agent in the city in 1422. This prosperity waned, however, after the end of the Hundred Years' War, as France's kings showered Lyon with privileges and drew to that city most of the trade between France and Italy. Geneva's trade reoriented itself toward regional commerce with Switzerland and the portions of Germany beyond it. Manufacturing was limited.

The shift of economic horizons toward Switzerland created the political opening through which Geneva gained its independence, for it built closer connections with the cities of the Swiss Confederation just when that entity was enjoying its greatest military glory and undergoing its most rapid territorial expansion. For a brief moment, "turning Swiss" became an attractive option for the inhabitants of the surrounding regions. By forging a pact of *combourgeoisie* with Fribourg and Bern, Geneva was able between 1519 and 1533, at a high cost in factional struggles, banishments, and executions, to throw off the overlordship of its bishop, who had ruled it throughout the Middle Ages, and to wriggle free from the growing domination of the expansionist dukes of Savoy, who had secured the surrounding territories, possessed certain rights of legal jurisdiction over the city, and established a virtual family monopoly over the episcopal see. In a sixteenth century characterized generally by the consolidation of large territorial monarchies, Geneva was the one city in Europe to win its independence and become a self-governing city-republic.

The military alliance with Bern and Fribourg also opened the way for the triumph of the Reformation, for Bern accepted Reformed Protestantism in 1528 and soon imposed it on all of its rural territories, employing as its chief agent in its French-speaking dependencies the aggressively confrontational Guillaume Farel (1489-1565). Protected by a Bernese safeconduct, Farel first came to Geneva to preach in 1532. He barely escaped with his life after the authorities called him in for questioning and a crowd gathered outside to chant "kill, kill this Luther!" Others soon took up the cause, and he was able to return within a few years under more propitious circumstances. Tumultuous scenes and provocative gestures drove the cause of reform forward. After a disputation organized in the summer of 1535 failed to convince the city fathers clearly to declare their preference for either the old or the new, an outburst of iconoclasm that stripped the city's churches of their images pushed them to act. In August 1535 the Mass was outlawed, most Church property was seized, and the departure of the Catholic religious communities from the city was negotiated. The first pieces of an austere civic reformation along Swiss lines soon followed: a radically simplified liturgy; the abolition of all holidays and feast days; tough laws against prostitutes, fornicators, dancing, and taverns; new schools; and a reorganized system of civic hospitals funded by seized Church property. Nine months later, after the French occupied Savoy and the Bernese took control of the neighboring Pays de Vaud, a general assembly of the city voted to "live henceforward according to the holy law of the gospel and the word of God as it is announced to us, wishing to abandon all masses and other ceremonies, Papal abuses, images, and idols . . . and to live in unity and obedience to justice."[2]

The Geneva whose gates John Calvin passed through for the first time in July 1536 was thus newly independent and newly Protestant. It was also, despite its vow to live in unity and obedience to justice, riven by faction and suspicion. Calvin had just turned twenty-seven years old.

Despite his youth and lack of formal training in theology, Calvin already had a breadth of learning and a depth of biblical knowledge that eclipsed that of all the permanent residents of this predominantly mercantile city whose prior ecclesiastical leadership had so recently been driven out. He had studied law at the universities of Orléans and Bourges and classical letters with the newly established royal lecturers in Paris, giving him both a solid understanding of jurisprudence and the underpinnings of an eloquence that ultimately even his enemies would recognize. After coming into contact with Protestant ideas during his student days, he had fled France in the wake of the 1534 Affair of the Placards and had taken refuge in Basel, where he had devoted himself to the independent study of theology and where he had just completed and published the first edition of his great summary of Protestant doctrine, the *Institutes of the Christian Religion*. Farel undoubtedly saw in this young lawyer-humanist-theologian the perfect person to help build up and defend the new Genevan church. Calvin later wrote that he had expected to spend just one night in Geneva on his way to Strasbourg, but that when Farel learned of his presence in town, he enjoined him to stay, threatening him that God would curse him

---

2. Borel-Girard, ed., *Guillaume Farel*, p. 333.

if he did not. This may be an accurate account of their encounter, or it may be an embellished version meant to suggest that Calvin was called to a clerical office for which he had no formal ordination. In any event, he stayed, accepting first a position as reader of holy scripture attached to the cathedral, then a parish ministry.

Calvin's first sojourn in Geneva lasted only two years. He and his fellow ministers pushed for a set of measures that required people to master a brief outline of the faith before being admitted to the Lord's Supper, created a system of ecclesiastical discipline exercised by "persons of upright life," and assigned the ministers the power to bar unrepentant sinners from the Eucharistic table. Many inhabitants balked at making the required confession of faith. The conflict over the issue convinced the city council to decree that nobody should be denied access to the Lord's Supper. When the council, dominated by a pro-Bernese faction, ordered the ministers to reintroduce special communion wafers as was done in Bern, Calvin, Farel, and some others insisted that it was their prerogative to determine the shape of the liturgy and disobeyed. They were summarily dismissed. Calvin spent the next three years in Strasbourg ministering to a small French refugee church and imbibing Martin Bucer's (1491-1551) ideas at his elbow. When nobody in Geneva could respond to a pamphlet written by the bishop Jacopo Sadoleto (1477-1547) urging Geneva to return to its ancestral faith, Calvin did. When the pro-Bernese faction fell from power in Geneva, the council implored him to return. After negotiating terms to his liking, he did so in 1541.

Calvin, who did not become a bourgeois of Geneva until 1559, always remained in his own mind first and foremost a Frenchman. He evoked the beauty of the country nostalgically in his sermons and retained an exile's fixation on the affairs of his native land. His mission, he clearly believed, was to all lands. He took part in German theological disputes and dedicated treatises to rulers throughout Europe. As for the Genevans, they were "a perverse and unhappy nation," he told his fellow ministers on his deathbed.[3] Central to his mission, however, was the task of bending stiff Genevan necks into the proper posture of humility to God in order to make the city a model community that might serve as an instrument for spreading the divine light more broadly. To that end he threw himself into the task of remaking Geneva's ecclesiastical institutions, manners, and morals.

Particularly important in any properly reformed church, Calvin

3. Calvin, *Lettres*, vol. 2, p. 576.

was convinced, was a consistory of elders and ministers with the power to reprimand and even to bar from communion those who unabashedly flouted Christian ethics or divided and defiled the Eucharistic community. Other reformers — Oecolampadius (1482-1531) in Basel, Bucer in Strasbourg — had said the same before him and had sought the establishment of such a system of church discipline in their cities, in vain. The ecclesiastical ordinance that Calvin drafted on his return in 1541 included a consistory. The initial wording of the ordinance was deliberately vague about the question of just who had the final say about who was to be admitted to or barred from the Lord's Supper. For the next fifteen years Calvin worked to establish the principle that the consistory wielded this authority.

At the same time, Calvin addressed pamphlets to the faithful living in Catholic lands urging them to make a clean break from what he considered to be the cesspool of Roman worship. If they could not refrain from public participation in the Mass without danger to their lives or livelihoods, they should emigrate to a place where they could. It was in this context that Calvin especially encouraged the Genevans to accept foreign refugees. The town was more inclined to do so than many other free cities at the time because, unlike in cities such as Basel, the guilds, always hostile to the threat of increased competition on the labor market, were not represented in municipal government. Migration to Geneva grew. As the newcomers were by and large committed adherents of Calvin's views, they increased support for his policies as they acquired the right to participate in municipal government.

Calvin used three chief means to transform Genevan manners and morals. The first was preaching. The ecclesiastical ordinances of 1541 prescribed twenty-six sermons a week divided among the city's three parishes and ministers. Calvin preached every Sunday and several times during the week, not necessarily in St. Pierre, his parish. His sermons combined the clear exposition of successive books of the Bible with topical remarks about the situation of the city or the world. When he observed forms of behavior that scandalized him as he went about the city, he did not hesitate to denounce them directly in his sermons. At times he criticized the city fathers and suggested that better ones be elected next time. In all, it has been estimated, he probably preached close to four thousand sermons in Geneva over twenty-five years. His commanding presence and sustaining or reproving words would have been familiar to all Genevans.

Calvin's second instrument was the consistory. This disciplinary body of about two dozen men was divided roughly equally between pastors and lay elders elected annually from among lists prepared by the Small Council. Its assigned mission as Calvin envisaged it was broad: to preserve the purity of the Eucharistic community, to bring sinners to shame and repentance, and to keep the good from being corrupted by the company of the bad. Cases came before it in a variety of manners. Some grew out of complaints by aggrieved or offended family members or neighbors. Others were identified by the elders. Most were called to the consistory's attention by unnamed secular officials. In the first years of its existence, most of the consistory's attention was devoted to ensuring that Genevans abandoned all Catholic devotional practices, attended sermons regularly, and learned Calvin's short catechism, mastery of which was reinstated as a requirement for admission to the Lord's Supper. Those who failed to learn the catechism were told to hire tutors. A barber who gave a man a tonsure was reprimanded for abetting Roman superstition. As the Genevans came to accept the new ecclesiastical order more fully, a good deal of the consistory's work came to be devoted to reconciling members of the church who had fallen out with one another. It worked to end domestic violence and brokered agreements between disputing parties that enabled them to avoid litigation. At the same time it watched to prevent offenses against Christian morality or at times simply the rules of basic civility. Numerous people were called before the body on suspicion of fornication, adultery, gambling, excessive drinking, or dancing in a manner that encouraged lascivious thoughts, which in practice appears to have been just about any manner. Smaller numbers of people were questioned on suspicion of commercial fraud or usury. One person was reprimanded for urinating in public without turning his back to the street. Finally, a not inconsiderable number of cases (6.5 percent in 1550) were devoted to upholding the dignity of the ministers against those who spoke ill of them or investigating those who complained about all the foreigners in town. For those found to have violated the norms of Christian charity, ethics, or civility, the consistory initially meted out three kinds of punishment. Most cases where the guilty parties showed themselves sufficiently contrite concluded with a private admonition before the consistory, usually delivered by Calvin himself. Unrepentant or more serious offenders were excluded from communion until they provided clear evidence of contrition and amendment. The most serious offenses against civic morals legislation were remanded to the secular authorities. Later on, certain offenses were also deemed to require public reparation before the entire congregation. The consistory was a powerful instrument for policing personal behavior.

The law was the third instrument that Calvin used to reform Genevan behavior, for while he considered temporal and spiritual governments to be separate domains with their own jurisdiction, he also believed that the two kingdoms were conjoined. The civil authorities were God's lieutenants on earth, and so had the obligation to defend the true religion. His legal training made him an invaluable advisor to the municipal authorities about the drafting of laws. He and his fellow ministers urged a variety of measures on them. Occasionally, they did not even wait for a new law to precipitate change, as when a new father presented his child for baptism in 1546 and asked to have him christened Claude, the name of a popular regional saint; the officiating minister refused and unilaterally named him Abraham, sparking a commotion in the church. The agitation was enough to convince the city council to ask Calvin to draw up a measure specifying by law the names that parents could not bestow on their children. The law when adopted included the names of the "idols whose cult had ruled this land" such as Claude and Suaire, those belonging to God alone such as Emmanuel or Sauveur, or "absurd and inept names that lend themselves to mockery" such as Toussaint, Croix, or Dimanche.[4] Other new laws of the 1540s prohibited singing dirty songs, forbade loitering in the streets during the Sunday sermon, and sought to restrict where inhabitants could drink or dine out to a limited number of establishments where no gambling was permitted, patrons were required to say a prayer before consuming what they ordered, and a Bible was made available to serve as the basis for edifying discussion. (This last measure was repealed after a month.) A broad morals edict of 1549 reinforced penalties for blasphemy, prohibited speaking ill of God's word or the city magistrates, banned dancing altogether, and enjoined "that nobody give themselves over to fornication, drunkenness, vagabondage, or foolishly wasting time, nor to debauching another, but that all work according to their capacity."[5]

Calvin and his fellow ministers also expected the magistrates to support them when their person or teachings were challenged. When in 1545 a manufacturer of playing cards named Pierre Ameaux remarked at a dinner

---

4. Richard, *Untersuchungen,* p. 186.
5. Rivoire and Van Berchem, eds., *Sources du droit,* vol. 2, p. 526.

party that Calvin was a wicked foreigner who deserved to be sent packing for teaching false doctrines, the council condemned him to apologize on his knees to Calvin in their presence. Calvin judged this insufficient and refused to preach until a more suitable punishment was decreed. Ameaux was condemned to make a public penance in which he carried a lit taper through the streets and called out for forgiveness at each intersection. When in 1551 an ex-monk working as a doctor in nearby Veigy, Jérome Bolsec (d. 1584/85), twice challenged Calvin's teachings on predestination at the weekly conferences, open to the public, where the town's ministers met to explicate and discuss passages of scripture, Calvin replied so extensively and powerfully to Bolsec that a municipal officer present arrested Bolsec on the spot for blasphemy. Certain of Calvin's letters suggest that he would have liked to see Bolsec put to death for his views in his subsequent trial for heresy. After several leading Swiss Protestant theologians indicated to the Genevan authorities that they did not find Bolsec's opinions objectionable, he was simply banished from the city. To comprehend episodes such as these, it helps to understand that the sixteenth century was a period in which individuals were intensely concerned about their honor, in which communities policed morals and considered blasphemy and heresy to be crimes that endangered the commonweal, and in which offenses of all sorts were punished harshly when detected. In 1562, a year for which the records are especially complete, fourteen people were executed in Geneva for their crimes: three for rape, three for homicide, three for serious or repeated theft, two for sodomy, two for witchcraft, and one for counterfeiting. Calvin, it must immediately be added, was especially unforgiving when his honor or teachings were challenged, for he saw himself as the expositor and prophet of God's word, and God was to be honored and served above all.

Hardly surprisingly, not everybody in Geneva appreciated the tougher laws and new consistorial oversight of their lives that the ministers encouraged, especially when the ministers were all non-Genevans. To many natives, it seemed as if their reformation had been hijacked by outsiders. A faction emerged within the city that identified itself as the *bons Genevoysiens* and began to resist the ministers' efforts to regulate behavior. A threatening note left in the pulpit of the cathedral lit into the "buggered renegade priests who have come here to ruin us." A group of journeymen sang scabrous parodies of the psalms through the streets by night. People called their dogs "Calvin" and Calvin "Cain." Calvin was profoundly alarmed by what he called the "madness" of those whose "unbridled licentiousness," "mischievous plots for the destruction of the faith," "gross contempt of God," and "impious conspiracies for the scattering of the Church" threatened to bring destruction to themselves and the community. He could not leave Geneva for a few days in early 1553 to attend a friend's wedding, he told the friend, because "the entire republic is at present in disorder, and they are striving to root up the established order of things."[6]

The decisive battle in the war between Calvin and those whom he called the "libertines" pitted him against Philibert Berthelier, the scion of an elite family whose father had been the first martyr in the city's struggle for independence. Berthelier, an initial supporter of Calvin, had quickly soured on him. From 1548 on, he was recurrently called before the consistory, first for saying that he once had drawn his sword in Lyon to defend Calvin's name but now would not clip his fingernails for him, subsequently for a series of more serious affairs: a drunken swordfight, an engagement that he broke off on discovering that his betrothed was not as rich as he first thought, an assault on several immigrants, reports that he was excessively familiar with a widow. In 1553, he decided that he wished to participate in communion once again. Rather than appear before the consistory to express his regret for his past actions, he approached the Small Council, believing that it had ultimate control over access to the Supper. The council, then under the control of a web of families hostile to Calvin, gave him permission to participate in the service. Calvin and his fellow ministers declared that they would leave town before they would permit this. The threat forced the council to back down and to persuade Berthelier not to present himself at church on communion Sunday.

Two years later the municipal elections gave Calvin's backers control of all four syndics' seats. Over the subsequent months, several members of the rival faction were purged from the Council of Two Hundred, and a sizable number of recent immigrants were admitted to the status of bourgeois, reinforcing the voting strength of the "faithful." As the "children of Geneva" saw power slip away from them, trouble broke out on the night of May 16. Encounters between members of the two factions led the cry to race through town that the time had come to kill the Frenchmen, which brought inhabitants into the streets with their arms. Leaders of the anti-

---

6. Witte and Kingdon, *Sex, Marriage and Family,* pp. 467f., quoting CO 14,455f.

Calvin faction helped to disperse the crowds after an hour, and nobody was injured. Calvin's supporters were nonetheless convinced of the existence of a treasonous conspiracy against the city. The leaders of the rival group were arrested and interrogated under torture. The investigation uncovered or produced the evidence for — that is always the uncertainty when torture is involved — a conspiracy to "overturn ecclesiastical discipline and the holy Reformation." Twelve death sentences were handed down. Four were executed. The others who were convicted managed to flee. They won considerable sympathy in the other cities of Protestant Switzerland with their tales of the mistreatment they had suffered, and Calvin's friends among the ministers of these cities warned him that the reports circulating about his role in these events were harming his reputation: he was said to have attended the torture sessions and to have approved all of the government's actions. He justified himself in a letter that he circulated to friendly ministers in which he denied that he had attended any of the sessions where torture was used; in any event, he said, the torture was moderate, and its employment was quite natural, for "the judges could not permit the plot to be denied when it was obvious."[7] One hears the voice of the trained lawyer here, for continental jurisprudence set the bar required to obtain a conviction high, and torture was often used in interrogations to extract the necessary confession. In the end, the threat that Geneva's good relations with Protestant Switzerland might be harmed passed when Emmanuel-Philibert of Savoy (1528-1580) led the imperial forces to victory over the French at Saint-Quentin, and the likelihood of his restoration to Savoy began to loom. Bern realized that its common interest with Geneva in resisting Savoyard territorial claims outweighed any rifts between them. In January 1557, the treaty of *combourgeoisie* between the two cities was renewed. The threat of isolation was over, and the triumph of the party favorable to Calvin in Geneva was secure.

As one of Calvin's early biographers observed about the 1555 tumult and its aftermath, "the discovery of the conspiracy led to a great advance for God's Church, for the populace was rendered more obedient to the divine word, the holy reformation was better observed, and scandals were duly punished."[8] In the wake of the affair, the consistory grew still more active. It summoned before it roughly one adult in eight each year around

7. Roget, *Histoire du peuple*, vol. 4, p. 323, quoting CO 15,830.
8. CO 21,79.

1560, and suspended from communion one in twenty-five. The ecclesiastical ordinances were revised to state that excommunicates who did not seek to mend their ways and gain readmission to the Supper would be subject to civil penalties, including banishment. Consistorial decisions were now reinforced by state authority. The dry statistics of historical demography offer proof that morals were indeed transformed. The city's parish registers from this era reveal rates of illegitimate births and of prenuptial conceptions of 0.12 and 1 percent respectively, the lowest rates ever reliably observed by European historical demographers. Godly visitors were enchanted by the behavior they observed. John Knox (ca. 1514-1572) famously called the new Geneva "the most perfect school of Christ . . . since the days of the apostles. In other places I confess Christ to be truly preached; but manners and religion so sincerely reformed, I have not yet seen in any other place."[9] "Everybody devoted themselves to the service of God now, even the hypocrites," wrote another chronicler.[10]

Not only were the city's manners and morals transformed; so too were its ruling class, population, and economy. Not one of the twenty-five members of the Small Council sitting when Calvin first arrived in 1536 was still living in Geneva when he died in 1564. The children of fully a third resided in exile. A new cohort of men had taken their place, many of them immigrants, grave, upright, and dedicated to upholding the city's reputation as a lamp unto nations. Between 1536 and 1564, perhaps ten thousand adult male refugees arrived in the city, plus an unknown number of women and children. While many subsequently moved on or returned to their homelands, enough stayed to swell the city's population to 21,000 people at the peak of the refuge around 1560 and 16,000 in its wake. Among the refugees were wealthy Italian merchants and skilled French artisans, who created the fine textile and clock-making industries that built the city's prosperity in the subsequent generations. Among them too were great master printers such as Robert Estienne (1503-1559) and Conrad Badius (1510-1560), upward of a hundred ordinary printing workers, and a wealthy entrepreneur from Calvin's hometown named Laurent de Normandie (d. 1569). Whereas Geneva had no printing industry to speak of before Calvin's arrival, no less than fifty printers opened shops, often short-lived, between 1550 and 1563. An average of sixty-one titles appeared

9. Knox, *Works*, vol. 4, p. 240.
10. Monter, *Calvin's Geneva*, p. 99, citing Roset, *Chroniques*, p. 377.

each year between 1559 and 1564. Most were works of Reformed theology, propaganda, or devotion. They were distributed across western Europe, especially to France, through a network of itinerant peddlers organized by de Normandie.

Shortly after the triumph of the pro-Calvin party, another of his hopes was realized when the city founded an institution of higher learning, the Academy, in 1559. Students crowded its lecture hall to hear Calvin lecture on theology. While there they familiarized themselves with the working of the consistory and the pattern of Genevan worship. In the following years large numbers were sent out from Geneva to become ministers to the churches that were multiplying in France. An English church existed in Geneva from 1555 to 1560, and an Italian church was founded in 1552 that would endure for several centuries. English and Italian Bibles were prepared and printed in Geneva.

As Reformed Protestantism spread throughout western Europe in the middle decades of the sixteenth century, Catholic observers had no difficulty diagnosing where the contagion began. Pierre Ronsard (1524-1585) wrote in 1562:

> In Savoyard fields sits a town
> Who by fraud has expelled her ancient lords,
> A miserable dwelling place of every apostasy,
> Of stubbornness, pride, and of heresy,
>
> Who (while kings were enlarging my boundaries
> And were fighting for honor far afield);
> Calling banished men to her damnable sect
> Has made me, as you see, puny and wretched.[11]

In less than three decades, this factionalized, relatively insignificant regional trading center had been transformed into a city that was judged by its admirers throughout Europe to be a model for its laws and ecclesiastical institutions and that was recognized by friend and foe alike as the chief base from which the most rapidly growing religious movement in Europe spread forth. Geneva's population had doubled. Its economy had been energized. Above all, its character had been transformed. A variety of Calvin's personal

---

11. Monter, *Calvin's Geneva,* p. 237, translating Pierre de Ronsard, *Continuation du discours des misères de ce temps,* in *Oeuvres complètes,* vol. 11, p. 55.

attributes help to explain how he could have exercised so much influence over a city in which he always felt himself a stranger: his legal expertise; his exceptional recall of the Bible; what his earliest biographers called his "truly prophetic vehemence," which he was not averse to unleashing in the face-to-face jousts of scriptural and legal argument that were so critical to carrying the day when key questions of theology and ecclesiastical organization were under discussion; the respect he enjoyed in other nearby Protestant cities, which he was able to mobilize when local voices challenged him within Geneva; and, above all, his awesome confidence that the views he defended represented nothing other than the pure word of God, combined with his profound fear that the least concession might open the door to rampant disorder, which led him to dig in whenever his teachings were challenged locally. Certain features of the city in which he operated also contributed to his success: the fact that Geneva was a newly independent city whose institutions were still young and malleable; the absence of any major centers of learning within it other than those created over time by Calvin and his allies; and the weakness of the guilds. The combination of the man and the moment added up to a dramatic illustration of how much influence a prophet can wield in propitious circumstances.

"Loved and Feared":
Calvin and the Swiss Confederation

Emidio Campi and Christian Moser

The extremely complex relations between Calvin and the Protestant areas of the Swiss Confederation cannot be expressed in simple terms. During his long years at work in Geneva, Calvin remained in close consultation with other Swiss reformers and their respective local political organs. Those years saw the making, breaking, and rekindling of friendships and correspondences, involving mutual support but also internal squabbles. Sympathy alternated with antipathy toward Calvin's efforts, ever in accordance with the prevailing situation and power structures.

While the theologians and public officials of the same territories often held differing views on Calvin, there was even a variety of positions on Calvin, embracing or rejecting him to various degrees, among the different factions within these groups. This essay provides an overview of Calvin's diverse relationships in the three main Protestant cities of the Swiss Confederation — Bern, Basel, and Zurich — illustrated with selected points of focus. Calvin's ties to other locations within the confederation, such as Neuchâtel, Biel/Bienne, Schaffhausen, St. Gallen,[1] and Graubünden, will be taken into account only in passing, if at all. These other ties will remain a matter for future detailed studies.[2]

---

1. Cf. Rüsch, "Beziehungen."

2. Gordon provides an overview of Calvin's relations with the Swiss Confederation in "Calvin and the Swiss Reformed Churches."

Bern and Vaud

Despite the fact that Bern's foreign policy — with the successful conquest of Vaud in 1536 — provided the basis of power for the establishment and consolidation of the Reformation in Geneva, Calvin painted an extremely negative picture of his historical relationship with Bern in his *Discours d'adieu aux ministres:* "The church [of Bern] has betrayed our church, and they have always feared me more than they have loved me there. They should only be aware that I died in the conviction that they feared me more than they loved me and that they now still fear me more than they love me. They were always afraid that I would trouble them in their doctrine of the Lord's Supper."[3]

While this statement of disillusionment was indeed but one side of the coin, Calvin was in fact involved in numerous disputes with Bern officials and theologians. This resulted from Calvin's influence on the church in the region of Vaud, which was occupied by Bern in 1536; from internal confessional squabbles within the Bern church; and from strong differences of church policy and the question of the relationship between church and state.[4]

Calvin was confronted with massive attacks and suspicions only shortly after the Lausanne dispute and the October 1536 establishment of the Reformation in Vaud.[5] These attacks were instigated by Pierre Caroli (ca. 1480–after 1545), a doctor of theology at the Sorbonne, who was installed as the first Reformed pastor in Lausanne in November 1536, leading to considerable irritation on the part of Pierre Viret (1511-1571) and his followers. The dispute broke out between the two city pastors the following January, when Caroli read from the pulpit theses in the defense of prayers of intercession on the part of the deceased, linked with polemic statements aimed at dissenters. Viret believed that he had to intervene and reminded Caroli of his obligation not to proclaim new doctrine without consulting his fellow pastors first. Caroli, however, who knew that his ideas were popular among the people and that the council was inimical to Viret, was un-

---

3. OS II,404. On the identity of the object of Calvin's criticism, which was not directly named, cf. CStA 2, 303, n. 13.

4. K. Guggisberg provides an overview of Calvin's relations with Bern in "Calvin und Bern."

5. For comprehensive views of the following, see Bähler, "Petrus Caroli," and Hundeshagen, "Partheiwesen," pp. 4-14.

impressed and began his own counterattack, in which he accused Viret, Calvin, and the other Geneva reformers of "Arianism," that is, anti-Trinitarian heresy. After being called to help by Viret, Calvin met with Caroli on February 17, 1537, and attempted, unsuccessfully, to defuse the accusation of heresy, leading to the postponement of the dispute's resolution to a synod to be held in Bern.

Calvin took this matter seriously. Immediately upon his return to Geneva, Calvin wrote to Kaspar Megander (1495-1545) and to the Bern pastors, defending himself against the accusation of Arianism and urging, for the sake of the church's unity, that the synod be held soon.[6] The opponents met, however, first on February 28 and 29 before the Bern consistory court *(Chorgericht)*. Caroli again accused the Geneva reformers of Arianism: "Many pastors, both in Geneva and in your lands, have been infected with the Arian heresy." He then read a long list of the names of the accused.[7] Calvin defended himself eloquently and again demanded that a synod examine the matter. The synod met on May 14 in Lausanne under the combined leadership of Kaspar Megander and Peter Kunz (ca. 1480-1544)[8] and exonerated Calvin of Caroli's accusations.[9] The deliberations, however, continued at the Bern Synod beginning on May 31, until a final verdict was issued on June 5 that conclusively vindicated Guillaume Farel (1489-1565), Calvin, and Viret, and expelled Caroli from the country.[10]

Caroli's accusations were grave and hit Calvin — who was by no means secure in his position in Geneva — hard, not only because Caroli would continue to make things unpleasant for him in the years to come,[11]

6. The pastors of Geneva to the pastors of Bern, ca. February 20, 1537, in Herminjard, ed., *Correspondance,* vol. 4, pp. 183-87, esp. p. 186, no. 610. Cf. also Calvin's letter to Kaspar Megander, ca. February 20, 1537, in Herminjard, ed., *Correspondance,* vol. 4, pp. 187-91, no. 611.

7. Cf. CO 7,308.

8. Cf. Calvin's report in CO 7,310-17.

9. Cf. Kaspar Megander's letter to Heinrich Bullinger and Leo Jud, May 22, 1537, in HBBW IV, 161f., no. 999. Cf. esp. 162.

10. Cf. the Bern council's letter to the Lausanne council, June 7, 1537, in Herminjard, ed., *Correspondance,* vol. 4, p. 238, no. 633.

11. After his dismissal, Caroli turned to France, where he reconverted to Catholicism. In 1539, he reappeared as a Protestant in Neuchâtel, but did not receive a position as a pastor. He then moved first to Metz and then to Paris. In 1545, he strongly attacked Calvin, Farel, and Viret in his work *Refutatio blaphemiae Farellistarum in sacrosanctam trinitatem.* Calvin replied in his *Pro G. Farello adversus Petri Caroli calumnias defensio* (CO 7,289-340). Cf. Stam, "Le livre de Pierre Caroli."

but also because his attacks in Bern did in fact fall upon fertile ground. It was clear to Calvin that the Bern council needed over four months to exonerate him, and that while the Bern officials did not reject the Francophone reformers, they eyed them with mistrust and skepticism. Kaspar Megander's lamentation to Heinrich Bullinger (1504-1575) about the activities of the "Galli" that led to upheaval — even if this was not aimed directly at Calvin — provides a clear witness,[12] while Myconius's criticism of Calvin's behavior showed that this skepticism went far beyond Bern alone.[13] This episode provided Calvin with a particular taste of things to come, in that the Bern council claimed the sole jurisdiction for itself and was not willing to have these problems resolved within the church. The official exoneration of the Geneva reformers, moreover, was not enough to clarify any misgivings related to their teachings on the Trinity. As early as August — only two months after their exculpation — the Bern council criticized Calvin and Farel for their reservations with regard to the terms *Trinity* and *person,*[14] and Calvin saw it necessary to justify himself in this matter before the Zurich church.[15]

Calvin had a welcome opportunity in September 1537 to endear himself to the Swiss churches and to dispense with their doubts, when Martin Bucer (1491-1551) and Wolfgang Capito (1478-1541) deliberated with the Bern pastors on the doctrine of the Lord's Supper and invited Calvin, Farel, and Viret to join them on the occasion.[16] The three friends were not only able to present the group with a Eucharistic creed,[17] as requested by Bucer, but were also able to explain the controversial aspects of their Trinity doctrine,[18] which played a major role in establishing them as the "triumvirate" of the Reformation in western Switzerland.[19]

---

12. Cf. Kaspar Megander's letter to Heinrich Bullinger, March 8, 1537, in HBBW VII, 93-96, no. 965; esp. 96.

13. Cf. Oswald Myconius's letter to Heinrich Bullinger, July 9, 1537, in Herminjard, ed., *Correspondance,* vol. 4, pp. 254-56, no. 640; esp. p. 255.

14. Cf. the Bern council's letter to Farel and Calvin, August 13, 1537, in Herminjard, ed., *Correspondance,* vol. 4, pp. 275f., no. 650.

15. Cf. the Geneva pastors' letter to the pastors of Zurich, August 30, 1537, in Herminjard, ed., *Correspondance,* vol. 4, pp. 281-86, no. 654.

16. Cf. the invitation of the Bern council of September 14, 1537, in Herminjard, ed., *Correspondance,* vol. 4, pp. 300f., no. 661. On the following, cf. Augustijn, "Farel und Calvin in Bern."

17. Text in CO 9,711.

18. Cf. CO 7,319.

19. Cf. Augustijn, "Farel und Calvin in Bern," p. 16.

Calvin, however, did not return home with a positive impression of the Bern church. In his letter to Bucer on January 12, 1538,[20] he not only complained about the dismissal of Kaspar Megander, a renowned reformer, but also strongly criticized the new church leaders. Sebastian Meyer (1465-1545), for example, was so forgetful, Calvin wrote, that he lost his train of thought after every third word of his sermons, and Peter Kunz, Calvin added, behaved like a mad beast.

The next time Calvin and Farel traveled to Bern, they did so under a very different set of circumstances. They no longer appeared as the official representatives of the Reformation in western Switzerland, but as dismissed pastors who had been expelled from Geneva.[21] Bern also played a part in this tragedy, which demanded that Bern church practice (in matters such as holiday celebrations and the use of unleavened bread for the Lord's Supper) be followed in Geneva as well. This roused Calvin to opposition, which in turn led to his clash with the Geneva council. Despite his complicated relationship with Bern, it seemed that everyone was inclined to let bygones be bygones when Calvin returned to Geneva in 1541. Calvin, for his part, sought to live in harmony and "brotherly goodwill" with Bern, which for its part had worked to make his return possible.[22]

The latent confessional antagonism reemerged in 1547, when strict followers of Zwingli in Vaud, led by André Zébédée, began to rise in opposition to the influences of Calvinistic theology.[23] This open confrontation was triggered by the publication of Viret's *De la vertu et usage du ministère de la parolle de Dieu et des Sacremens dependans d'icelle*.[24] In its pointedly written dedication to the Bern council, Viret came out against any excessive influence by the authorities on matters of the church. While his treatise hardly veiled its criticism of Bern's church policy and practice, it defended the Calvinistic doctrine of the Lord's Supper and the church discipline ineluctably connected to it.[25] The Zwinglian theologians of Bern

---

20. Herminjard, ed., *Correspondance,* vol. 4, pp. 338-49, no. 677.

21. Cf. Calvin and Farel's defense before the Bern council, in Herminjard, ed., *Correspondance,* vol. 4, pp. 422-26, no. 705.

22. Cf. Calvin's letter to Martin Bucer, October 15, 1541, in Herminjard, ed., *Correspondance,* vol. 7, pp. 289-94, no. 1053; esp. p. 293.

23. Cf. on the following Bruening, *Calvinism's First Battleground,* pp. 183-94.

24. This was published in 1548 by Jean Gérard in Geneva.

25. Cf. Viret, *De la vertu et usage,* p. 336.

felt vindicated in their continuing skepticism with regard to Calvin's doctrine of the Lord's Supper, and were concerned about the future of Zwingli's legacy. The Bern council was alarmed by the incipient dispute in Lausanne and was cognizant of how its own church had been increasingly marred by deep inner conflict, which led to the dismissal of Simon Sulzer (1508-1585) and Beat Gering (d. 1559). In this context, the council also decided to instigate an inquiry into Viret's stance. Viret feared for his position in Lausanne and "prepared for anything that the Lord wished to decide" for him.[26] Calvin, for his part, observed this development in disbelief and understood it as a great danger for the church.[27] The conflict, which Zébédée pursued with great passion, continued for over a year. Viret's exoneration came with particular thanks to Heinrich Bullinger's intermediary words on his behalf, but also as a result of Calvin's ability to assuage the fears of those pastors concerned with Zwingli's legacy in his treatise in opposition to the Augsburg Interim[28] and the doctrine of the Lord's Supper that it represented.[29]

The so-called Zébédée Affair depicts how sensitive Bern — with an awareness of its own Zwinglian tradition — was to differences of doctrine and practice. Calvin, moreover, became painfully aware of the great resentment that still persisted with regard to his doctrine of the Lord's Supper. This, in turn, may well have contributed to his belief in the necessity of a pan-Swiss agreement in this matter. And yet even this project, which, with the Consensus Tigurinus, would prove a success, was not enough to eliminate all doubts.[30]

In 1549, pastors with a Calvinistic orientation received another blow from the Bern authorities, when they decided to do away with the pastors' weekly exegetic-dogmatic colloquia, or to limit them to four times each year, as a means of nipping future dogmatic disputes in the bud. The authorities' demonstration of power constituted for Calvin, without any doubt, an illegitimate foray into the internal affairs of the church. He was,

26. Cf. Viret's letter to Calvin, May 3, 1548, in CO 12,695, no. 1015.

27. Cf. Calvin's letter to Farel, April 30, 1548, in CO 12,690, no. 1013.

28. CO 7,545-674. The Augsburg Interim decreed in 1548 by Charles V, Holy Roman Emperor, as imperial law, was to constitute a temporary resolution of the church situation. It was, however, met with bitter opposition.

29. Cf., for example, the generous evaluation of the Bern Zwinglian Eberhard von Rümlang, which Viret passed on to Calvin on February 6, 1549 (CO 13,178, no. 1136).

30. On the Consensus Tigurinus, cf. "Zurich," below.

however, especially stricken by the fact that it was the two prominent Bern pastors Wolfgang Musculus (1497-1563) and Johannes Haller (1523-1575) who not only legitimized this move, but in fact had initiated it themselves.[31] No two positions could have been any further apart with regard to the relations between the authorities and the church.

As part of the Bolsec Affair,[32] the doctrine of predestination was a further aspect of Calvin's theology that came under the scrutiny of friends and opponents alike in Bern. After the arrest in Geneva of Jérôme Bolsec (ca. 1520-1584) in October 1551 for his public attacks on Calvin's doctrine of predestination, Bern,[33] alongside Zurich and Basel,[34] urged a measured approach. Bolsec was expelled from Geneva in December and moved — of all places — to Thonon in Bern territory. From there, he continued his attacks in coordination with allies such as André Zébédée. On September 18, 1554, Calvin complained to Bullinger that a number of pastors from the Bern area were depicting him as a heretic worse than the papists,[35] while the Geneva pastors, at the same time, complained to the Bern council that Bolsec and his confederates did not even shrink from cursing Calvin as the Antichrist.[36] The reaction of the Bern council showed Calvin — who, in 1552, had had to defend himself against the accusation that he had been agitating in Vaud[37] — unmistakably what sort of reputation he enjoyed in Bern: the Geneva council was to ensure that the pastors of Geneva would end their criticism of Bern and its church.[38] The increasingly obvious difference between the Bern state church and Calvin's theology, in the end, led to a ban on sermons on predestination[39] and the Lord's Supper in accordance with the Cal-

---

31. Cf. Calvin's letter to Wolfgang Musculus, October 22, 1549, in CO 13,433, no. 1294; Viret's letter to Calvin, November 4, 1549, in CO 13,443, no. 1300.

32. Cf. Holtrop, *Bolsec Controversy*.

33. CO 8,238-42.

34. CO 8,229-34 (Zurich); CO 8,234-37 (Basel).

35. Calvin's letter to Heinrich Bullinger, September 18, 1554, in CO 15,233, no. 2011.

36. Bern council, October 4, 1554, in CO 15,251f., no. 2020; cf. also the letter of the pastors of Geneva to the pastors of Bern, October 6, 1554, in CO 15,256-58, no. 2023.

37. Cf. Calvin's letter to the Bern council, ca. February 17, 1552, in CO 14,284, no. 1604bis.

38. Bern council's letter to the Geneva council, November 17, 1554, in CO 15,313f., no. 2047. Cf. also CO 15,312, no. 2046.

39. Cf. Bern council's letter to the pastors of Vaud, January 26, 1555, in CO 15,405, no. 2096.

vinist rite.[40] The use of Calvin's *Institutes* in the Lausanne Academy was also viewed as "*intolérable*."[41]

Before these measures, Bern had demonstrated its unity with Calvin and the other Swiss Reformed churches in the legal proceedings against the anti-Trinitarian Michel Servetus (1511-1553), and had supported Calvin's actions.[42] Some in Bern, however, were speaking out against the execution of heretics and for religious freedom. It was Niklaus Zurkinden (1506-1588) who was the most outspoken of these figures, and who serves as the most vivid example of how, in the sixteenth century, friendships could overcome explicit theological and political oppositions: despite clearly divergent points of view and many clear verbal exchanges reflecting this, Zurkinden and Calvin remained friends their entire lives.[43]

The differences, shown in these examples, between the theology and church politics of the Calvinists and the Bern church led in 1558 and 1559 to the peak of these tensions when Pierre Viret again demanded stronger church discipline with the option of excluding offenders from the Lord's Supper. The dispute escalated to such a degree that Viret, along with forty like-minded pastors, was dismissed, leading to a full-scale exodus to Geneva. Calvin played an insignificant role in the affair, having already described this clash as unavoidable in August 1558.[44] His focus and primary area of interest would then shift westward to France.

Basel

In 1535, following the Affair of the Placards,[45] Calvin arrived in Basel as a young and unknown scholar. There, he wrote under the pseudonym "Martianus Lucianus" for well over a year, and was able to find the quiet

---

40. Cf. Bern council's letter to the reeves, January 26, 1555, in CO 15,406, no. 2097.

41. Cf. Bruening, *Calvinism's First Battleground*, p. 220, n. 35.

42. Cf. Bern council's letter to the Geneva council, October 6, 1553, CO 8,818, and Bern council's letter to the Geneva council [October 1553], CO 8,818f.

43. Cf. Bähler, *Nikolaus Zurkinden*.

44. Cf. Calvin's letter to Johannes Camerarius, August 29, 1558, in CO 17,313f., no. 2946.

45. The October 1534 Affair of the Placards, in which placards against the Roman Catholic Mass were raised in the vicinity of the royal court, led to a wave of persecution and flight in France.

that he needed for his studies and to complete the first edition of his *Institutes*.[46] Of his personal contacts during this period, that of Simon Grynaeus (1493-1541), with whom Calvin maintained a continual correspondence in later years, was of particular note. Calvin in fact dedicated his 1539 Commentary on the Epistle to the Romans to Grynaeus, in appreciation for their conversations during his first stay in Basel, in which they discussed, most extensively, the questions and problems of exegesis.[47] Grynaeus's death in 1541 left behind a gap in Calvin's personal ties to Basel, which Oswald Myconius (1488-1552), the chief of the Basel church, was not able to fill. The relationship between the two reformers was seriously damaged early on, when Myconius, from Calvin's point of view, was all too ready to believe Caroli's accusations.[48] The debates and events most relevant to our discussion did not, however, occur during Myconius's term of office, but during that of Simon Sulzer, whom Calvin had already known from his time in Bern. These debates revolved around religious freedom in the wake of the Servetus affair, Geneva's dispute on excommunication, and Basel's position in the second dispute on the Lord's Supper.[49]

Massive opposition to Calvin already began to mount in Basel during Servetus's trial[50] in Geneva. This opposition was supported less by renowned representatives of the Basel church than by humanistic religious refugees at or in the vicinity of the university, whose orthodoxy had always been viewed with doubt by the exponents of the Swiss Reformed churches. The leaders of this so-called Basel Circle included Sebastian Castellio (1515-1563)[51] of Savoy, who, in 1545, had fallen out with Calvin in Geneva, and Celio Secondo Curione (1503-1569)[52] of Piedmont, who came to the Lausanne Academy in 1542 and who began his tenure at the University of Basel as a professor of rhetoric in 1546.

---

46. On Calvin's relations with Basel, cf. Wernle, *Calvin und Basel*, and Plath, *Calvin und Basel*.

47. Cf. COE 13,3. On the dedication to his Commentary on the Epistle to the Romans, cf. Kuropka, "Calvins Römerbriefwidmung."

48. Cf. "Bern and Vaud," above.

49. On the following, cf. Plath's thorough depiction in *Calvin und Basel*.

50. On Servetus and his trial, cf. Bainton, *Hunted Heretic*; Friedman, *Michael Servetus*; Hillar, *Case of Michael Servet*; Hillar and Allen, *Michael Servetus*; Zuber, *Les conflits de la tolérance*.

51. Cf. H. Guggisberg, *Sebastian Castellio*.

52. Cf. Kutter, *Celio Secondo Curione*.

After Calvin detailed his point of view in a letter to Sulzer on September 9, 1553,[53] Sulzer promised him the support of the Basel church.[54] This was in fact confirmed in Basel's evaluation as prepared by Sulzer, Markus Bertschi (1483-1566), Johannes Jung (d. 1562), and Wolfgang Wissenburg (1496-1575).[55] Calvin was, however, also aware of the fact that the opinions in Basel were by no means as unanimous as suggested in the evaluation. On November 22, Calvin revealed to Bullinger his plan for a publication directed toward his critics — and those in Basel in particular.[56] The first fruit to be reaped in the progressing dispute over the execution of heretics and freedom of religion appeared in the *Historia de morte Serveti*,[57] likely to have been written by Castellio himself in December 1553. Calvin, for his part, justified his actions in his *Defensio orthodoxae fidei de sacra trinitate contra prodigiosos errores Michaelis Serveti*, which according to its cover page was to demonstrate that "heretics are to be punished by the sword" and especially that "this godless person was rightly punished in Geneva."[58] Calvin wrote this, as he himself explained, as a means of defending himself against the accusations and stemming the further diffusion of Servetus's beliefs.[59] Calvin was forceful in his understanding that one must take the most extreme of measures to avoid further damage when the church — as in the Servetus case — is shaken at its roots.[60]

Early March 1554 saw the publication of an alternative to Calvin's views in a small but epoch-making pamphlet entitled *De haereticis, an sint persequendi*. Neither the supposed main authors (Martin Bellius, Georg Kleinberg, and Basilius Montfort) nor the printer (Georg Rausch of Magdeburg) were known to contemporaries at the time. The publication in fact was a product of the Basel Circle and is likely to have been chiefly the work of Sebastian Castellio, who called readers to embrace Christ's

---

53. CO 14,614-16, no. 1793.

54. Simon Sulzer's letter to Calvin, September 18, 1553, in CO 14,622f., no. 1801.

55. The Basel evaluation in CO 8,820-23.

56. Calvin's letter to Bullinger, November 22, 1553, in CO 14,671, no. 1854.

57. Cf. Plath, *Calvin und Basel,* pp. 88-93.

58. Cf. the cover page, CO 8,453: "Defensio orthodoxae fidei de sacra trinitate, contra prodigiosos errores Michaelis Serveti Hispani, ubi ostenditur haereticos iure gladii coercendos esse, et nominatim de homine hoc tam impio iuste et merito sumptum Genevae fuisse supplicium." The work itself: CO 8,453-644.

59. Cf. CO 8,459-61.

60. CO 8,477.

gentleness and to exercise a reserved hand against heretics because the danger existed that false charges of heresy could be raised or that heretics could be punished more harshly than necessary.[61] Castellio underscored his call for moderation in an anthology of different authors and texts — including, ironically enough, two of Calvin's own quotes[62] — combining to negate the right of the authorities to execute heretics.

The pseudonymity of the authorship was not enough to prevent Calvin from suspecting the Basel Circle immediately upon its publication,[63] nor from depicting the book as being "full of unbearable blasphemies"[64] and its authors as "brazen scribes" who "not only obscure the light of pure doctrine with the fog of heresy, and rob the simple and less educated of their reason through their evil lunacies, but also take the liberty of destroying the entire religion through the unholy freedom of doubt."[65] This debate continued with the publication of Theodore Beza's *De haereticis a civili magistratu puniendis* and Castellio's response *De haereticis non puniendis*, in which both points of view were highlighted yet again.

This discussion, only summarized briefly here, on the execution of heretics and the freedom of religion, demonstrates that Basel of the mid-sixteenth century — unlike Bern, which developed into a center of opposition motivated by church politics — grew into an "intellectual" center of opposition. Anchored in other theological premises, these opponents cast into question and actively fought central aspects of Calvin's thought and action.[66]

In the midst of the Servetus trial, another dispute arose in Geneva, one that was also of relevance to Calvin's relationship with Basel.[67] When Philibert Berthelier, who had been excluded from the Lord's Supper, petitioned the council for his readmission and the request was granted despite

---

61. Castellio, *De haereticis,* pp. 12f.

62. Castellio, *De haereticis,* pp. 107f. The quotes derive from the dedication for the Commentary on Acts and from the first edition of the *Institutes.*

63. Cf. Calvin's letter to Bullinger, March 28, 1554, in CO 15,93-96, no. 1935.

64. Cf. Calvin's letter to the congregation in Poitiers, February 20, 1555, in CO 15,435-46, no. 2118; here 440f.

65. CO 15,200.

66. Curione, for example, also opposed Calvin's doctrine of predestination in a treatise with the programmatic title *De amplitudine beati regni Dei* (Poschiavo 1554). Cf. Plath, *Calvin und Basel,* pp. 164-72.

67. Cf. Plath, *Calvin und Basel,* pp. 94-111.

Calvin's opposition, this led to a quarrel between the council and the church over the right of excommunication. As was often the case, the parties involved requested evaluations from other Reformed cities of the confederation. Although the power of excommunication was held by the authorities of all these cities, Zurich, for one, supported Calvin's position.[68] Basel, where Johannes Œcolampadius (1482-1531) is known for not having been able to push through his order of church discipline,[69] was more reserved on the matter. While Sulzer worked to stand by Calvin by daringly interpreting the Basel excommunication order ("Basler Bannordnung") as a matter for the church to decide, he was in fact met with resistance. The evaluation requested by Basel consisted in the end of a copy of the "Basler Bannordnung" alone — thus avoiding the actual question at hand.[70] Taking into account the balance of power in Basel, the evaluation could have been worse for Calvin. Still, he expressed only his disappointment: "They do not provide us with their counsel but only send their laws without seeking to take a stand."[71] Calvin also showed disappointment with Sulzer, whose promises — all that could be obtained at the time — did not convince Calvin.[72] In late 1553, Calvin was faced with a sobering balance of his relationship with Basel: the opposition of the Basel Circle combined with the half-hearted (as Calvin saw it) support of the Basel church as led by Sulzer.

Sulzer's position in the second dispute over the Lord's Supper[73] led to a further cooling of relations.[74] When the Hamburg pastor Joachim Westphal (ca. 1510-1574) attacked the Consensus Tigurinus in two polemic treatises, Calvin wanted to reply on behalf of all Swiss churches although he could see how difficult this would in fact turn out to be.[75] On October 6, 1554, Calvin sent the *Defensio* that he had prepared to Zurich. Bullinger was to examine it and then work to gain support among the Reformed cities of the confedera-

---

68. The Zurich evaluation in CO 14,699-703.

69. Cf. Kuhr, *Macht des Bannes.*

70. Basel council's letter to the Geneva council, December 23, 1553; printed in Plath, *Calvin und Basel,* p. 282.

71. Calvin's letter to Bullinger, December 31, 1553, in CO 14,722f., no. 1884; here 722.

72. Cf. Calvin's letter to Bullinger, December 31, 1553, in CO 14,722f., no. 1884; here 722.

73. On the controversy, cf. Bizer, *Geschichte des Abendmahlsstreits;* Tylenda, "Calvin-Westphal Exchange"; Tylenda, "Calvin and Westphal."

74. Cf. Plath, *Calvin und Basel,* pp. 173-92.

75. Cf. Calvin's letter to Bullinger, April 29, 1554, in CO 15,123-26, no. 1947; esp. 125.

tion.[76] After reading the manuscript, the pastors of Zurich asked that it be revised, and Bullinger told Calvin that he doubted that they would receive the support of Basel.[77] This turned out to be correct: Sulzer was not willing to openly support Calvin and Bullinger. Once asked by Bullinger for his views, when the *Defensio* did not enter into circulation as a common position of the Swiss churches, as had been planned, but as Calvin's own work, Sulzer did not mask his displeasure. He condemned Calvin's acerbity and feared that old divides were purposely being pried back open. In his opinion, in order to preserve the peace, the Consensus Tigurinus should never have been published in the first place.[78] Calvin had no understanding for Sulzer's views; as he expressed it to Bullinger: "I have always feared that Sulzer would remain cold in order to be able to remain neutral. But I had in fact expected something better or at least less witless."[79]

Zurich

Ever since his first time in Geneva and through the end of his life, Calvin closely followed the theological, church, and political events in Zurich, at times investigating these developments in depth; this came in addition to his other interests and tasks, but with increasing dedication and remarkable endurance. Neither Bern, which was politically allied with Geneva, nor Basel, a city of scholars — not to mention Luther's Wittenberg — constituted as great an attraction to Calvin as did Zurich. There were certainly many common interests. Calvin traveled to Zurich five times (three of which with Farel) to discuss political and church affairs. In addition to Heinrich Bullinger and his family, in whose pastoral residence he sojourned, Calvin came to know a large number of Zurich theologians, including Leo Jud (1482-1542), Rudolf Gwalther (1519-86), Konrad Pellikan (1478-1556), Theodor Bibliander (1505-1564), and Konrad Gessner (1516-1565), and later, Peter Martyr Vermigli (1499-1562), whom Calvin held in particularly high esteem. These contacts soon led to extensive correspondences, which were

---

76. Cf. Calvin's letter to Bullinger, October 6, 1554, in CO 15,255f., no. 2022.

77. Cf. Bullinger's letter to Calvin, October 25, 1554, in CO 15,296f., no. 2036; esp. 296.

78. Cf. Sulzer's letter to Bullinger, March 7, 1555, in CO 15,491f., no. 2141; Sulzer's letter to Bullinger, March 23, 1555, in CO 15,521, no. 2160; Sulzer's letter to Calvin, March 28, 1555, in CO 15,531f., no. 2168.

79. Calvin's letter to Bullinger, June 5, 1555, in CO 15,640-42, no. 2218; here 642.

encouraged by strong personal ties of sympathy and characterized by an unusually intensive exchange of thought on theological, church, and political issues, as well as the correspondents' literary and personal plans. That Calvin's correspondence with Bullinger and others in Zurich — to judge by the number of letters sent — was only exceeded by his correspondence with Farel and Viret,[80] demonstrates the high esteem in which Calvin held his Zurich friends.[81] This is also evidenced by the frequent parallel letters sent by the Geneva councilors to their Zurich colleagues. A view to Calvin's relationship with the Zurich church and its theologians can thus help shed light on several significant aspects of Calvin and his influence.[82]

Calvin's correspondence with the *antistes* (head of the church) of Zurich — with five letters still preserved — from his first period in Geneva casts a spotlight on the conflicts in which Calvin was involved between 1536 and 1538, while also helping to understand his efforts to gain favor with his Zurich colleagues as allies. This correspondence revolved around the aforementioned dispute with Pierre Caroli in Lausanne on the doctrine of the Trinity and the reorganization of the Reformed churches of Vaud, and around the clash between the Geneva pastors and the city council over the ceremonies, the worship service, and the Lord's Supper, and the tensions between different factions of the city council.[83] Calvin particularly welcomed, in this regard, the help of Bullinger and his church, whose influence extended well beyond eastern Switzerland. Zurich was early to recognize Calvin's significance for Reformed theology and the Reformed church. In 1536, Konrad Pellikan, a highly renowned scholar of Hebrew at the Schola Tigurina (Zurich's "superior school"), praised the *Institutes* in a letter to Joachim Vadian (1484-1551) in St. Gallen, in which he lauded Calvin's work for its clear theological content.[84] The following year, Leo Jud

---

80. Cf. Bruening, *Calvinism's First Battleground,* p. 178.

81. Calvin wrote, for example, a total of 115 letters to Bullinger, and Bullinger wrote 162 letters to Calvin between 1538 and 1564.

82. In addition to the literature dedicated to the topic, listed below, for Calvin's relations with Zurich and Bullinger, cf. Rüegg, "Beziehungen Calvins"; Kolfhaus, "Verkehr Calvins mit Bullinger"; Büsser, *Heinrich Bullinger,* vol. 2, pp. 115-43.

83. Cf. Burger, "Werben um Bullingers Beistand"; Burger, "Calvins Beziehungen zu Weggefährten in der Schweiz"; Stam, "Verhältnis zwischen Bullinger und Calvin"; Bruening, *Calvinism's First Battleground,* pp. 61-91.

84. Cf. Pellikan's letter to Joachim Vadian, April 21, 1536, in VadB V 325-27, no. 888; esp. 326.

— a colleague of Zwingli and pastor at Zurich's St. Peter's Church — expressed, in the preface to his catechism, his admiration for Calvin's deep piety and great scholarship.[85] Bullinger, however, continued for the time being to avoid involving himself in Genevan affairs, and did not use his influence in Bern to support Calvin. It took strong motivation to get him to speak out. When Calvin and Farel were faced, in the spring of 1538, with a united opposition and both pastors were expelled from Geneva, they turned to Zurich for help. Bullinger then finally decided to send a letter of recommendation to Niklaus von Wattenwyl (1492-1551), the mayor of Bern, albeit with an interesting reservation: "Their zeal is much too great. They are, however, holy and scholarly men, who, in my opinion, one must forgive for much."[86]

The wish, expressed in these first letters, for theological and practical-political ties to the Zurich church, took on a more definitive shape during Calvin's time in Strasbourg, a time in which he was practically forced, time and again, to turn his eyes toward Zurich. Bucer's indefatigable attempts to mediate between Lutherans and Zwinglians in the matter of the Lord's Supper, and Calvin's participation in religious colloquies in Hagenau, Worms, and Regensburg, in which he came to know other Protestant views, roused his hopes for their unification. The second edition of the *Institutes* (1539) and Calvin's *Petit traité de la Sainte Cène* (1541) both attest to his attempts to overcome the dispute over the Lord's Supper by using more precise formulations than had Bucer. He occasionally wrote to Leo Jud and Bullinger in this vein and told Farel of the theological significance of this correspondence for Protestantism as a whole.[87] In addition to a reflection of daily events, these letters prominently featured theological discussions, especially with regard to the sacraments. This included intimations of the polarization between Lutherans and Zwinglians, which was not at all necessary in Calvin's view and which should thus be brought to an end. In a concise dispatch to the *antistes,* Calvin made it clear that he sought to reach an understanding with his Zurich correspondents.[88]

---

85. Kolfhaus, "Verkehr Calvins mit Bullinger," p. 28; Stam, "Verhältnis zwischen Bullinger und Calvin," pp. 39f.

86. Bullinger's letter to Niklaus von Wattenwyl, May 4, 1538, in CO 10b,195, no. 114.

87. Calvin's letter to Farel, February 26, 1540, and February 27, 1540, in CO 11,23f., no. 211.

88. Calvin's letter to Bullinger, March 12, 1540, in CO 11,27-29, no. 213.

By then, the political situation in Geneva had changed again. In October 1540, the councilors decided to ask Calvin to return, relying on support from Basel, Bern, and Zurich. The significance of Calvin's theology and efforts at unity, as perceived by the Bullinger Circle, was manifested in the letters sent by the Zurich pastors to their Strasbourg colleagues and to Calvin, encouraging him to return to Geneva.[89] The human ties and everyday proximity, brought to light in later letters through their nearly colloquial exchange of ideas, were not yet present in the correspondence of the Strasbourg years. The trust placed in Calvin by Zurich's theologians in contributing to his return would, however, seem to have solidified the basis for their friendship as correspondents once and for all, making their previously sporadic correspondence into a solid institution.[90]

The years 1541 to 1549 were affected by three closely related problems relevant to Calvin's relations with the Swiss Confederation: the conflicts with Bern in matters of church politics; the agreement with Zurich on the doctrine of the Lord's Supper; and efforts to form an alliance of Protestant areas, together with France. Although Calvin recommended his activity as a reformer in Geneva, his *Ordonnances ecclésiastiques* and *Catéchisme* provided the Geneva church with a new face that would differ from that of other Reformed churches of the confederation. Tensions soon arose with Bern, which was influenced by Zwinglianism, and whose area of sovereignty extended to the gates of Geneva since Bern's occupation of Vaud. Disputes broke out regarding theological matters, including church customs, excommunication, and the Lord's Supper in particular.[91] The Bern authorities feared that Calvin was edging too strongly toward Lutheranism, which increasingly weakened his reputation there. A synod was convened in Bern in March 1549 to tackle these growing difficulties; Calvin was, however, not allowed to appear there personally for fear of hostilities. The year 1549 thus saw a "nearly complete freeze in church relations between Geneva and Bern."[92] Calvin hoped that he could reach a theological understanding with Bullinger that would make it possible to end the conflict with Bern. The situation with regard to foreign affairs in the Holy Ro-

89. Letter of the Zurich pastors to the pastors of Strasbourg, April 4, 1541, in CO 11,183-85, no. 293; letter of the Zurich pastors to Calvin, April 4, 1541, in CO 11,185-88, no. 294.

90. Cf. Calvin's response to the pastors of Zurich, May 31, 1541, in CO 11,229-33, no. 318, esp. 232f.

91. Cf. "Bern and Vaud," above.

92. Gäbler, "Zustandekommen des Consensus Tigurinus," p. 325.

man Empire with the establishment of the Augsburg Interim (1548) encouraged vigilance and unity, while, conversely, a potential alliance of the Swiss confederates with King Henry II of France (1519-1559) opened up the possibility of assisting the Protestants in France, who had come under considerable pressure. Once Bern and Zurich refused to furnish mercenaries, however, Calvin sought to campaign personally in Zurich for a renewal of the mercenary alliance. Calvin (along with Geneva) hoped, in the end, for help from Zurich in an attempt to slacken ties to Bern as a means of maintaining relations throughout the entire confederation. Seen as a whole, Calvin's intent on coming to a consensus with Zurich in the important theological question of the Lord's Supper was "in terms of politics and church politics, a lashing out at Bern."[93]

Calvin did not see his hopes fulfilled with regard to church politics and politics in general, hopes that were primarily tied to the conclusion of a theological agreement on the Lord's Supper. Zurich did not in fact join in an alliance with France. Bern continued to oppose any solutions attempted by Geneva. On the other hand, Geneva and Zurich were at least able to agree in full on the Lord's Supper, an agreement that both parties in fact went on to uphold. This was the result of a long, chiefly private theological discourse between Calvin and Bullinger from 1547 to 1549. Both theologians eschewed no effort in this, exchanging numerous letters and ideas for a solution to the problem and meeting three times in Zurich with the assistance of Farel. A compromise made this agreement theologically possible, taking a number of Zwingli's main views into account and determining the presence of Christ, alongside the granting of salvation, to be the work of the Holy Spirit.[94] There is no point in asking whether Calvinism prevailed over Zwinglianism or whether Calvin gave up his primary position in order to make this possible. It is far more important to emphasize the future impact of the text: the agreement between Geneva and Zurich would lead to a completely new type of church, the Reformed Church, which, within Western Christianity, solidly opposed Roman Catholicism as well as Lutheranism and other outgrowths of the Reformation.

The 1551 printing of the Consensus Tigurinus, as the text has been

93. Gäbler, "Zustandekommen des Consensus Tigurinus," p. 328.

94. Cf. Gäbler, "Zustandekommen des Consensus Tigurinus"; Janse, "Calvin's Eucharistic Theology"; Rorem, *Calvin and Bullinger on the Lord's Supper.* The Consensus Tigurinus can be found in CO 7,735-44.

known since the nineteenth century,[95] gave way to an unanticipatedly hefty polemic and lengthy dispute between Calvin and the German Lutherans, the quarrelsome Hamburg pastor Joachim Westphal in particular. In the dispute, Calvin, in close collaboration with Bullinger, vehemently defended the Consensus.[96] One can clearly see how the relations between the Genevan and the Zurich reformers intensified and deepened during the second dispute over the Lord's Supper, so that one can go beyond a long period of mere mutual admiration and actually speak of a friendship between the two.[97] While this led to a deepening of the chasm between the German and Swiss Reformation, Calvin, who had been held under suspicion in German-speaking Switzerland, especially for his ties to Bucer, was then able to secure his place among the Reformed churches of the confederation.

This friendship did not, however, exclude differences of opinion in a number of matters, as demonstrated in the correspondence between Geneva and Zurich on the Bolsec affair, which first concerned the Geneva church and then all of the Swiss Reformed churches.[98] After Bolsec's arrest, Bern, Basel, and Zurich were asked for their opinions on the matter. In their evaluation, the pastors of Zurich urged moderation and compromise.[99] As can be seen in a letter to Calvin from Bullinger, the Zurich pastors were closer to Bolsec than to Calvin. Bullinger did not seek to hide this disagreement with Calvin and replied in typical manner: "Believe me that there are some who are vexed by your sentences in the *Institutes* on election, and are led by them to the same conclusion drawn by Hieronymus from Zwingli's book *De providentia,*" that God is the creator of sin.[100] This discussion turned increasingly bitter. Calvin, for example, wrote to Farel concerning Bullinger: "I complained lately of the theologians of Bâle, who, as compared with those of Zurich, are worthy of very great praise. I can hardly express to you, my dear Farel, how much I am annoyed by their rudeness. There is less humanity among us than among wild beasts."[101]

---

95. The original Latin was titled "Consensio mutua in re sacramentaria."

96. Cf. "Basel," above.

97. Rüegg, "Beziehungen Calvins," p. 89.

98. Cf. also the above comments on the perception of the affair in Bern and Basel.

99. Letter of the Zurich pastors to the pastors of Geneva, November 27, 1551, in CO 8,229-31; letter of the Zurich pastors to the Geneva council, December 1, 1551, in CO 8,232f.

100. Bullinger's letter to Calvin, December 7, 1551, in CO 14,214f., no. 1565; esp. 215.

101. Calvin's letter to Farel, December 8, 1551, in CO 14,218f., no. 1571; esp. 218 (= Calvin, *Letters,* vol. 2, pp. 313f.)

Even after the dispute was resolved in Calvin's favor, when Bolsec was expelled from the city, Calvin still was not able to let things stand as they were. He wrote to Bullinger: "Although you disappointed my expectations, I nevertheless gladly offer you our friendship. Before the others I will maintain silence as if I was entirely satisfied."[102] While the disagreement between Calvin and Bullinger subsided,[103] they continued to maintain differing opinions with regard to predestination.[104]

There was, however, no difference of opinion in the much more difficult matter of Michael Servetus.[105] Both Zurich and the other Swiss Protestant churches were asked for their evaluations. The necessity of the death penalty in punishing Servetus's crime was expressed clearly, albeit indirectly.[106] Servetus was declared a heretic, and the Geneva council was urged to carry out its duty in the matter. The accusation that Servetus had, for decades, been incorrigible in publicly attacking the foundations of the Christian faith not only corresponded with the generally held — as well as the Catholic — understanding of the matter, but was also grounded in imperial law. Indeed, since the edict issued in 380 by Theodosius I (347-395), *Cunctos populos,* the avowal of the orthodox doctrine of the Trinity was viewed as a foundation of the Christian West and played a prominent role in civil law. Servetus's punishment was also anchored in the *Constitutio Criminalis Carolina,* the criminal law order introduced by the empire in 1530. The Zurich evaluation thus corresponded with the consensus of the time, which was questioned only by a few outsiders, often individuals in danger of persecution themselves.[107]

We will lastly turn to a matter that was decisive in the relationship between Geneva and Zurich, Calvin and Bullinger: their common efforts on behalf of refugees of faith. The help extended by Geneva and Zurich in the sixteenth century to Reformed Christians under attack in Italy, France, England, Hungary, and Poland derived primarily from Calvin and Bullinger's true empathy and strong partisanship with regard to the fates

---

102. Calvin's letter to Bullinger, late January 1552, in CO 14,251-54, no. 1590; esp. 253.

103. Cf. Calvin's letter to Bullinger, March 13, 1552, in CO 14,302-5, no. 1612.

104. Cf. Walser, *Prädestination bei Heinrich Bullinger;* Locher, "Bullinger und Calvin," pp. 23-28; Muller, *Christ and the Decree,* pp. 39-47; Venema, *Heinrich Bullinger and the Doctrine of Predestination.*

105. Cf. also "Basel," above.

106. CO 8,555-58.

107. Cf. "Basel," above, on the Basel Circle.

of the persecuted. The generous reception of these refugees often had long-term positive effects on their host cities. Just to name a few examples from England and Italy: the "Marian exiles" who resided in Zurich during the reign of "Bloody" Queen Mary I included a group of gifted men who would later hold High Church and academic positions under Queen Elizabeth I and would contribute decisively to the spread of Reformed theology in their country. A refugee congregation grew in Geneva, which most prominently included John Knox (ca. 1513-1572), Scotland's future reformer. Bullinger and Calvin had both positive and negative experiences with the Italians who had had to flee their home country due to their faith. Bullinger's favored theologian Petrus Martyr Vermigli and Calvin's personal friend Galeazzo Caracciolo (1517-1586), as well as the Diodati and Turrettini from Lucca and others, all enriched their new home and the Geneva church with their extraordinary talents for years to come. There were, however, rifts in Zurich with Bernardino Ochino (1487-1564), the former general vicar of the Capuchins, and in Geneva with Valentino Gentile (ca. 1530-1566) and Giorgio Biandrata (1516-1588). The care extended by the Zurich *antistes* to the Reformed refugees from Locarno is quite well known, as are Calvin's indefatigable efforts on behalf of the Waldensians, whose grave situation was, as to be expected, first felt in Geneva, but who then received support and found succor in both cities.[108] Calvin and Bullinger's support of Reformed Christians in France was even more extensive. Bullinger continually supported Calvin's indefatigable efforts, whether with material or literary assistance, or with petitions and common delegations, even though the two friends did not always agree on the type of assistance that was appropriate.[109]

Summary

Dissent generally leaves behind deeper historical traces than does consensus. This should indeed be taken into account with regard to Calvin's relations with the Swiss Confederation. At least since Calvin returned to Geneva in 1541, no representative of the Reformed churches or of the municipal authorities could cast serious doubt on Calvin's fundamental sig-

---

108. Cf. Bächthold, "Volk auf der Flucht."
109. Cf. Mühling, *Heinrich Bullingers europäische Kirchenpolitik,* pp. 187-224.

nificance for the Reformation in Geneva and western Switzerland. This did not, however, necessarily entail unconditional support for his work, as we have seen in the examples discussed in this essay. Calvin by no means enjoyed "home-field advantage" in Switzerland, but in fact often met with skepticism or even open opposition.

His relations with Bern were those most riddled with conflict. As a reflection of his direct area of influence in Vaud, the sovereign territory of Bern, the contradictions between Calvin's theology and understanding of the church and Bern's flavor of municipal church administration had a direct and unmitigated effect on their mutual relations. Calvin was especially confronted with the confessional tensions of his era in Bern. While Bern's attitude toward Calvin was strongly influenced by the confessional power struggle there, Calvin also met with the opposition of strict Zwinglians within the Reformed movement, who were fully dedicated to the preservation of Zwingli's legacy.

Calvin's relations with Basel were of a completely different nature. The Basel church, influenced by the reserved Simon Sulzer, was inherently well disposed to Calvin, while he saw the church as lacking in zeal, courage, and effort. The Basel Circle under Castellio and Curione was a stronghold of stark opposition that attempted — with both eloquence and scholarship — to provide alternatives to Calvin's theology.

Finally, Calvin found in Zurich a true comrade-in-arms, Heinrich Bullinger, who remained loyal to Calvin despite initial reservations and occasional theological differences and differing positions with regard to church politics. Bullinger's Zurich church maintained its own points of view with regard to Calvin, but consistently allowed him the leeway to follow his own path in the face of changing conditions in Geneva. The Consensus Tigurinus remains to this very day an expressive symbol of the mutual respect and the emerging personal friendship between Calvin and Bullinger.

This overview of Calvin's relations with the Swiss Reformed cities of Bern, Basel, and Zurich thus demonstrates most strongly — as laid out in Calvin's words used in the title of this essay — that Calvin was indeed both "loved and feared" in the Swiss Confederation of his time.

Translated from German by David Dichelle, Leipzig

Calvinism in Europe

Andrew Pettegree

When the great historian of twentieth-century Protestantism Emile G. Léonard (1891-1961) attempted to sum up the essence of Calvin's achievement, he considered it the creation "of a new type of man, the Calvinist." Such a man was characterized by his moral rectitude and sense of vocation — a sense of vocation that sustained adherents of the new churches through suffering and tribulation. Others, such as the American historian Robert Kingdon (b. 1927), laid stress on the Calvinist churches' capacity for social solidarity and organization. In the middle years of the sixteenth century, the structures and disciplines Calvin had successfully imposed in Geneva were exported to a number of countries, where this new church order became a hallmark of the church.

It is certain that for Protestants in many parts of Europe, Calvin was an inspirational figure and Geneva an ideal of the true church. But it was never Calvin's intention to organize an international church or insist on the Genevan model as normative. When asked by admirers elsewhere in Europe how they should conduct themselves as Christians, Calvin often gave surprising answers. When in 1554 a French exile community at Wesel in the Rhineland asked Calvin whether they should conform themselves to the local Lutheran rite, as they had been asked to do, Calvin advocated compliance. It was better to accept Lutheran church order, he argued, than to lose the chance of a church altogether. To admirers in the French refugee church in London four years before he had been even more blunt. Do not, he told them, make "an idol of me, and a Jerusalem of Geneva."

These are words that all students of Calvin's movement should remember when they consider the extraordinary success of churches inspired by the Swiss Reformation in the second half of the sixteenth century. Churches that took their doctrinal inspiration or models of organization from Geneva and Zurich were established in England and Scotland, the Netherlands, and large parts of Germany. Calvinism had a profound impact on the established Protestant churches of eastern Europe. But none of these churches was a slavish imitation of Calvin's Geneva. Nor could they be, for what was suitable for a small city church could not easily be transposed to a large state or nation.

Modern scholars of Calvinism are therefore far more inclined to stress the diversity of the movement and the subtlety with which Calvin's precepts and the Genevan model of church government were adapted to new places and circumstances.

Almost inevitably, Calvin's greatest initial impact was in the land of his birth, France. Calvin's ministerial colleagues in Geneva, were, like him, exiles from France. The promotion of true religion in their homeland was, for many, a consuming preoccupation. Almost from the time that Calvin was first settled back in Geneva in 1541, the reformer and his colleagues turned out a stream of exhortatory writings, urging fellow believers to abandon the Roman Church and witness to their faith. For Calvin, a self-conscious and somewhat aesthetic intellectual, to have discovered a popular voice as a vernacular writer was one of many surprises of this part of his career. But he did indeed prove to be a polemicist of rare talent, ably assisted by other colleagues such as Pierre Viret (1511-1571) and Guillaume Farel (1489-1565).

The writing campaign of the 1540s and 1550s transformed Geneva's profile in the Protestant world. Calvin's sermons and writings were spread through France by a network of traveling salesmen, a hazardous trade underwritten by Calvin's friend the entrepreneur Laurent de Normandie (d. 1569) and, more surprisingly, the Bourse Française, a body ostensibly charged with supporting the poor French refugees in the city. The circulation of these writings was a clear provocation to the French authorities, and in 1551, the king, Henry II (1519-1559), issued a draconian edict forbidding all contact with Geneva. But a trade conducted under the cover of the normal interchange of goods and books was hard to control, and Geneva's publishing industry grew steadily.

It is nevertheless hard to believe that this busy evangelical activity would necessarily have brought any great change in France without a major transformation in the political situation at home. In 1554 and 1555, small evangelical communities were established in Orléans, Paris, and elsewhere, encouraged by ministers dispatched from Geneva. But persecution continued, and the end of the Franco-Habsburg war in 1559 raised the prospect of an intensification of the campaign against domestic dissent. Then at a tournament to mark the peace, the king was fatally wounded. His son, Francis II (1544-1560), was inexperienced and much under the influence of his uncle, the Duc de Guise. In December 1560, he died too. This double catastrophe for the French monarchy provided French evangelicals with their opportunity. From 1559 they became increasingly assertive. By 1562, some two thousand churches had sprung up around France, and large parts of the nobility had converted. Church leaders demanded that their religion be given public recognition, demands given urgency by increasingly provocative public demonstrations of strength: open-air services, public psalm singing, and even violent attacks on Church fabric and Catholic sacred objects. Such conduct inevitably also inflamed Catholic opinion. By 1562, France was hurtling toward civil war.

It is instructive to consider Calvin's attitude to these events. On the whole, he viewed the descent into conflict with great misgivings. When churches sought his advice, he cautioned patience and submission. It was only with great reluctance that he dispatched representatives from Geneva to the first national synod of the French churches, held in Paris in 1559. Calvin consciously distanced himself from the more ambitious nobles who plotted against de Guise, preferring to cultivate the fickle and foolish Anthony of Navarre (1518-1562) — an error of judgment that cost the movement dearly. But Calvin was also increasingly sick during these years. When, in a final effort to stave off armed conflict, Catherine of Medici (1519-1589) summoned a colloquy to attempt reconciliation between the conflicting faiths, it was Theodore Beza (1519-1605), Calvin's younger colleague, who led the Protestant delegation. Beza was instinctively more sympathetic to French Protestant activists; his uncompromising defense of the faith at Poissy effectively closed the door on a negotiated solution.

In these circumstances it is hardly surprising that the churches that emerged in France in these turbulent years were far from a pale imitation of the Genevan model. The establishment of new churches was inevitably shaped by local circumstances. Where the local magistrates were sympathetic, the new churches often gave them an explicit role in church government. Others, in places where the church was in a minority, gave an enhanced role to the deacons, the order of church government charged in Geneva only with administration of support for the community's poor. The church had grown so rapidly that there were far too many congregations for each to be provided with a minister from Geneva, and some of those who offered themselves for the new Calvinist ministry in France were of decidedly dubious quality and character. The French National Synods were frequently obliged to publish lists of unsatisfactory ministers that they had stripped of their office. These decrees were accompanied by a physical description, in case the deposed ministers should attempt to pass themselves off to a new church under an assumed name.

The task of building a church in a nation of fifteen million inhabitants was inevitably more complex than the maintenance of discipline in a small city-state such as Geneva. The result was that while the French church benefited from the leadership of Genevan-trained ministers and owed an obvious debt to Genevan texts, not least the Bible and metrical psalms, it also developed its own responses to the challenges of church building.

The first civil war of 1562-63 ended in a settlement that was decidedly disadvantageous to the new Huguenot churches. Protestant nobles were to be permitted to establish Protestant churches on their own lands, but otherwise the congregations were limited to one church per bailliage. This was a terrible handicap to the urban congregations that had provided the dynamic core of the church's very rapid recent growth, and support for Calvinism in these cities and provincial towns began to ebb even before the St. Bartholomew's Day Massacre of 1572 dealt it a decisive blow. The massacre all but eliminated organized Calvinism in northern France. The faith lived on in the French Midi, remote from royal control, in towns where Calvinism had established an early ascendancy, such as Montauban, Nîmes, and Montpellier. Paradoxically, this adverse turn of events served to revive the influence of Geneva. The massacre of leading personnel in 1572 had destroyed the influence of those who challenged the Genevan-inspired national church structure of hierarchical synods. Nothing more was heard of Jean Morély (ca. 1524–ca. 1594) and his more democratic congregational model. The tribulation of 1572 also revived the spirit of patience and resignation that Calvin had preached in the early decades of trial and persecution. Together, these factors ensured the survival of French Calvinism.

The final years of Calvin's life, from 1559 to 1564, had witnessed an utter transformation of the religious landscape in his French homeland. But the situation in other parts of Europe was hardly less dramatic. The year 1559 was a true *annus mirabilis.* In November 1558, Mary (1516-1558), the Catholic queen of England, died, leaving as her heir a new queen, Elizabeth (1533-1603), brought up in the Protestant tradition. In 1559, it became clear that England would once again abolish the Mass and restore a Protestant church settlement. These events in turn provoked in Scotland a revolt against French Catholic domination of the government. The result was here too the installation of an explicitly Protestant church settlement. The death of Mary also dramatically weakened the position of her husband, Philip of Spain (1529-1598). In 1559, he departed his northern territories in the Low Countries and returned to Spain, leaving a grumbling nobility and a nascent evangelical movement keen to emulate the example of the new Protestant churches in England and France. The result, after years of increasing paralysis in the administration of the Netherlands, was a revolt against Spain that would ultimately culminate in the establishment of a free Calvinist state.

These events, all sparked by the turbulence of 1559 and all closely interrelated, would lead to the transformation of the international map of Europe and the establishment of the Swiss Reformed as a second major church tradition, alongside the Lutheran churches of Germany, Scandinavia, and central Europe. But these new churches were not a faithful imitation of the Genevan model, nor even of the national church established in France. Each took a strikingly different course.

In England, Elizabeth left little doubt that her rejection of Catholicism would be wholehearted. The daughter of Ann Boleyn (1507-1536) was a child of the English Reformation. Her closest advisors were veterans of the bold experiment in Protestantism pursued during the reign of her brother, Edward VI (1537-1553). European reformers, Calvin among them, hastened to offer congratulations and much unsolicited advice. But Elizabeth proved stubbornly reluctant to be shown the way to reform by continental patriarchs; Calvin's approaches, in particular, were brusquely rejected. The church settlement that emerged in England owed much to the theological inspiration of the Swiss tradition, which had shaped the beliefs of all those promoted to positions of influence in the new church. But the Swiss model of church government was emphatically rejected.

There were several reasons why this outcome was probably inevitable. Calvin was not particularly well informed about English events. During the reign of Edward VI it was Heinrich Bullinger (1504-1575) and Zurich that exercised the most profound influence on behalf of the Swiss. Geneva's influence grew during Mary's reign, when a colony of English Protestant exiles was established in the city; but this came with a price, for among the Genevan exiles were several whose radicalism would be offensive to the new queen's conservative instincts. Chief among them was John Knox (ca. 1514-1572), who chose 1558 to publish his singularly inopportune *First Blast of the Trumpet against the Monstrous Regiment of Women.* Intended as a denunciation of Mary, its obvious general implications cast a shadow over Geneva's relations with Elizabeth.

So although Calvin strove, with kind words and dedications, to undo the damage done by Knox, he was only partially successful. Elizabeth would not hear representations on behalf of the Genevan reformers, and for her bishops Heinrich Bullinger remained the continental advisor of choice. The Genevan church order, with its model of church government and congregational discipline, became, in consequence, the preserve of those who urged further reform of the English church settlement. This further inflamed the queen, who regarded church government as an aspect of her prerogative. These critics of the church, sometimes described as Puritans, tried on several occasions to promote reform of church government — sometimes, provocatively, through legislation in Parliament. It only gradually became clear that the queen regarded the church settlement as a final, not a first, step.

Despite these setbacks Calvin's teachings exercised a most profound influence over the Elizabethan church. Whatever Elizabeth's own personal view, the English read Calvin avidly: his sermons, biblical commentaries, and the *Institutes* were all swiftly made available in English editions and frequently reprinted. More editions of Calvin's writings were published in England during the second half of the sixteenth century than in any other part of Europe, including Geneva and his native France.

The eagerness to read and imbibe the theological works of Calvin spread across the range of religious opinion in the English church, embracing both the church's strongest defenders, such as John Jewell (1522-1571), and its eager critics. Not without reason English historians talk of a "Calvinist consensus" underpinning the Anglican Church settlement — a consensus that embraced its theological precepts, if not agreement with respect to church organization. It was only in the seventeenth century that this consensus was seriously threatened by the rise of Laudian ceremonialism, to many uncomfortably redolent of popery. The role that this clash over church ceremonies played in poisoning relations between the crown and the people demonstrates how deeply ingrained the habits of Anglican worship and liturgy had become.

Scotland represents Calvinism's most unlikely triumph. Until the middle years of the century, Scotland had been little troubled by heresy. This was a sparsely populated country divided between the Lowlands, with a number of small but lively commercial trading towns and fishing ports, and the remote Gaelic-speaking Highlands. The Stewart dynasty had little reason to compromise its loyalty to the pope, particularly when the English Reformation gave Scotland's continued support a greater strategic importance. Robust English attempts to make Scotland a client state only drove the fiercely independent ruling class more firmly into the embrace of Catholic France, a longstanding ally in counterpoint to the powerful southern neighbor. When James V (1512-1542) died after the battle of Solway Moss in 1542, it was to France that Scotland turned to protect the interests of the infant heir, Mary (1542-1587).

So things might have remained but for the events of 1559, which brought both the change of religion in England and turmoil in France. These events emboldened a small clique of Scottish noblemen to agitate against the French regent, Mary of Guise (1515-1560), and they received powerful support from an equally tiny group of Protestant preachers led by the indefatigable John Knox. Spurned in England, in 1559 Knox returned to his native land, preaching a Genevan-style reform. A sermon in June at the university city of St. Andrews inspired his congregation to the forcible removal of Catholic images from the city's churches and cathedral. Ministers and nobility were soon allied in arms, though pitifully weak against the French garrison holding Edinburgh castle. Now the English government played a crucial role. Seeing the opportunity to destroy French influence and secure the northern border, Elizabeth and her ministers took the bold step of dispatching north a blockading fleet. The French were persuaded to withdraw, and the rebels took power.

This was, in effect, a military coup, unsupported by any great wellspring of support among the populace. The establishment of a new Protestant church rested on these insecure foundations; but it was a success that was in many respects Calvinism's most complete and thorough. In 1559, a specially convened Reformation Parliament introduced a new church order modeled closely on that of the English church at Geneva. Knox became the church's dominant spirit, soon at odds with Mary, now returned from France to assert her right to rule.

This proved a combustible mix, but in the meantime the Scottish nobility also exacted a heavy price for their support of the new church settlement. Before the Reformation a large part of the property of the Church had passed into lay hands, and the landowner possessors of these rights had no wish to surrender them. A deal was struck whereby the Church had to content itself with a third of the income of this property: the "third of benefices." Thus although the hegemony of the new Calvinist church was theoretically unchallenged, its authority in practice depended on the development of a cadre of educated ministers, who could provide leadership from the pulpit. The emergence of such leadership was a matter of generations rather than years. But from the beginning the new church made every effort to articulate the full institutional structure of a Calvinist church order, with deacons to support the poor and elders to support the ministers in the exercise of consistorial discipline. This reformation of manners was a difficult undertaking in towns and fishing villages where levels of literacy were low, but the ministers stuck to the task, and by the seventeenth century Scotland was deeply shaped by its new church tradition. The Highlands also experienced a profound and surprisingly successful engagement with Calvinism. Here, in a largely traditional society, the example of the clan chief often determined religious allegiance.

The sixteenth-century Low Countries were a very different society. This was one of the most heavily urbanized parts of Europe, its proud and sophisticated towns home to a highly developed educational tradition. Not surprisingly, the populations of these cities evinced a great curiosity for Luther's teachings, and it was only determined action by Charles V (1500-1558), hereditary ruler of the Netherlands, that prevented a more widespread adoption of a Lutheran Reformation. Instead, the Netherlands witnessed a prolonged and at times brutal repression of heresy. Those who did not submit were forced to flee abroad.

It was here, in exile, that the foundations of the Dutch Reformed Church were laid. Dutch exile congregations gathered in London, in Wesel, and at Emden. They adopted a church order patterned on that of the Swiss churches, strongly influenced by both Zurich and Geneva. In the early 1560s, members of these churches turned their attention to the conversion of their homeland.

The attempts to establish secret congregations back in the towns of Antwerp, Bruges, and Ghent were met with brutal retribution: the Dutch contributed their fair share to the annals of those whose sacrifices were recorded in the martyrologies of Jean Crespin (1520-1572), John Foxe (1517-1587), and Adriaen van Haemstede (ca. 1525-1562). Faced with the prospect of a terrible death, the numbers ready to join the congregations remained small. But, as in France, the Dutch churches would get their opportunity through a change in the political situation. Philip's departure to Spain left the government in the hands of his half-sister, Margaret of Parma (1522-1586). The local nobility resented their lack of influence and chose to take up the cause of religious policy as a means of putting pressure on the regent. The grandees had shown little previous interest in Protestantism, but if they thought that heresy was merely an issue to be exploited the tactic backfired badly. When Margaret, in the spring of 1566, was forced to concede a temporary halt to persecution, thousands returned from the exile towns to claim the new freedoms. Months of excited open-air preaching led to more radical action: an attempt to win permanent concessions by "cleansing" the Catholic churches for the use of the new congregations.

In the short term these acts of iconoclasm proved counterproductive. Appalled by the violence, the nobility withdrew their patronage of the rebels. Margaret was able to restore control, and those who had joined the new congregations were forced to take flight once more. But in retrospect 1566 and the years in exile that followed mark the decisive point at which Calvinism took charge of the disparate forces of Dutch evangelism. Reorganized in exile and adopting a model church order closely patterned on that of the French national church, the Calvinists made common cause with the sole survivor of the aristocratic rebellion, William of Orange (1533-1584). Henceforth the Calvinist church would be at the heart of the struggle against Spain.

In 1572, William of Orange led a new invasion of the Netherlands. The comprehensive assault failed everywhere but in Holland, which thus became, quite accidentally, the fulcrum of resistance. The support of the Reformed congregations, particularly those overseas, was crucial to sustaining the struggle, particularly when the Spanish made every effort to subjugate the Holland towns in rebel hands. The price for this support was that Calvinism became closely identified with the fight against Spain. The returning exiles quickly took possession of the principal churches in the insurgent towns, and expelled the remaining Catholic priests. William of Orange, irenic by nature, expressed misgivings, but at this stage of an increasingly brutal struggle the churches and their friends abroad were indispensable allies and had to be indulged.

The geographical limits of the new northern state emerged only after two decades of hard military struggle. It was battles and sieges that determined that former centers of Protestantism in the south would eventually return to Spanish allegiance. But when Antwerp fell in 1585 a large part of its skilled workforce departed for the north. This, and Antwerp's subsequent eclipse as a trading metropolis, laid the basis for the Dutch economic miracle of the seventeenth century. But the character of the Calvinist church in this new state was decidedly idiosyncratic. The Calvinists defined the face of the public church and only they were permitted official status, the fruits of their part in the establishment of the new state. But the magistrate rulers of the new Dutch Republic were determined not to exchange Catholic persecution for Protestant theocracy. They resisted all efforts on the part of the ministers to make Calvinist church membership mandatory for all the population, and insisted that the Reformed ministers, as state employees, should make the sacraments of baptism and marriage available to all citizens. The church, despite much grumbling and frequent ritual protests on the part of their synods, gradually accommodated themselves to this situation. Although about half of the population attended the Reformed Church, only about 10 percent chose to become full members and submit themselves to church discipline. A surprising number of the inhabitants of the Dutch Republic adhered to other Protestant or dissident congregations, or remained stubbornly loyal to Catholicism; all of these choices were tacitly tolerated. This informal but surprisingly stable toleration became a fundamental part of the makeup of this most unusual commercial state, its public face shaped by the austerities of Calvinist style, its private attitudes shaped by the pragmatism of a mixed and heterogeneous population.

Such compromises, it might have been thought, would also come naturally to the patchwork of princely states that made up the German-speaking Holy Roman Empire. Here, in Luther's homeland, the decisive issues had already been settled by the time that Calvin's church was first becoming an international movement. The victory of Charles V in the Schmalkaldic War, and his later compromise in the Peace of Augsburg (1555), had awarded German states the right of religious self-determination, dividing the empire on a permanent basis into Lutheran and Catholic states. But this apparently flexible compromise proved extremely brittle when the influence of Calvinism began to make itself felt in the empire. Not many German princes were minded to shift from their family's established Lutheran allegiance. But those that did caused deep fissures in a settlement that could accommodate two, but not three, confessions.

The greatest threat to German Lutheran hegemony was posed by the decision of the elector palatine, Frederick III (1515-1576), to convert his lands to Calvinism. This brought to the Reformed confession not only a critical and strategic Rhineland state, but a second intellectual powerhouse, since the distinguished medieval University of Heidelberg lay within Frederick's dominions. The Heidelberg Church Order of 1563 was an important milestone in the development of the Calvinist church in Germany, while the Heidelberg Catechism, published in the same year, would become the normative document of Reformed churches in many parts of Europe and later in North America. The Heidelberg Confession and Catechism were the achievement of Zacharias Ursinas (1534-1584) and Caspar Olevianus (1536-1587), two of the formidable band of international scholars attracted to Heidelberg by its new status as the fulcrum of the Reformed scholarly tradition.

Despite this intellectual pedigree, German Calvinism did not have a happy history. The conversion of the Palatinate had a seriously destabilizing effect on the German religious settlement and on the politics of this sensitive and strategic part of Europe. Frederick III barely avoided an attempt at the Diet of 1566 to condemn his religion as falling outside the protection of the Augsburg Peace, an unthinkable humiliation for one of the seven imperial electors. Ten years later, the new elector, Ludwig VI (1539-1583), abruptly converted his lands back to Lutheranism, prompting a significant exodus of teachers and students from the University of Heidelberg. Leadership of the Calvinist cause devolved on his younger brother, the adventurous John Casimir (1543-1592), already deeply involved in schemes to bring military support to the French Huguenots. These schemes were encouraged by, among others, Elizabeth of England, who always preferred to wage war by proxy and thus sponsored Casimir rather taking on herself the mantle of protector of continental Reformed churches. Casimir's military skills, however, never matched his ambitions, and the search for a convincing military alliance proved elusive. As Calvinism spread through a string of smaller principalities in northern Germany, the tensions engulfed the Lutheran confession, where orthodox defenders of Luther's teachings turned against more eclectically minded theologians who favored Melanchthon's more irenic rewording of the Augsburg Confession (1530), the *Variata* of 1540. The charge of crypto-Calvinism proved toxic and in some cases fatal for a number of those embroiled in bitter controversies at Wittenberg and elsewhere. Relations between the faiths reached their nadir in this period: the divisions between the two Protestant confessions were now too absolute to be easily bridged by syncretic theology. It was also the case that by this point the Lutheran allegiance of many ordinary citizens in German cities and principalities was fixed and deep seated. Very few of the German city-states showed any propensity to switch to the Reformed confession. And when the elector of Brandenburg, Johann Sigismund (1572-1619), announced his own conversion to Calvinism in 1613, any attempt to convert his dominions was strongly resisted by both the clergy and the political nation. Calvinism in Brandenburg remained largely confined to the court and to the university at Frankfurt-an-der-Oder.

To balance this unsatisfactory history, in eastern Europe Calvinism achieved a surprising, and in the case of Hungary, an enduring success. Hungary's initial contact with Swiss reform came through Heinrich Bullinger at Zurich, rather than Calvin, and it was Bullinger who in 1567 provided the decisive document of Hungarian Calvinism, the Second Helvetic Confession. The fierce preaching and organizing zeal of Peter Melius (1536-1572) converged with the anti-Habsburg sentiment of the nobility to open the way for a dynamic church that flourished under the benign influence of the prince of Transylvania, Stephen Báthory (1533-1586). Calvinism never enjoyed a monopoly in Hungary. Legislation in 1568 proclaimed toleration, so long as the four major churches in the region did not introduce further doctrinal innovation. But such a settlement, coming at a moment of dynamic growth for Calvinism, helped the new church more than its established Lutheran or Catholic competitors.

The same might be said of the situation in Poland, and, to a lesser extent, Bohemia. In Poland successive waves of refugees from the religious conflicts in western and central Europe had established a de facto diversity, such that only a formal proclamation of religious toleration could bring a semblance of order. Thus although Calvinism was a relative latecomer, this was a context in which the Reformed confession could thrive, particularly as it profited from the strong advocacy and organizational flair of the charismatic reformer John a Lasco (1499-1560). Lasco, who returned to his native land after a peripatetic career as a reformer in England and Germany, brought both the experience he had accrued organizing the refugee churches in London and Emden and considerable social prestige as a leading figure in the Polish nobility. Although Lasco died very shortly after his return to Poland, Calvinism flourished. By the end of the century there were some two hundred churches in Poland and another two hundred in Lithuania. Bohemia, with its established allegiance to the heirs of the Hussite tradition, was less susceptible to aggressive proselytizing, but nevertheless played host to scholars and theologians of a moderate hue.

By 1617, the centenary of the Reformation, the German Palatinate had once more been restored to Calvinism. At celebrations to mark the centenary at the University of Heidelberg, the theologian David Pareus (1548-1622) was moved to assert an extraordinary claim for the primacy of the German city within the Reformed tradition: Heidelberg, he proposed, could now be seen as the mother of all Calvinist churches. The hubris of this assertion would be all too swiftly exposed, as the elector's impetuous intervention in the Thirty Years' War led to both his own deposition and the investiture of his lands by imperial troops. The great library of Heidelberg was removed as plunder to Rome, where much of it still remains. But for all the turmoil and bitter experiences of these difficult years, these turbulent events reveal one final aspect of the Calvinist family of churches: their capacity, in times of trouble, to come to the aid of suffering coreligionists. This identification with the wider cause of the church was a notable feature of international Calvinism during all the critical moments of the churches' first century. This sense of solidarity was manifested in a massive outpouring of sorrow and anger at the time of the St. Bartholomew's Day Massacre: prayers were said, fasts undertaken, and moneys raised to assist the dispossessed ministers and congregations. The same sense of solidarity was demonstrated again when Geneva itself was threatened by the forces of the duke of Savoy in 1589, 1590, and 1602. An international fundraising effort brought contributions from many parts of Europe. The same international sympathy could be evoked when Louis XIV (1638-1715) moved to expel his Huguenot subjects at the end of the seventeenth century.

Such a sense of international brotherhood was an enduring motive for those who welcomed exiles and refugees, in England, Germany, and in parts of central Europe, and often protected the newcomers against the bitter complaints of indigenous artisans. The newcomers in turn often evinced a strong enduring loyalty to the cause of the church in the lands they had left behind.

The web of connections that linked Calvinists in many parts of Europe — scholars, statesmen, pastors, and ordinary citizens — was a tangible factor in promoting a distinctly confessional view of international politics. Such people were often in the vanguard of urging active military action to confront what they perceived as the malign force of Catholic imperialism. In England the godly were early advocates of war against Spain, striving to persuade a reluctant Queen Elizabeth that the nation's interests were best served by bold action to help Protestants abroad and thus frustrate the purposes of Philip II and Spain. In the early seventeenth century, they struggled to persuade an even more reluctant James VI and I (1566-1625) to embrace the cause of the Palatinate. In the seventeenth-century Dutch Republic, refugees from the southern provinces were always among the most vocal in opposing any attempts to make peace with Spain.

If international Calvinism was thus a tangible political force, it was also in less turbulent times a bond that united scholars, pastors, booksellers, and active Christians in a shared community of belief, and, perhaps as important, a shared code of values. The Puritan instinct could be off-putting and self-absorbed — a sense that if only a few were to be saved, the self-consciously godly were destined to be among the elect. But it also encouraged a seriousness of moral striving, reflected in piety and biblical education that embraced the whole family, and a culture of charitable works. This sense of intellectual brotherhood and shared experience of religion was an enduring legacy of the Calvinist century and a fitting tribute to a founding father whose patient teaching and exposition of the Christian life was directed to all those seeking a path to God.

Calvinism in North America

James D. Bratt

An old story about the founding of America puts English Calvinists on the ground floor of that enterprise. In this account the "Pilgrim fathers," separatists from the Church of England, and their much more numerous, non-separating Puritan kin are the architects of a uniformly devout New England, which in turn becomes the model of the independent nation divinely destined to arise on the New World's shore. By logical transition, then, the United States was set upon Calvinistic foundations.

The reality turns out to have been much more complicated. Recent historians have discovered how variegated the settlers of New England were (the Puritans having comprised at most one-third of the whole) and how unusual New England was as a British colonial settlement in North America. The earlier-established Virginia turns out to have been more typical of the lot, and thus the proper home of the authors of the great documents and feats of American independence. But even in the conventional tale the Puritans' theology was always a sticking point quickly left behind for more widely valued qualities. It was the Puritans' solid character, or their contributions to liberty and education, all somehow emerging despite their distasteful predestinarianism, that won Americans' affection.

The revised story of America's origins thus gives a better forecast of Calvinism's destiny on the North American continent. Always controversial for the rigor as well as the substance of their theology, vastly outnumbered by populist denominations like the Methodists, and an embattled minority even when they have been the establishment, Calvinists have nonetheless exerted an outsized influence in the development of American politics, academia, and national self-conceptions. They have been the leaven in a now-resistant, now-absorptive loaf. Their external influences have come despite — or perhaps because of — chronic internal fissuring, for from the start Calvinists in North America have split along lines of ethnicity, polity, and theological interpretation. Prospering as a minority, they have become many minorities, each shaping and being shaped by the niche where they have landed.

The Puritan Legacy

The Calvinism that came ashore in New England in the 1620s and 1630s had already been altered from continental standards by the exigencies of England's protracted process of church reformation. Neither outlawed nor in power, English Calvinists negotiated an indeterminate space by building congregations that were in part voluntary associations of the like-minded. This gave rise to the localistic polity that would be one of the most powerful legacies of Puritanism in America. A second would be a habit formed in England that became standardized in America: the expectation that full church membership be accorded only upon the applicant's testimony of a personal experience that settled any doubts about his or her election. In this manner the Puritans in New England aimed at making the visible and invisible churches as synonymous as possible. At the same time their churches were state-supported to the exclusion of all others. If zeal for purity and broad public sway proved to be unstable associates, the combination contained a great deal of America's religious future, which lay in the separate, even rival, elaboration of these two impulses.

Two other Puritan tensions also reverberated down through the American future. Their insistence on experiential conversion potentially amplified the authority of the human soul in things religious, a precedent unfailingly invoked by later generations of searchers and freethinkers. On the other hand, from the Cambridge (Massachusetts) Synod of 1648 to Connecticut's Saybrook Synod in 1708, the Puritans moved toward establishing the Westminster standards[1] as collective authority and so resolutely

1. The enactments of the Synod of Westminster (1645-1652) included the Westminster Confession (1647), the Larger and Shorter Catechism, and mandates for worship and church

asserted God's sovereignty over all things. Many who would leave established Congregationalism nonetheless took along this theology into their new fellowships. Likewise, a tension between piety and intellect marked Puritanism from the start. It is no accident that Harvard College, founded just six years after the Puritans' first landing in 1630, evolved over the eighteenth century into the American bastion of Enlightenment rationalism, or that virtually every one of the oldest Puritan congregations was Unitarian by the mid-nineteenth century. On the other hand, the exuberant revivalism that swept America from 1740 to 1840 drew from models and sources in classic Puritanism. The earnest heart and the formidable systematic head of John Calvin carried over to the New World in this manner, and in this potent combination.

The Puritans aimed at thorough reformation not only in church but in state and society as well; theirs would be a "Bible commonwealth" founded upon a social compact between people who were at once fellow citizens and fellow church members. Until its original charter was revoked in 1684, Massachusetts restricted the franchise in colony-wide elections to full church members. Yet the new charter formalized what had been the practice all along in local affairs, awarding the vote according to a property qualification that many could meet. The "democracy" of the famous New England town meeting should not be misunderstood, however; it aimed not to poll between discordant opinions but to establish and enforce communal consensus. Dissent was more begrudged by necessity than legitimated by right.

Still, cultivation of a responsible public ethos was high on the list of Puritan priorities — and high on the list of their accomplishments as well. Though the clergy were barred from civil office, they typically worked in close cooperation with the magistracy to shape a society that was at once formally secular and deeply Christian. Key instruments to this effect were not only churches, which all inhabitants were required to attend, but also the schools that appeared in nearly every town. Thus literacy, piety, and social duty were each promulgated via the other. Commerce played a more ambiguous role. On the one hand, New England's townships of small

---

governance. While these "Standards" together were adopted by most of the world's English-speaking churches of Presbyterian governance, the New England churches affirmed just the Confession and Catechisms, as have many other bodies within the worldwide Calvinist tradition.

farmers and artisans generated a thoroughly, if modestly scaled, commercial nexus in which nearly everyone participated. On the other hand, a rough egalitarianism combined with suspicions of covetousness and luxury to keep market exploitation under control and to make the achievement of material prosperity as much a cause for introspection as for self-congratulation. Most of all, New England's social behavior was marked by remarkably low levels of violence; its laws singled out crimes of aggression over those involving property, sexuality, or libel.

The Puritans took divine election to apply not only to individuals and churches among them but also to New England as a "nation." This too gave as much occasion for lament as for celebration, so that the distinctive genre of colonial New England literature became the jeremiad — sermons recounting the myriad ways in which the chosen people had fallen short of their calling. The very punishments that God was visiting upon them for these infractions became signs of hope, however — proof that God had not withdrawn his covenant from them. The rhetorical cycle traced out in the jeremiad would endure a very long time and at a very deep level in the American psyche, as the range of what counted as God's chosen nation gradually expanded to include, first, those adjacent territories where the children of New England spread in the search for land and opportunity, and later (but only in the 1820s), the United States as a whole. The sense of national election could work to launch evangelism campaigns and crusades for social justice — and to launch holy wars against enemies. Not accidentally, the most epochal conflict in U.S. history, the Civil War (1861-65), joined those two prongs in fatal combination, as a war to thwart Southern disobedience became a war to abolish slavery. The fiercest and most accomplished rhetoric in that war on the Northern front came from New England ministers who consciously styled themselves as "sons of the Puritans." Ironically, their equals on the Southern side were self-consciously Calvinistic Presbyterians.

Unfortunately, God's "New Israel" also had "Canaanites" near at hand to deal with. The grimmest annals in New England history recount the Pequot War (1637-38) and King Philip's War (1675-76) — proportionate to population, some of the costliest episodes in American military history. Land pressure, complaints about trade, and racism all played their part in causing the conflicts, but the sanction for genocide that Puritan leaders drew out of scripture in these instances soaked their faith in the blood that condemns, not redeems. The more familiar Salem witch craze

(1692) turned the hunt for the Lord's enemies inward, and its twenty victims count as the predictable sacrifice of an insular community trying to dam its tide of afflictions. The quiet anomaly of Salem is that such episodes did not occur more often in the region. For that New England's learned ministry and magistrates are due credit, as they usually nipped the folk mania of witch-hunting in the bud.

The Great Awakening

By the 1730s, under the strains of rapid economic growth and demographic dispersion, the New England pulpit triggered a new religious era that later historians would call "the Great Awakening." Resoundingly Calvinistic sons of the region like Jonathan Edwards (1703-1758) set this stage, and upon it trod the British-born missionary George Whitefield (1714-1770), who spread the new model of heart religion across all the colonies. Combining theatrical charisma with a new emphasis upon the proximity of Christ's redeeming mercies, Whitefield simplified the exacting measures of Puritan conversion into a ready, wholesale plan. Still, Whitefield's was a Calvinistic gospel — he broke with his erstwhile Oxford friends, John Wesley (1703-1791) and Charles Wesley (1707-1788), over their Arminian[2] understanding of justification — and the Awakening can be understood in part as a wave of Calvinistic reform. It brought its converts to vital religious commitment; it multiplied colleges (Dartmouth and Brown in New England, Princeton in New Jersey, sundry academies in the South) to train ministers for further evangelization. As in Calvin's own time, it raised its adherents' religious sights beyond their native locale to an international vista. Yet the Awakening was Calvinistic only in part, for the Arminian Methodists on the Wesleyan side would eventually outnumber the converts Whitefield left. Furthermore, the most numerous fellowship among his progeny, the evangelical Baptists, however much they held to Reformed theology, repudiated the public sweep of magisterial Calvinism.

Baptists had been present in British North America from an early date, especially in Rhode Island, where so many dissenters from the New

---

2. A school of thought named after the Dutch theologian Jacobus Arminius (1560-1609) that amplified the role of human will and initiative in the process of salvation, over against the orthodox Calvinist position ratified by the Synod of Dort (1618-19).

England establishment fled or were exiled. Tolerated, they did not much multiply there. The zeal of the Awakening radically altered the scale of things. New Light (pro-revival) New Englanders began to form their own churches under the principles of strict local control and renewed insistence upon experiential conversion as test of full membership. (That had eroded with the spread of the "Half-Way Covenant"[3] in the New England establishment from the last third of the seventeenth century.) Many "Separates" then took the logical next step of requiring believer baptism and leaving Congregationalism entirely. The movement spread steadily across New England from 1750 on but really flourished on the backcountry frontier, especially in Virginia and the Carolinas, where it was brought by New England missionaries. Theologically these Separate Baptists took a soft Calvinist line, insisting on agreement only in "essentials," but mandated exuberant experience and strict discipline of life and fellowship as the definition of true Christianity. They met and gradually intermingled with Particular Baptists, who had been evangelized by the more consistently Calvinistic Philadelphia Association, founded in 1707 by streams of Welsh immigrants. Together, the Baptists' lay leadership and localist polity made them self-sufficient as communities. Their hostility to established churches left them oscillating between radical libertarianism and world-renouncing quietism[4] during the American Revolution, and their ethical sobriety made them one of the most effective instruments of social discipline on the post-revolutionary frontier without their assuming much claim upon or for the public order.

The Presbyterians, the third large body of Calvinists in colonial America, also expanded rapidly over the eighteenth century, bolstered by immigration as well as revival. By Independence some 150,000 Scots and Ulster folk had poured into the colonies, typically settling along the Appalachian backcountry from Pennsylvania south. Religiously their communities showed stout Westminster orthodoxy alongside vivid folk religion, and strong church assemblies jostling with prickly individualism in a libertine environment. This Scots-Irish phalanx soon came into tension with

---

3. The Half-Way Covenant, affirmed by the Boston synod of 1662, opened the sacrament of baptism to children of parents who themselves had been baptized but had not experienced regeneration as was required for full church membership, so long as these parents professed believing knowledge of Christian doctrine, promised to obey church authority, and manifested a proper way of life.

4. An attitude distancing oneself from worldly affairs, particularly politics and warfare.

homegrown Presbyterians who had become allied with New England Congregationalists of semi-Presbyterian polity. The alliance favored revivals and regional autonomy, less so doctrinal uniformity and synodical controls. The issue was joined in the subscription controversy at the Synod of 1729, which passed an Adopting Act that required clergy to affirm the spirit though not the letter of the Westminster Standards, as the immigrant, pro-subscription party wished. The battle resumed with the Awakening, and the anti-revival Old Side split from the more evangelical party at the Synod of 1741. The two were eventually reconciled in 1758 on New Side terms: subscription on doctrinal essentials, relative regional autonomy, and attention to the evangelical spirit as well as the formal education of clergy. Both the split and the reconciliation were propelled by the Log College, founded outside Philadelphia by William Tennent (1673-1746) to provide ministerial training on-site to avoid the hazards of traveling to and (in his mind) absorbing the spirit of Scottish universities. Ulster-born but a New Sider, a champion of heart religion but also of theological education, Tennent helped mediate the two poles, just as his son Gilbert Tennent (1703-1764), a fire-breathing revivalist, soon settled down to good order in his Philadelphia pulpit.

Helpful in the church's reconciliation but much more influential in the new nation about to be born was John Witherspoon (1723-1794), a Scottish pastor brought to New Jersey in 1768 to preside over the college founded at Princeton. His evangelical past did not prevent Witherspoon from purging the curriculum after Jonathan Edwards was installed there and substituting for it the moral-sense ethics and common-sense epistemology of the Scots Enlightenment. If this conciliation of rationalism and revivalism muted the implications of Calvinist doctrines of sin, it served admirably to pump political leadership into the American Revolution. In fact, Princeton produced more officeholders on all levels of the infant nation than did any other American college. Witherspoon's political Calvinism emphasized the responsibilities of public service, and the centrality of law to both legitimate and stabilize the revolutionary process. Witherspoon's most distinguished student was James Madison (1751-1836), principal architect of the U.S. Constitution. The document reflects the naturalized Calvinism that Madison took away from Princeton: utterly secular, trusting in no redemptions, arraying structural mechanisms to control indelible self-centeredness.

Theological and Regional Divergences
in the Nineteenth Century

Once national independence was definitively secured at the end of the Napoleonic wars, Princeton returned to its original intent of producing ministers, founding a separate theological seminary that also became a font of undiluted Calvinist orthodoxy. Leading the enterprise for half a century from his arrival on the faculty in 1822 was Charles Hodge (1797-1878): professor of systematic theology, the vastly learned editor of perhaps the foremost academic journal in the nation, a force for moderation in denominational councils, but an unbending advocate of what he took to be the timeless faith of the church. His system combined François Turretin's Reformed dogmatics, Francis Bacon's induction as theological method, commonsense realism as philosophical frame, and earnest polemics against any deviation from this profile. Hodge's regime would endure at Princeton until the modernist quarrels of the 1920s and then live on in the scholastic wing of American fundamentalism. Yet, for much of the nineteenth century, Princeton minted more ministers — and thus more professional leaders in local communities across the country — than did any other school in the land, cultivating in society as well as in church a respect for learning, a culture of sober realism and civil respect, and a model of piety fulfilled in institutional service.

Post-revolutionary adjustments in New England were very different. Loyal Congregationalism perceived a tide of unbelief and licentiousness at loose in the young republic and rekindled the revival enterprise against it, redoubling their efforts when their churches were disestablished in Connecticut (1817) and Massachusetts (1833). They entered a Plan of Union (1801) with their old New York Presbyterian allies to practice comity in planting churches across New York and the Midwest. They brought additional allies into a remarkable phalanx of national voluntary agencies to promote education, Bible and tract distribution, and the reformation of public morals. This "Presbygational" complex aimed to rebuild the old Puritan holy commonwealth by voluntarist means, and it achieved remarkable success. Separately and together these Calvinist bodies founded more colleges and published more books and Bibles than did any other church, including the Baptists and Methodists who greatly outnumbered them. Their agency budgets compared respectably to those of the federal government, and their network of local affiliates rivaled those of the greatest organizers of the age, the political parties.

Yet the Presbyterians at Princeton, along the border states, and in the South became increasingly troubled by these efforts and banded together in 1837 to end the Plan of Union, evicting the New School congregations formed under its aegis from the Presbyterian Church. The Old Schoolers cited, besides errors of polity, a theological degeneration in the inheritance of the sainted Edwards. Edwards himself had so altered the Puritans' covenant theology to qualify his as a neo-Calvinism. Conversion amounted to a "divine and supernatural light" being imparted immediately to the affections, there implanting an entirely new sensibility that wrought in the redeemed a new vision of reality and a new motivation for conduct — a "true virtue" that consisted in "love for being in general," free of the calculated self-interest dear to Enlightened moral theory. Such love was impossible for those still dead in their trespasses, Edwards said; yet these too had free will to do as they pleased. They simply could not by their own volition wish to please God.

Edwards's followers modified this system further to accommodate the voluntarist-individualist canon of the new democracy. Samuel Hopkins (1721-1803) deemphasized the bonds of original sin, which Edwards had robustly reasserted, while translating the master's ethical rule into a command for "disinterested benevolence." This necessitated love for the least regarded, Hopkins declared, and he made good on his word by preaching against slavery from his pulpit in Newport, Rhode Island, a center of the American slave trade. New England's revival passions thus always bore moral urgency. That combination peaked in the next generation at the hands of Nathaniel William Taylor (1786-1858), professor at Yale Divinity School, and Charles Finney (1792-1875), master evangelist of the Yankee diaspora. Out of revival urgency the two laid the entire guilt of sin at the door of each individual's will, and taught the power of that will to submit immediately to the moral law of God, which constituted true conversion. This Charles Hodge denounced as worse than Arminian — as Pelagian.[5] On the other hand, Boston Unitarians spied in Taylor and Finney a hyper-Calvinism fixated on guilt and depravity and prone to legalism. In either case, Finney's revivalism launched a fleet of social reformers to crusade against all of America's sins, including slavery.

---

5. A theologian active ca. 400 CE, Pelagius taught salvation by human merit and decision, thus not by divine grace. Arminians deem grace to be necessary for salvation though accessible by human-initiated decision.

That activism helped prompt the Presbyterian split of 1837. The staunchest Calvinists among the Baptists voiced their own complaints at the same time, reasserting divine election in theology and the strictest localism in polity to forestall the erection of a new "religious establishment" by a Yankee "hydra" consumed with human pride and imperial ambition.[6] These Particular or Primitive Baptists found New School deviations among fellow Baptists especially troubling, and their own campaigns via press and pulpit spread a resolute, populist form of Calvinism across the border states and rural South out to the plains of Texas.

Presbyterians in the South moved to withstand Northern critiques by discovering new doctrine. At the hands of James Henley Thornwell (1812-1862), a pastor and professor of theology at Columbia, South Carolina, the notion of "the spirituality of the church" sharply demarcated civil from ecclesiastical spheres and limited the church's corporate authority to the latter. Not accidentally, slavery being deemed entirely a civil institution, Thornwell's position exempted the foundation of Southern society from the church's judgment. This did not prevent him, however, from writing the *Address to All the Churches of Jesus Christ throughout the Earth* (1861), by which Presbyterians in the newfound Confederacy warranted ecclesiastical separation from their Northern brethren and gave fulsome support to their region's cause. Although Thornwell himself came to think that the South's military reverses reflected divine punishment upon some abuses of the system, his denomination never doubted that their slave regime had biblical warrant and that Northern abolitionism necessitated all sorts of departures from orthodoxy. Their social outlook combined with rigorous Westminster confessionalism and Baconian commonsense hermeneutics to make the Presbyterian Church in the United States (PCUS) a strategic leader in the New South that emerged out of postwar Reconstruction, assimilating such change as was necessary within a matrix of tradition and order.

Leavening influences from Presbyterians above and Baptists below accentuated the disproportionately Calvinist aura of New South culture. Military defeat, economic straits, and the weight of a burdensome past reinforced the current of fatalism that was already strong in Southern lore and letters. "Calvinist" became the literary shorthand for this complex,

---

6. *Address to the Particular Baptist Churches of the "Old School"* . . . , in Bratt, ed., *Antirevivalism*, pp. 69-77.

which in fact derived as much from stoic and aristocratic sources as from Reformed theology. If skepticism about the illusions of progress helped rationalize the racial segregation of the South, warnings against pride and ambition could have been well used in the booming industrial North. Old School Presbyterians had warranted the Civil War upon constitutional grounds, while New Schoolers were more invested in it as a crusade to eliminate slavery. Notably, military and political triumphs eroded old theological tensions, and the two wings reunited in 1870 upon a moderate Calvinist base. The Congregationalists, who had been more uniformly of the crusader mind during the war, proceeded to become the friendliest ground for theological liberalism once the war was over.

In fact, more and more Northern Protestants in the final quarter of the nineteenth century became convinced that religion needed to innovate to match change in society and economy. As old theological distinctives faded, the traditionally Calvinist denominations became absorbed in a generic Protestant culture marked by prosperous respectability at home and a zeal for spreading "Christian civilization" abroad. Thus in eight of the nine presidential elections from 1884 through 1916, the Democratic candidate was a Presbyterian — Grover Cleveland (1837-1908), William Jennings Bryan (1860-1925), and Woodrow Wilson (1856-1924). That each held political and theological attitudes clearly at odds with the others' illustrates the limits of denominational salience in the era. What religious historian Sydney Ahlstrom (1919-1984) said of the transit of Puritanism is equally true of the fading Calvinism of the Gilded Age: it showed a "crucial susceptibility . . . to transmute its power into secular impulses . . . virtually sacrific[ing] itself on the altar of civic responsibility."[7]

African Americans and Canadians

Presbyterian experiences in two other nations illustrate the limits and lure of the American compromise. The freed African Americans of the post–Civil War South were indeed a people set apart, organizing separate churches when whites refused to fellowship with them as equals. For black Presbyterians, who were far less numerous than their counterparts among the Baptists and Methodists, this posed a severe challenge, since they had

7. Ahlstrom, *Religious History of the American People,* p. 348.

typically worshipped (in segregated seating) at white churches prior to the war. Their numbers grew to about seventy congregations by 1898 when, with Jim Crow at its peak, they formed an independent body, only to rejoin the PCUS as a separate and subordinate synod from 1917 until 1951. The factors that kept Presbyterian numbers low in the African American community — the insistence upon an educated ministry and "good order" in worship — also boosted their disproportionate leadership in the community's life, North as well as South. Presbyterianism both pointed the way toward the respectability that black achievers yearned for in the face of white denials of the very possibility and agitated politically to make sure that neither side became comfortable in any state short of justice. Thus the escaped slave turned Presbyterian minister Henry H. Garnet (1815-1882) became one of abolitionism's most radical orators in the decades before the Civil War. After liberation Francis J. Grimké (1850-1937) — born to a South Carolina slaveholder, educated at Princeton Seminary, and Garnet's successor at the leading black church in Washington, D.C. — was numbered among the foremost Presbyterian clergy in the nation, black or white. Grimké was feared for his logic and learning by anyone admitting to second-class arrangements for reasons of race.

The Calvinist experience in Canada was much more placid and fit readily into the pan-Protestant culture that took hold everywhere in that nation outside Quebec from 1830 to 1930. Canadians were more orderly than the Yankees they decidedly did not want to emulate: the Methodists were more serene, the Baptists more uniformly Calvinistic, and the Presbyterians more closely tied to developments back in Scotland whence most of them had emigrated. The Free Church secession (1843) in that motherland registered strongly across the water, holding the sympathies of more Canadian Presbyterians than not by the time of Confederation (1867). Yet the seceders too had affinities for establishment, and the erosion of the Anglican hold on that status in Canada led both Presbyterian sides to functionally fill that gap. They did so with a quieter version of the American New Schoolers' campaigns for evangelism and regulation of public mores. They followed a like inclination for alliance building. Most Canadian Presbyterians were in one house by 1875, then proceeded through long negotiations with Methodists and Congregationalists into the United Church of Canada in 1925. Much less theological backlash attended this process than was the case for even smaller ventures in the United States, partly because Protestants in Canada felt called to enter a common front against consolidated Roman Catholic Quebec, partly because church-state collaboration in educational policy promoted cooperation across denominations in forming universities.

Calvinists in Protestant Fundamentalism

The roots of Protestant fundamentalism in America lie in protests against any policy of accommodation. Charles Hodge's son, Archibald Alexander (1823-1886), and Benjamin Warfield (1851-1921), who eventually succeeded both Hodges on the Princeton faculty, published a robust assertion of scriptural authority in 1881; fundamentalists derived from it one pillar of their theology, a doctrine of biblical "inerrancy." The other pillar would be dispensational premillennialism,[8] a wholesale remapping of eschatology that broke with traditional Reformed understandings of continuity in God's purpose and people but strongly reaffirmed divine sovereignty as well as biblical authority in an era that had begun to doubt both. Prime representatives of this doctrine were conservative Presbyterian clergy, including its chief publicist James Brookes (1830-1897)[9] and its missions theorist Arthur T. Pierson (1837-1911).

Meanwhile, the rigorist ethic of "holiness" that was equally definitive of fundamentalism had a Reformed wing parallel to the more numerous Wesleyans and Finneyites in that movement. Named after the English conference site where its teachings were elaborated, Keswick holiness taught that an "in-filling" by the Holy Spirit would enable the believer to live "victoriously" over sin. The motivation to evangelism that drew off Keswick heroics, millenarian urgency, and confidence in scriptural truth readily blended with the work of mainline church executives like the Presbyterian

8. The doctrine that Christ's return will precede (hence "pre") rather than culminate (as "post"-millennialism teaches) the thousand-year reign of perfection promised in some New Testament passages. Dispensationalism, popularized by John Nelson Darby (1800-1882) of the Plymouth Brethren in Great Britain, understands God's work in history as dividing into seven distinct phases, with the current epoch of the "church" or "grace" being sharply distinguished from that of "Israel" and soon to come to a catastrophic end.

9. A Presbyterian pastor long situated in St. Louis, Brookes presided over the Niagara Bible Conference, one of the principal avenues for disseminating dispensational premillenarian teachings. Brookes's many writings further popularized the movement, as did the definitive Scofield Reference Bible edited by his disciple, Cyrus I. Scofield (1843-1921).

Robert Speer (1867-1947) to make the generation before World War I the great age of American missions. The Presbyterians were particularly effective in China, Korea, and Brazil; the Baptists were everywhere; the Congregationalists took pride in having started the movement a century before.

But controversy from the mission fields washed back into the United States to help trigger the attack upon the theological modernism from which fundamentalism proper was born. The principal Baptist and Presbyterian denominations in the North underwent tempestuous assemblies in the 1920s from which small, resolutely Calvinist bodies emerged, unable to tolerate further membership in what they took to be theologically compromised churches. The General Association of Regular Baptist Churches grew out of a rupture in Northern Baptist circles and continues to the present, combining traditional Calvinism with dispensational eschatology and strict behavioral codes. More notable for its intellectual sophistication was the Presbyterian quarrel provoked by Princeton Seminary professor J. Gresham Machen (1881-1937), whose *Christianity and Liberalism* (1923) cast the two terms of its title as entirely different religions. The denominational courts faulted him, however, for supporting a separate mission board from theirs, leading to Machen's 1936 departure to form the Orthodox Presbyterian Church (OPC). Holding to an unaltered understanding of their historic standards, the OPC's Westminster Theological Seminary in Philadelphia cast itself as the true descendant of the "old Princeton" of Hodge and Warfield.

Fifty years later the drama was replayed among the Southern Presbyterians when conservatives, protesting loose theology and political involvement on the part of the PCUS, withdrew into the new Presbyterian Church in America (PCA). Their founding statement replicated the title of Thornwell's *Address,* and their conservative politics were never far from view. The PCUS in turn opened negotiations to reunite with their Northern counterparts, who had assimilated a number of smaller Presbyterian bodies already in 1958. The North-South union was accomplished in 1983, producing the Presbyterian Church (U.S.A.). Given similar unions occurring on the Congregational side, the counterplay between ecumenical unity and separation for purity formed the principal twentieth-century plotline in the American churches with the oldest Calvinist roots. The unions have not halted the steady loss of membership that the ecumenical bodies have suffered since the late 1960s, nor the relative strength gained by the purists via separation. On the other hand, those purists gained most who have decked their Calvinist theology with generic evangelicalism; thus the PCA is far larger than the OPC. In all these maneuvers, the oldest tension in American Presbyterianism has played out, but across both sides of the current divide. The ecumenical PCUSA breathes the socially activist New School, loose-subscription spirit; yet like eighteenth-century Old Siders it is adamant about proper polity, and its seminaries today affirm Reformed tradition as the proper bed of theological instruction. The PCA, on the other hand, proclaims its doctrinal orthodoxy but promotes an evangelical spirit and allows internal variations on a New Side model. The OPC resembles the small sects sprinkled across the American Presbyterian past, tenacious for the issues that defined them in a distant time or place.

Impulses from Dutch and German Communities

Some of the freshest impulses on the twentieth-century scene came from German and Dutch Reformed communities that had been present in America from colonial days but remained at the edge of British-derived developments. A major voice sounded already in the 1840s in the person of John Williamson Nevin (1803-1866), a native-born Presbyterian who quit those circles in disgust over the split of 1837 and joined the faculty of the German Reformed seminary at Mercersburg, Pennsylvania. Faulting Old School scholasticism and New School revival alike, Nevin found in contemporary German theology an inspiring recovery of the church in its confessional heritage, its historical evolution, and its role in Christ's continuing presence on earth. Nevin resurrected for American Protestantism (and to the disbelief of his teacher, Charles Hodge) Calvin's Eucharistic theology and saw in sacrament, confession, and liturgy the means of believers' lasting union with Christ and with each other. Castigating the entire "Puritan" heritage as rationalistic, subjectivist, and sectarian, Nevin's Mercersburg theology offered a dramatic departure on the American scene — nicely enough, in the name of recovering stability and tradition. His offering proved premature but Philip Schaff (1819-1893), his German-educated colleague at the seminary, showed how mediating theology could work on the postwar scene. Moving to the New School–founded Union Seminary in New York City, Schaff became the supreme scholar-statesman of the Protestant mainline, directing a new Bible translation and the English publication of the church fathers, among myriad other projects.

Mercersburg's deeper impulse began to be recovered in the 1930s as mainline Protestants talked of church union but also of recovering an authentic voice for the church, free of cultural conformity. In one merger the German Reformed in the United States joined with the immigrant children of the Evangelical Synod formed out of the post-Napoleonic Reformed-Lutheran union in the motherland. That synod happened to be the American home of the two strongest theologians on the mid-century scene, Reinhold (1892-1971) and H. Richard (1894-1962) Niebuhr. In their "neo-orthodoxy," the cultural captivity of the church found its keenest critics, and Barthian dialectical theology its American counterpart. Without affirming the letter, Reinhold asserted the spirit of Augustinian theology and the voice of Calvin himself. It was not in the offerings of secular rationalism, technocratic fixes, or assimilated religion that the world crises of economic depression, total war, and Cold War could best be fathomed, thundered Reinhold, but in a restored understanding of sin — original sin, structural sin, the hidden self-interest of the good citizen, and the pious mantle of the churchgoer. Reinhold's appeal especially touched the rising generation in American academia and government, steeling them to endurance in the cause of free civilization while alerting them to their own compromises and illusions. H. Richard's attentions went principally to the church, for which he constructed not only a critical but a constructive ethics of responsibility that would dominate mainline discourse into the 1970s. In the process he also worked as a pro-Calvinist church historian, rehabilitating Edwards and the Awakenings as the golden thread of the American Protestant heritage. His vision was fulfilled (and Nevin's spirit perhaps provoked) when the German Reformed and Evangelical Church merged with the Puritan-descended Congregationalists.

Although they claimed to transcend it, the Niebuhrs clearly worked on the mainline side of the Protestant divide. Dutch Reformed voices helped rehabilitate fundamentalism's children who emerged from underground in the 1960s as "neo-evangelicals." The Reformed Church in America, planted in seventeenth-century New Netherland, had taken a guarded part in pre–Civil War evangelical collaborations, staying on the Old School side of theological debates but serving its own ethnic enclave. It was more enthusiastic for the missions enterprise later in the century and the Prohibition crusade at home. As part of its home missions extension it had helped Dutch immigrants in the 1840s to 1850s who settled in the farmlands of western Michigan and central Iowa, but since a crucial portion of the new arrivals had just passed through a bitter secession from the established Reformed Church in the Netherlands, suspicion of a quasi-established American Protestantism spread in the *kolonies* and led to the formation of a separate Christian Reformed Church (CRC). It hewed to the strict confessionalism of the Seceded Church in the Netherlands and drew in a majority of the newcomers to America.

The pietist orthodoxy of the CRC was soon modified by the neo-Calvinist influences of Abraham Kuyper (1837-1920), a multitalented Dutch visionary who founded a university, two newspapers, and a political party, on his way to becoming prime minister of the Netherlands early in the twentieth century. Kuyper's project had two purposes: to awaken orthodox Calvinists from their pietistic slumbers to intentionally Christian participation in every domain of modern life; and, as a strategic part of that labor, to mount a wholesale critique of secularism and theological liberalism that would expose their inadequacies and warrant integral Christian options instead. These proposals had two corollaries that Kuyper freely granted: an explosion of the Enlightenment — but also an old Christian — notion of human objectivity in the articulation of knowledge and public policy, and a frank pluralism by which adherents of each "worldview" received their fair share of public space and respected that of others as a matter of Christian principle, not just out of begrudging toleration. Kuyper's dicta, no less than his example in founding a distinctively Christian university, galvanized any number of Christian Reformed youth to academic labors, most notably philosophers on the order of Cornelius Van Til (1895-1987), Alvin Plantinga (b. 1932), and Nicholas Wolterstorff (b. 1932). Their work exploded the Baconian commonsense approach that neo-evangelicals had inherited from nineteenth-century Princeton and replaced it with a presuppositionalist method that by century's end dominated American evangelical discourse — and opened it to creative interaction with some types of postmodernism that Kuyper's critique of power and pretensions to neutrality had anticipated by a century. At the same time, Kuyper's mandates for full-spectrum political and cultural engagement pushed the Christian Reformed out of their ethnic enclaves after World War II and inspired evangelical activism after the collapse of the Cold War consensus in the 1960s. This Kuyperianism could cut Right as well as Left, generating something of an evangelical liberation theology in critique of American domination abroad, but also militating against an expansive state and defending the organic orders of creation in a manner very friendly to the Christian Right's "family values" agenda of the past quarter century.

Along with the Niebuhrians and Kuyperians have sounded some surprising voices from the Calvinist residuum of the erstwhile mainstream. The 2005 Pulitzer Prize for fiction went to *Gilead*, the story of a soulful Presbyterian minister by the doughty Presbyterian author, Marilynne Robinson (b. 1947). Her earlier collection of essays, *The Death of Adam*, stands in a long line of American mediations on the hollowness within the nation's experiment and on the possibility — explicitly averred in Robinson's case — that John Calvin had the essential things right, and not only for believers' eternal salvation but for moderns' life together. A fellow Presbyterian, pastor-novelist Frederick Buechner (b. 1926), has walked more mellow paths to inspire a new birth of interior spiritual reflection. Calvin's *Institutes* opined that the knowledge of God would lead to self-knowledge; Buechner and his followers have taken Calvin's other option, searching the self to open unto God. The Genevan's impact on the American psyche, politics, and cultural criticism has evidently not run out. If his predestinarian reputation will never endear him to American hearts, his long train of disciples still leavens American lives.

Calvin's Understanding and Interpretation of the Bible

Wulfert de Greef

We are not the first ones to read the Bible. Many have indeed gone before us. And just like them, it is our goal to understand what the Lord God is telling us through his word. Calvin strove to be "of use" to others in everything that he wrote or said on the topic of understanding the Bible. In the present essay, I focus on the most important topics relevant to Calvin's understanding and interpretation of the Bible, in the hope that this too may be of service to readers.

Calvin's Understanding of the Bible

The Central Role That the Bible Played for Calvin

The Bible played a central role in Calvin's life and work. On April 25, 1564, Calvin dictated his testament to a notary, in which he described himself as a servant of the word of God in the Geneva church.[1] He explained that he strove, in accordance with the grace that God had granted him, to proclaim God's word in its pure form and to interpret scripture accurately, in both his writings and his speech. Calvin preached in Geneva for many years. He began his work as a preacher after Guillaume Farel (1489-1565) persuaded him to work on the reformation of Geneva in August 1536.

1. French text: CO 20,298-301; Latin text: CO 21,162-64.

From 1538 to 1541, years that Calvin spent in exile in Strasbourg, he preached to a small congregation of French refugees. He returned to Geneva in 1541 and was active as a preacher there until his death in 1564.

Calvin was involved in leading a particularly large number of worship services, held in Geneva on Sunday and other days of the week. And Calvin was also a teacher. The first task that he took on in Geneva, even before being called to preach, was the interpretation of the Pauline letters in the St. Pierre Church. Later, he interpreted the Bible for students in his lectures, at first concentrating on the New Testament, but later turning to the Old Testament as well. He often explicated a portion of the Bible in Friday morning meetings for other preachers.

We still have many of Calvin's interpretative texts today. His sermons were written down stenographically by Denis Raguenier (d. 1560) beginning in 1548 for later expansion and, in some cases, publication as well. His lectures began to be recorded and published in 1556. And Calvin wrote a variety of commentaries as well.[2] He must have put time into interpreting the Bible every day, if it was at all possible. He did this both in Geneva and during his time in Strasbourg, when he lectured on New Testament exegesis in the Gymnasium.

When Calvin described himself as a servant of the word of God, he lent expression to the central role that the Bible in fact played for him. He came in contact with the Bible and the church during his childhood. At first he was supposed to study theology but, as circumstances had it, he turned to law instead. During his time in Orléans in 1528 and 1529, he met his cousin Pierre Robert Olivetanus (1506-1538), who possibly had a positive impact on him with regard to reading the Bible. It is not insignificant that Calvin, in the preface to his Commentary on the Psalms, spoke of his "sudden conversion" in connection with "*docilitas*."[3] He explained that God moved him to learn from scripture from that point on. This was characteristic for Calvin as a preacher and teacher; after his conversion, he allowed God and his word to show him the way.

Even before he became active in Geneva, Calvin was involved in translating for the Olivetan Bible, the first edition of which appeared in

2. He wrote commentaries on all the books of the New Testament except for 2 and 3 John and Revelation. Calvin also wrote commentaries on Genesis, Exodus through Deuteronomy, Joshua, the Psalms, and Isaiah in the Old Testament.

3. CO 31,21.

Serrières near Neuchâtel in 1535. In the letter appearing in the edition to "emperors, kings, princes and to all peoples subject to the sovereignty of Christ,"[4] Calvin pled strongly for the centrality and authority of the Bible. Calvin was also strongly involved in the revised editions of the Olivetan Bible. He wrote a letter "To the Reader"[5] for the 1546 edition, in which he used colorful language in praising the Bible as a priceless treasure.

The Bible as the Word of God

Calvin never wrote a treatise on his understanding of scripture and seemed not to have deemed this necessary. In 1536 or 1537, the *Confession de la Foy*[6] appeared in Geneva, written with a good certainty by Farel, a creed that it was hoped the people of Geneva would adopt. The first article of the creed stated that scripture would be the sole measure for faith and that one should be led only by that which scripture taught. Calvin consistently upheld this principle; he thought, spoke, and wrote on a scriptural basis, thus clearly demonstrating how important the Bible was for him.

For Calvin, the particular significance of the Bible was closely connected to God. He understood God as having spoken to us — and as still speaking to us — through the Bible. Calvin saw this as the fundamental difference between Christians and the adherents of other religions.[7] He viewed the knowledge that God has spoken to us as an important fundament, one that, in terms of the Bible, occurred through the medium of human effort. The prophets were thus instruments of the Holy Spirit, proclaiming that which they had received from God. If we seek to progress with regard to holy scripture, we must thus be convinced that what the Bible teaches us is not of human origin but comes from the Holy Spirit. We do not have ourselves to thank for this understanding; it is God, teaching us through the Holy Spirit, who is the actual author of the Bible.

In his *Institutes,* Calvin spoke of the authority of scripture.[8] He recognized that any number of arguments could help to prove the credibility

4. CO 9,787-90.

5. CO 9,823-26.

6. CO 22,85-96.

7. See Commentary on 2 Tim. 3:16 (CO 52,382-84) and Sermon on 2 Tim. 3:16-17 (CO 54,283-87).

8. See *Inst.* I,7-8 (CO 2,56-69).

of the Bible. But however good these arguments might be, they were not enough to prove this in a way that is sufficient to overcome all of our doubt. It made no sense to view the authority of scripture as depending on the authority that the church accorded it. This meant turning the world upside-down, as the church was indeed built upon the teachings of the prophets and apostles. The credibility of the Bible was anchored in God himself, who spoke to us through scripture. The prophets and apostles deferred to God: that which is proclaimed in the name of God can only attain authority through God alone when he convinces us of the certainty of his word through the Holy Spirit.[9]

The Equal Significance of the Old and New Testaments

In the second century CE, Marcion (ca. 85-160), who was condemned as a heretic, did not wish to recognize the authority of the Old Testament since, from his point of view, the Creator God was a different God from that of the gospel. Since the ancient church, this has been up for discussion. Calvin, however, was of the view that the Bible knows only one God, who remains the same with regard to his interaction with his people. Calvin thus deemed the Old Testament to be equal in value to the New Testament, even as he admitted certain differences. While he, as a teacher, began by interpreting the New Testament, at a certain point he also began to focus on the Old Testament as well. His first commentaries were written on the New Testament, focusing only later on the Old Testament. Each Sunday morning, he would interpret a book of the New Testament in an unbroken *lectio continua* from week to week. For his midday worship sermons, he often chose a psalm instead.

Calvin pointed out that the first Christians could have had no other Bible than the Old Testament.[10] The gospel that was proclaimed to them was indeed based in the Old Testament. Apollos used scripture to prove to the Jews that Jesus was the Christ (Acts 18:24-28). Calvin explained that the Law and the Prophets provided so much clarity that Apollos was able to point to Jesus Christ as the promised Messiah.[11] He was not a new lawgiver

---

9. See *Inst.* I,7,5 (CO 2,60). He states that the Holy Spirit teaches us within that scripture is *autopistos* (reliable in itself); Van den Belt, *Authority of Scripture*.

10. See, for example, Calvin's Sermon on 1 Tim. 4:12-13 (CO 53,411).

11. Commentary on Acts 18:28 (CO 48,439). See also Commentary on Acts 28:21-23 (CO 48,568f.).

but a true interpreter of the Law received from God,[12] upholding the authority of the Law in its entirety. The gospel thus contained nothing new in comparison with the Old Testament. Paul proclaimed the gospel that God had promised through the prophets of the Bible. The writings of the apostles thus contained none other than the genuine interpretation of the Law and the Prophets in that they focused on how Old Testament matters appeared in the New Testament.[13]

It was an important part of Calvin's understanding of the Bible that the Old Testament was not subordinate to the New Testament but was in fact to be seen as the fundament upon which the New Testament rested. When Calvin stated that the gospel contained nothing new, he did not wish to downplay the significance of the New Testament but in fact sought to underscore the solidity of the gospel and the surety of salvation.[14]

In the sixteenth century, Calvin was not the only one to speak out on the importance of the Old Testament. He was, however, the one whose influence has been the greatest in this regard through to our own day.

The Bible as the "School of God"

Calvin often spoke of the Bible as the "School of God,"[15] a metaphor that was known to him from the Christian tradition. In Calvin's view, if we really wanted to learn something from the School of God, we needed to follow the instruction that God gave us through his word. Calvin was able to apply the image of a school to the church as well. Just as one listens only to that which the teacher teaches in a well-organized school, the church can be instructed only by the Spirit in the word. For Calvin, this referred not only to the instruction from God received through proclamation and in the personal study of the Bible, but also to the work of the Holy Spirit whose task it was to ensure that this instruction of the word would come to fruition in our everyday lives.

Calvin connected the instruction we receive from God in the Bible

---

12. See Commentary on Matt. 5:27 (CO 45,179); cf. Commentary on Matt. 5:17 (CO 45,171-72).

13. Commentary on 2 Tim. 3:17 (CO 52,384).

14. See Commentaries on 1 Pet. 1:10 (CO 55,215), 1 Pet. 1:12 (CO 55,219), and 2 Pet. 1:19 (CO 55,455).

15. See Blacketer, *School of God*, pp. 37-40.

with the term *wisdom,* as the Bible was, in his view, the school of the true and fulfilled wisdom.[16] The wisdom received from the Bible was thus closely tied with one's understanding of God and oneself. From 1539 on, Calvin explained the importance that he gave to wisdom in the first sentence of the *Institutes:* "Nearly all the wisdom we possess, that is to say, true and sound wisdom, consists of two parts: the knowledge of God and of ourselves."[17]

Calvin used the image of a school for the world that is created by God as well. A view of God's creation should also lead us to a true understanding of God, as God revealed his wisdom in creation (Rom. 1:20).[18] He said, however, that it was of our own doing that this instruction did not enable us to go beyond a vague idea of God, preventing us from being able to excuse ourselves before God.[19] This is why God chose another way to teach us, that we may follow his word.

In his sermons, Calvin often explained that if we believe that we possess great knowledge we are not really listening to what God is telling us. This means that our pride is an obstacle to us. If we do not become small and modest, we can never become good students of God. Calvin also stressed that we remain students of God our entire lives. This may seem foolish to the eyes of the world, but it is wise to the eyes of God.

The Bible Is of Importance to Us

Calvin was driven by the idea that the Bible is of importance to us. And when he drew attention to this, he used words from Jesus Christ, the evangelists, and the apostles, all of whom knew the Old Testament as the Bible.

Calvin often used the term *useful* to describe how the Bible is important to us. He borrowed the term from 2 Timothy 3:16-17, in which Paul speaks of the usefulness of scripture: "All scripture is inspired by God and is useful for teaching, for reproof, for correction, and for training in righteousness, so that everyone who belongs to God may be proficient, equipped for every good work."[20] As an exegete, Calvin sought to follow

---

16. See, for example, Calvin's "Letter to the Reader" of 1546.

17. See CO 1,279 and CO 2,31.

18. See Commentary on 1 Cor. 1:21 (CO 49,326-27) .

19. See Calvin's introduction to his Genesis commentary (CO 23,5-12).

20. See also Calvin's "Letter to the Reader": "Scripture is not given to us of course in

this path and have his work be of use.[21] He was not concerned about glorifying himself. He sought instead to help others understand scripture and, in this way, to build the church.

Calvin used the term *instruction* or *training* with particular frequency.[22] He borrowed this term from Paul, who tells Timothy that scripture is useful, particularly for its instructive nature. In this manner, Calvin also focused on the interpretation of scripture, seeking to tell us what scripture wants to teach us through the explication of each part of the Bible.

The Bible is thus God's instruction that is important "for us." Calvin's work was seeped in this "for us," as it is brought to one's attention in the New Testament.[23] In Romans 4, Paul references Genesis 12, which explains that Abraham's faith counted toward his righteousness. This story was not told just to honor Abraham, but also for "our sake." Calvin drew attention to Paul's admonition to us to make use of the examples given us in scripture.[24] In Romans 15:4, Paul refers to Psalm 69:10, after which he speaks in general on the writings of the Old Testament: "For everything that was written in the past was written to teach us, so that through endurance and the encouragement of the Scriptures we might have hope." Calvin referred to the special significance of this text; nothing that God said was insignificant or fruitless. We should thus strive to learn from all that has been written in scripture.[25] To close, I would like to mention 1 Peter 1:10-12, in which Peter points to the significance of the prophets. Calvin explained that the prophets spoke on the future status of the kingdom of Christ in order to serve us. In this way, they set the table for us that we may "feed on the provisions laid on it."[26]

---

order to satisfy our foolish curiosity or in order to serve our honor. But Paul said that it was useful, but what for? In order to provide us with good teaching, to console us, to motivate us, and to make us whole in all our good works. Let us therefore use scripture toward this goal" (CO 9,825).

21. Cf. Fritz Büsser's remark: "This word serves as a golden thread through the literary works of the Reformer" (translating Büsser, *Calvins Urteil*, p. 133).

22. D'Assonville, *Der Begriff "doctrina" bei Johannes Calvin.*

23. Cf. Reventlow, *Epochen der Bibelauslegung*, vol. 1, pp. 63-68 (= Chapter 3: "Das Alte Testament im Neuen Testament," Section 3: "Die Schrift ist geschrieben 'um unsretwillen': Paulus").

24. See Commentary on Rom. 4:23-24 (CO 49,85-87).

25. See Commentary on Rom. 15:4 (CO 49,271).

26. Commentary on 1 Pet. 1:12 (CO 55,218).

God Descends to Us and Chatters with Us

Calvin often said that God speaks to us in a special way.[27] He sets aside his majesty, as it were, and adapts himself to us in order to speak to us. Calvin compared God with a nurse who speaks with a small child in a different way than with adults. God "chatters" with us in a language that we understand.[28]

In terms of speech in human language, we might imagine people who have been appointed by God to speak in his name. When Calvin, for example, interpreted a psalm, he was not only able to explain what David wanted to tell us as a prophet, but also what God or the Holy Spirit is teaching us. Calvin recognized that we deal in the Bible with human writers with their own personal styles. Ezekiel, for example, was more thorough in his use of words than were Isaiah and Jeremiah.[29] Calvin proceeds in his Bible interpretation in a fashion similar to his academic commentary on one of Seneca's writings (1532).[30] In his explications of the Bible, he used everything he knew from his rhetorical studies with regard to the understanding of texts.[31] He had an eye for all the various stylistic figures that were used in the Bible and that did not serve simply to embellish the text but that expressed what the text had to say in the best way possible.[32]

When it comes to God speaking in human language, we should think of a God who adjusts his manner of speaking to our ability to understand. This applies equally to the imagery that is used by God and for God. God takes on another form in these images, and is able to appear as a husband who burns with love for his wife (Zeph. 3:17) or compares himself with a mother who carries her child (Isa. 46:3). In this familiar imagery, God can be seen to descend to meet us. In a certain sense, he distances himself from

27. See Balserak, *Divinity Compromised.*

28. See Calvin's Sermons on Deut. 5:22 (CO 26,387), Deut. 30:11-14 (CO 28,574), and Deut. 33:3-7 (CO 29,121-22); cf. Commentary on Gen. 35:7 (CO 23,469); Treatise "Against the Libertines": "In the gospel God thus takes on the role of a nurse" (CO 7,169); Sermon on Job 22:18-22 (CO 34,316) and on Job 38:18-32 (CO 35,398).

29. Lecture on Ezek. 3:11 (CO 40,83); cf. Lecture on Ezek. 12:4-6 (CO 40,256).

30. See Battles and Hugo, eds., *Calvin's Commentary on Seneca's De Clementia.*

31. Cf. Opitz, *Calvins Theologische Hermeneutik,* p. 94: "As a help to understand scripture, grammar and rhetoric had the same function that they had in the Commentary on Seneca's De Clementia."

32. See, for example, Commentary on Ps. 22:18-19 (CO 31,229).

himself to come closer to us in order to win our hearts. As apt as these images may be, they are, however, not sufficient in themselves. God's love far surpasses that which one can express in terms of love or inclination with human imagery.[33] The anthropomorphic discussion of God in the Bible is also a case of human speech that does not accurately say what God is. "Why does God say that he has eyes, ears, and a nose? Why does he clothe himself with human feelings? Why does he say that he is enraged or sorrowful? Is it not because we do not understand God in his inscrutable majesty?"[34] The result of our feebleness is that God must speak to us in human terms so that we may understand who he is with respect to us.

More than once, Calvin noted in his exegesis that God takes on human feelings.[35] This is closely connected with God's "babbling." But Calvin seemed to contradict himself when he pointed out that we always have to understand that God is free of such feelings.[36] It is indeed quite difficult for us to figure out what Calvin meant. While Calvin described this portrayal of a God with human feelings as an inauthentic manner of speaking about God, he wished to maintain a clear distinction between God and humankind. We can see this particularly in the way Calvin spoke about God's remorse. When people are full of remorse because their actions had another effect than expected, they will think better of it and act differently.[37] This cannot, however, be the case with a God who sees all. He cannot have remorse like a human being. And still, Calvin said, it is of great importance that the Bible speaks of God in human terms. We could otherwise understand nothing about God. God "chatters" with us in the Bible when he takes on human feelings. They play a role in God's interaction with us. God adapts himself so that we can get to know him in his relationship to us.[38] It is therefore necessary that we understand precisely what is

33. See Lecture on Zeph. 3:16 (CO 44,72-73), Commentary on Isa. 46:3 (CO 37,154-55) and Isa. 63:9 (CO 37,398-99); cf. Sermon on Isa. 31:1b-5 (SC III,92): "God surpasses in terms of love the affection of all fathers and mothers; they can only cast a mere shadow on God's goodness."

34. Sermon on 1 Tim. 2:3-5 (CO 53,151).

35. For example, Commentary on Exod. 32:10 (CO 25,87).

36. For example, Lecture on Hos. 11:8 (CO 42,442).

37. See *Inst.* I,17,12-14 (CO 2,164-67), Sermon on 1 Sam. 15:8-11 (CO 30,95-96) and 1 Sam 15:24-29 (CO 30,134-35).

38. See, for example, Sermon on Deut. 25:13-19: "Il est vray que Dieu n'est point suiet à passions, il ne s'esmeut point à la façon des hommes: mais pour nous monstrer combien il a nostre salut pour recommandé, et que nous ne le comprenons pas, sinon qu'il se transfig-

meant when one speaks of God in human terms, which applies, to be sure, to God's human feelings.[39]

Calvin's Interpretation of the Bible

A Matter of the Writers' Intentions

Calvin followed certain rules in his interpretation of the Bible. Interpreters of the Bible primarily need to focus on the question of what the original writers meant to say *(mens scriptoris)*. Calvin wrote this on October 18, 1539, in a letter to Simon Grynaeus (1493-1541), who taught Greek in Basel. A few years earlier, they had discussed the question of what exactly characterizes good commentary. They had agreed that an exegete should write clearly and concisely what the author meant to say without the necessity for any extensive explanations. When he wrote to Grynaeus that exegetes should avoid extensive explanations, he was thinking of the distinction that he wished to make between his commentaries and the *Institutes*. In the commentaries, he sought to provide a clear and concise summary of what the authors had meant to say, while in the *Institutes*, he delved into certain matters *(loci communes)* in detail.[40] In order to make it clear that this was in fact his intent, he included the letter to preface his Commentary on Romans (1540).[41]

Calvin upheld the notion in his sermons, lectures, and commentaries that an exegete, when interpreting the Bible, needed to follow that which the author meant to say. This was based in the view that language is a means for people to put their thoughts into words.[42]

A knowledge of Hebrew and Greek is necessary in order to be able to pay close heed to what the authors of the Bible wished to say. In line with the humanist movement's call to return to the sources, the exegetes of the

---

ure, par maniere de dire: et qu'il se presente à nous, en sorte que nous apprehendions quelques passions en luy" (CO 28,246).

39. See, for example, Commentary on Gen. 6:6 (CO 23,118) and Gen. 35:7 (CO 23,469).

40. Muller, *Unaccommodated Calvin*.

41. See CO 10b,402-6.

42. See Commentary on 1 Cor. 14:11 (CO 49,520) with a reference to Aristotle's *De Interpretatione*.

sixteenth century focused on the original biblical texts. In addition to his Greek, Calvin's Hebrew was so good that he was able to determine the meanings of the words independently. Whenever words had several different meanings, the context was able to clarify the correct meaning. At times, other texts with the same words would be taken for comparison as well. But Calvin always focused on the meaning of the texts within their contexts.[43]

Calvin also found it important to heed what other exegetes had to say.[44] Indeed, God did not grant any one single person full insight into all things. One had much to learn from others as an exegete, and only had to depart from the ideas of others when this became necessary and useful. Calvin was well versed in the biblical interpretation of the church fathers, medieval exegetes, Jewish interpreters, and his own contemporaries, though he seldom mentioned their names.[45] When different exegetes had different explanations for a word or text, Calvin listed these views and then went on to explain which one was the best in his own opinion.

The Literal, Historical Meaning

For centuries, biblical exegesis distinguished between literal and spiritual interpretations, which was itself a distinction founded in scripture. In 2 Corinthians 3:6, Paul describes himself as the servant of a new covenant, a covenant not of the letter but of Spirit, as the letter kills while the Spirit gives life. Paul is thinking of Jeremiah 31, which states that God promises, in a new covenant, to write his law through the Spirit onto the hearts of the people.

In the third century, Origen (ca. 185-254) spoke for the higher, spiritual meaning of the text *(sensus spiritualis),* as the literal understanding of scripture often met with objection. His view led to the distinction between literal and spiritual scriptural interpretation. The spiritual interpretation

---

43. Cf. the Second Helvetic Confession *(Confessio Helvetica Posterior)* of 1566, Chapter 2: "But we hold that interpretation of the Scripture to be orthodox and genuine which is gleaned from the Scriptures themselves (from the nature of the language in which they were written, likewise according to the circumstances in which they were set down, and expounded in the light of unlike passages and of many and clearer passages)."

44. See Letter to Grynaeus (CO 10b,405).

45. Lane, *John Calvin.*

was divided into three modes: allegorical interpretation referred to the significance of the Old Testament texts for the faith of Christians and for the church; tropological, or moral, interpretation related to the meaning of the text for the actions of Christians; and anagogic interpretation spoke of the hopes of Christians.

Calvin rejected this, which was established in medieval exegesis *(quadriga)* as a distinction between the literal and spiritual interpretation. In his view, the differentiation gave rise to the impression that a literal understanding of scripture was nonspiritual, and that only a spiritual explanation would suffice to reveal the true significance. Calvin sought to keep the word and the Spirit connected; just as we communicate our thoughts to each other by using words, God reveals himself to us in his words, adapting this to our human form of communication. The Holy Spirit awakens in us a reverent reception of the word. Exegetes therefore have to listen carefully to the text and reflect on what the author attempted to compose in words. A search for a deeper, spiritual meaning of the text, underlying the words, would therefore be in error. Calvin sought the simple, natural meaning of the text, making clear that he wished to adhere closely to the meaning of the words.

We can characterize Calvin's interpretation as *literal* and *historical,* terms that we use to indicate the great care that he paid to the meaning of the words in the historical context. For Calvin, the literal meaning of the words *(sensus litteralis)* was closely connected with the historical meaning *(sensus historicus)*.[46] The importance of the historical context for Calvin attained particular clarity in his understanding of the interpretation of the Old Testament texts that are cited in the New Testament.

Calvin made a few important notes in this regard in his biblical lectures on Hosea.[47] He first explained that we should look to the original situation of the Old Testament texts in order to reach the right understanding of them. He, furthermore, pointed out that there are different reasons to quote these texts. They might be incorporated as an attestation, but might also serve as allusions or other comparisons. When they are used as attestations, we need to investigate the meaning of the text in the context of the Old Testament in order to discover the simple and true meaning of the text. We need not, on the other hand, be as precise in cases where the citations

46. See, for example, Calvin's interpretation of the Psalms.
47. See Lecture on Hos. 13:14 (CO 42,493).

are used in allusion to individual words in the New Testament. And if such citations are in fact comparisons, it is no longer necessary to determine how each aspect of the text fits in with the New Testament passage in which it is quoted. We then only have to focus on the one aspect that clarifies the connection between the original text and the meaning that the quoted text had.

The importance of the historical context in Calvin's Bible interpretation also is evident in his exegesis of Galatians 4:22-31, in which Paul writes that Abraham had two sons, one with Hagar the handmaiden and one with Sarah. From this perspective, Hagar's son was born of the flesh, while Sarah's son was born of the promise. For Paul, this has a deeper meaning: there were two covenants, the one of Mount Sinai, which brought about slaves, as represented by Hagar; and the heavenly Jerusalem, which remained free. In Galatians 4:24, Paul uses a Greek word that can be translated as "deep meaning," a word that has entered modern languages as the word *allegory*. As we have already pointed out, the allegorical sense of language was part of the spiritual sense of the medieval *quadriga*. It would thus seem that Paul, in his work on the Old Testament, did not limit himself to that which we are told about Hagar and Sarah, but delved deeper to discover a more profound, hidden meaning. Calvin, however, did not agree with this.[48] He did not believe that Paul was doing what Origen and others later would do, for whom the literal meaning was too mundane and who therefore sought after a deeper, secret meaning of scripture. Calvin rejected this method of exegesis in which the spiritual meaning was supposed to lie hidden beneath "the bark of the letter." In his view, this would only open the floodgates for arbitrariness. Calvin, in contrast, stood for a simpler understanding of scripture *(sensus simplex)*. This simple sense of the words was for him the literal and true meaning of the text. According to Calvin, Paul was not seeking to transform the Genesis narrative into an allegory, but noting instead God's particular guiding role throughout history. He adapted the events that once occurred in the house of Abraham to the situation of the church of his times. For Calvin, this did not constitute a contradiction with a simple understanding of scripture. The house of Abraham was, from his perspective, the church of the time, and it was therefore fully legitimate to view important and remarkable events from the history of the church as models or paradigms for the contemporary church.

Calvin was not interested in allegorical interpretation, as the search

48. See CO 50,236-42.

for deeper meaning entailed a disregard for history and a reality behind reality. Calvin held fast to the historical character of the Old Testament. What Paul wrote in Galatians 4 was thus, strictly speaking, not an allegorical interpretation. Calvin instead used the word *anagoge:* "And an anagoge of this kind is not alien to the true, literal meaning when a comparison is made between the Church and the family of Abraham." In addition to *anagoge,* Calvin also used the term *type.* Events that occurred in the church could then be significant to us as examples or types. He aligned himself with that which Paul wrote on individual occurrences from throughout the history of Israel in 1 Corinthians 10:1-11, which can serve us as examples for God's judgment. Calvin explained that discussions of these types would not work to deny the past, but would only carry forward a thread from the past to the present. Calvin vehemently challenged those for whom Israel was a mere shadow of the church. The blessings and punishments that Israel received from God were, in their opinion, only a shadow of what would become full reality with the advent of Christ. Calvin characterized this view as pernicious foolishness, insulting not only the holy fathers, but even more so God himself. Calvin explained that the people of Israel only represented a likeness of the church to the extent that it was itself in reality the church.[49]

Calvin worked with great care on his exegesis of the Old Testament. He placed his analysis in the historical context, which he used as a basis to explain what the text had to say. While he recognized that he interpreted the Old Testament as a Christian, this did not mean that he referred to the New Testament alone for his understanding of Old Testament texts. He did this only when there was good reason for this, for example, to explicate an Old Testament passage better. He saw particular meaning in how the New Testament showed the way the Old and New Testaments fit together. This would guide him in his attempts, in his exegesis, to connect the Old Testament with the New Testament.[50]

The Old Testament and the New Testament Form a Single Body

One important facet of Calvin's biblical exegesis was his view that the Old and New Testaments were to be understood as a single body. He also rec-

49. See CO 49,460.
50. See the following section "The Covenant and Jesus Christ."

ognized how important it was that we maintain a correct view of the agreement and differences between the two Testaments. In the second edition of his *Institutes,* Calvin wrote that "authors" had focused to a great degree on the differences between the Old and New Testaments but had not brought about full clarity. While this was a sufficient reason to expand on this topic, he saw himself forced by the Baptists as well to do so, who had not recognized the spiritual significance of the Old Testament. Calvin opined that, in their "foolish prattle," they had thought of the people of Israel just as they would a herd of swine, fed by God in this world with no hope of heavenly immortality. This was why he dedicated a chapter in the second edition of the *Institutes* to "the agreement and the difference between the Old and New Testament."[51] In this, he focused on the agreement, or better put, the unity of the two Testaments, as any differences were of lesser nature. He phrased his point of view clearly and concisely in that the "covenant made with all the patriarchs is so much like ours in substance and reality that the two are actually one and the same. Yet they differ in the mode of dispensation."[52]

One and the Same Covenant All throughout the Scriptures

Calvin joined Huldrych Zwingli (1484-1531) and Heinrich Bullinger (1504-1575) in placing his focus on the covenant as a means of highlighting the agreement of the Old and New Testaments, often referring to Abraham within this context. God extended the validity of his covenant with Abraham to all of his descendants. The covenant of the Old Testament was therefore a sign of the special relationship between God and Israel. This also extended to the term *adoption* that Calvin often used in connection with the covenant.[53] He also often referred to the covenant as

51. *Inst.* VII (1539; CO 1,802-30). In the final edition of the *Institutes* (1559) Calvin replaced what was originally one single chapter with two chapters. the first deals with the agreement between the Old and New Testaments (*Inst.* II,10 = CO 2,313-29), while the second focuses on the differences between the Testaments (*Inst.* II,11 = CO 2,329-40). The content, by contrast, changed little after 1539, as did Calvin's understanding of the connections between the Testaments.

52. CO 1,802 and CO 2,329. Quotations from the *Institutes* (1559) refer to *Institutes of the Christian Religion* (1559), trans. by F. L. Battles (Philadelphia/London, 1960).

53. See, for example, Calvin's Commentary on John 8:33 (CO 47,203).

a covenant of grace, a grace not founded in any merit of Israel but in God's mercy alone.[54]

When God granted Israel the Law atop Mount Sinai, this did not entail the introduction of a new covenant since the covenant with Abraham was eternal and could not be broken.[55] But because so much time had passed and the people had grown careless, it had become necessary to renew this covenant. It was carved in stone tablets and written in a book so that the special grace that God granted the Abrahamic lineage would never be forgotten.[56] With respect to the meaning of the Law, Calvin stated first and foremost that the Law works like a mirror.[57] He invoked the image of a man with a face so dirty that everyone laughed at him without his knowing why. When someone brought him a mirror and he saw himself, he wanted to wash. The Law teaches us about what we are. Calvin said that we are forever newly dependent on the grace of God, and that God's Law is also of importance for society because the will of God applies to everyone. But the most important significance of the Law is to act as a norm for a life in accordance with God's will. Calvin often pointed out, moreover, that the Law has its place within the framework of the covenant,[58] and most important, that God loves us, wants to be our Father, and always seeks to be close to us.[59]

With regard to God's covenant with Israel, Calvin often cited the words: "I will be your God and you will be my people." The first part of this "legal formulation"[60] was an attestation to God's love. In the second part, Israel was called upon to live as God's people aspiring to God's love. Should Israel fail and not conduct itself as the people of God, there would always be the opportunity to repent. At times, it seemed as if the relationship between God and Israel had failed completely because Israel had bro-

---

54. For example, *Inst.* II,11,11 (CO 2,337); *Inst.* III,17,15 (CO 2,602f.); Commentaries on Gen. 34:7 (CO 23,458), Gen. 49:28 (CO 23,609), and Ps. 9:12 (CO 31,102).

55. See, for example, Lecture on Jer. 31:31-32 (CO 38,688).

56. Commentary on Exod. 19:1-2 (CO 24,192).

57. Hesselink, *Calvin's Concept of the Law,* p. 219.

58. If we view the Law as a collection of commandments that we must follow, the Law is deemed to be stripped naked *(nuda lex)*. The Law is instead "graced with the covenant of free adoption." See *Inst.* II,7,2 (CO 2,254).

59. Calvin continually emphasizes this in his twenty-two Sermons on Ps. 119 (CO 32,481-752).

60. Cf. *Inst.* II,10,8 (CO 2,317), in which Calvin states that God used this phrasing when he concluded a covenant with his servants.

ken the covenant. God would then be free to break the covenant as well — but he did not do this. God said that he would establish an everlasting covenant (Ezek. 16) or that he would form a new covenant with them (Jer. 31:31).[61] Calvin pointed out that "new" did not mean that this was a different covenant, but that nothing would change with regard to the substance of the covenant, only with regard to the form. In this new covenant, God would write his law onto the hearts of the people through the Spirit, guiding them toward obedience.[62]

The Covenant and Jesus Christ

The covenant is also very closely connected to Jesus Christ. God promised to bless all peoples through Abraham and "his seed." In Galatians 3, Paul establishes that the word *seed* refers to Christ.[63] This entailed, as Calvin put it, that God realize this promise in Jesus Christ. Although Christ had yet to come when God made his covenant with Abraham, the covenant was still established with a view to Christ. This is why Calvin often spoke of Christ as the foundation of the covenant. The advent of Christ strengthened the covenant, which had existed for centuries, rendering it solid and secure.

The Law that God granted to Israel through Moses also pointed forward to Jesus Christ, in Calvin's view. In this regard, Calvin alluded to the promises in which God said that he would be ready to forgive sin, and to the cultic laws in which God revealed, as in a mirror, that which he grants us in Christ. Without Christ, the ceremonies and sacrifices would only be a pointless spectacle. For his part, Jesus Christ brought his own death into connection with the covenant, as Calvin maintained. He said that Jesus spoke of "the new covenant in my blood" (Luke 22:20). Calvin explained that the word *new* referred to the comparison with the sacrifices of the Old Testament, which had to be made again and again, whereas Jesus Christ sacrificed himself once for all time.[64] We thus have a covenant founded in the sacrifice of Jesus Christ that remains with us to the end of the world.

61. In this connection, see Calvin's interpretation of Ezek. 16:59-60 (CO 40,391-93), Jer. 31:31-33 (CO 38,686-92), and Ps. 132:12 (CO 32,348-49).

62. See his interpretation of Jer. 31:31-33 (CO 38,686-92).

63. See Commentary on Gal. 3:14-16 (CO 50,210-13).

64. Commentary on Luke 22:20 (CO 45,711).

With regard to the covenant and Jesus Christ, Calvin established that we must also note the importance of the special relationship between King David and Jesus Christ. God indeed placed the covenant into David's hands that he had established with Abraham and confirmed with Moses, so that the covenant would always remain intact.[65] In his interpretation of Psalm 89, Calvin emphasized how strongly God maintained his focus on the salvation of the people in his covenant with David; God would always grant his grace to the people for the sake of the king. David and Christ would remain closely connected as the result of God's promise that David would always have successors, and of the complete fulfillment of this promise in Jesus Christ, a son of David. David's kingdom and house were, in his view, a shadow image of Christ's authority as Lord. Calvin repeated this link between David and Christ in his interpretation of the psalms and the prophets in which the house of David is mentioned.

The Newness of the New Testament

Calvin was emphatic about there being only one single covenant throughout the scriptures with the Old and New Testaments representing a single body. And yet, there was still a difference between the two Testaments, a difference not with regard to the actual substance but with regard to form. Although Calvin stressed that the New Testament did not proclaim anything new, more than once he stated that the gospel was of particular significance as the magnificent proclamation of the revealed Christ, in whom all of God's promises were fulfilled.[66] This is why Calvin chose to refer to the New Testament as the gospel, or *evangelium*. According to Calvin, the "authors" who thought that the gospel was timeless and who viewed both the prophets and the apostles as servants of the gospel missed the difference between the two Testaments: "Christ, although he was known to the Jews under the law, was at length clearly revealed only in the gospel."[67]

Calvin often explained that God revealed himself at a higher level in the New Testament than in the Old Testament, where he viewed God to be

---

65. Commentary on Isa. 55:3 (CO 37,285).
66. Commentary on Rom. 1:2 (CO 49,9). See also the introduction to his Commentary on Matthew, Mark, and Luke (CO 45,1-4).
67. Title of *Inst.* II,9 (CO 2,309).

84

present in shadows and images.[68] In the New Testament, on the other hand, God no longer revealed himself from afar but was openly and personally present in Christ. This is why, as Calvin explained, we Christians are preferred over the Israel of the Old Testament. In Christ, we are permitted to see God face to face. And with the veil now open, we can now be on more intimate terms with God. God shed more light on us through Christ as the sun of righteousness. Calvin explained, moreover, that we are now able to get to know God much better in terms of his grace, which is more solid and secure in Christ, and in terms of the life eternal.

Calvin also found it significant that, in the New Testament, God no longer focused solely on Israel but was indeed open to all peoples. This was new but by no means a strange development, since the prophets had already spoken of it. With the resurrection of Jesus Christ, the difference between Jews and heathen disappeared. Calvin often expressed the idea that the church had taken the place of Israel. With this manner of speech, however, he adapted himself to the situation after Christ when the heathen who joined the people of God were so numerous that they indeed took the place of the Jews.[69] Calvin repeatedly noted that we, as heathen, entered into Israel through Jesus Christ,[70] while continuing to speak of the same covenant in both the Old and New Testaments. We then became able, along with Israel, to take part in God's grace, salvation, and blessings, and to share the same hope, constituting a single church together with Israel. Calvin's frequent use of the word *church* in his interpretation of the Old Testament was indeed remarkable, and thus characterized Israel as the people of God, but this surely does not reduce the status of Israel. Calvin was able to shift between speaking of Israel as the people of God and as the church within his interpretation of the same psalm. For him, both terms meant the same thing.

What Did Calvin Mean by "Spiritual"?

The word *spiritual* played a major role in Calvin's Bible interpretation. The Baptists saw the Old Testament as being devoid of spiritual meaning. Cal-

---

68. Calvin derived his ideas about the different stages of church development from Gal. 4:1f. (CO 50,223-26).

69. See Commentary on Rom. 11:25 (CO 49,226) and *Inst.* II,11,12 (CO 2,338).

70. See, for example, Commentaries on Ps. 67:3 (CO 31,618) and Ps. 87:4-5 (CO 31,802-3).

vin countered this by emphasizing that the Old and New Testaments both made reference to the very same covenant. He characterized this covenant as one not only of mercy but also as a spiritual covenant, to which the patriarchs had belonged as well.[71]

In his use of the word *spiritual*, Calvin was influenced by Paul, who in 1 Corinthians 10 connects spiritual food and spiritual drink with the manna and the water from the rock that the Israelites received on their journey through the desert. Paul uses the word *spiritual* to describe one's relationship with Christ, who grants us spiritual and eternal life through the Spirit.[72]

Calvin explained that the covenant was a spiritual covenant from the very beginning, one that entailed the promise of spiritual and eternal life.[73] For Calvin, the unified body of the Old and New Testaments derived from God himself, who remained the same throughout the centuries of his interaction with his people; the salvation that he envisioned from the beginning has also always remained one and the same. Calvin described this salvation as the spiritual and eternal life, providing a means of overcoming sin and death.

Calvin often emphasized that the kingdom of God is a spiritual kingdom.[74] He often repeated, in this regard, that the Jews had lost from view the spiritual character of the kingdom.[75] They had sought the kingdom of Christ in this world, and thus limited their search to this world. When Calvin, by contrast, stressed the spiritual dominion of Christ, he seemed to remove the kingdom from this world. This was, however, not in fact the case. When he spoke of the spiritual character of the kingdom, he primarily meant to say that the kingdom of God is not a matter for us but instead one consigned to God himself. God's kingdom is thus closely linked to Jesus Christ, and takes on its form through Christ alone. It is thus of further significance that God, in building his kingdom, would go beyond the limitations of this world. God was up to facing the forces of sin and death, which had to be overcome if one was truly to begin with something new.

---

71. *Inst.* II,10,7 (CO 2,317).

72. See Commentary on 1 Cor. 10:1-4 (CO 49,451-56).

73. See *Inst.* II,10,13 (CO 2,322).

74. See, for example, *Inst.* II,15,3-5 (CO 2,363-66), Lecture on Jer. 31:12 and Jer. 33:15 (CO 38,659-62 and CO 39,67).

75. See, for example, Commentaries on Gen. 49:10 (CO 23,598) and Isa. 35:1 (CO 36,590), Sermons on Dan. 7:27 (CO 41,83-84) and Isa. 14:2 (SC II,36,24-27).

God is in Christ focused on the renewal of the entire creation. The chaos that was brought about by the forces of sin and death could then be overcome, and everything would become new again. Calvin added that we can hardly imagine what exactly this would entail, and that the prophets used imagery in their description of the new world that God would call into being, imagery that fit well into our scope of imagination. But these images are not sufficient to describe the salvation that is so vast that it will not fit within the framework of the transience that now hems in our lives. When Calvin tried to express what the images used by the prophets meant to say, he could say no more than that God's blessings will come to us from all sides. The whole earth and everything within it is to serve our well-being. Everything will become completely new again.[76]

Jesus Christ as the Goal of Scripture

In the aforementioned letter "To the Reader," Calvin referred to Jesus Christ as the goal of the Law and the essential content of the gospel. He added that the point of engaging with scripture was to recognize Christ, and that the slightest departure from this would be in error.[77] Calvin's words referred to scripture as a whole, including the Old Testament. One must, however, note that his interpretation of the Old Testament did not prominently feature mention of the name Christ. He instead focused his attention, time and again, on God. He wanted us to understand who God is for us, and that God is the same throughout scripture. Calvin's exegesis was theocentric, which did not, however, mean that Christ was not of importance as well. Calvin interpreted the Bible as a Christian for Christians. This applied to his interpretation of the Old Testament as well; God is always the God and Father of Jesus Christ, even when the name of Christ is not mentioned.

Calvin saw that it was important for us to know Jesus Christ in order to understand the Old Testament. Those who would not find Christ in the Old Testament would never come to recognize the truth, even if they

---

76. See, for example, Commentary on Isa. 30:25 (CO 36,525). Cf. Calvin's interpretation of Isa. 32:19; 35:5-6; 35:7, 9; and Isa. 61:5 and Isa. 65:13-14 (CO 36,554; 593-95; 597; CO 37,229; CO 37,426-27).

77. See CO 9,825.

should work their entire lives toward this understanding.[78] Christ was thus the goal and soul of the Law. Whatever the Law taught, stipulated, and promised was pointed toward Christ.[79] Calvin said that Moses and Elijah appeared on the mountain of the transfiguration as representatives of the Law and the Prophets. Their appearance thus meant for us that the Law and the Prophets would have no other goal than as Christ.[80] Without Christ as the sun of righteousness, the Law and the entire word of God would remain in the dark.[81]

In his interpretation of the New Testament, Calvin inquired several times into how the Old Testament testified to Christ.[82] He admitted that there were only a few passages in which Moses clearly denoted Christ. In later days, many took Calvin to task for developing a new interpretation of a number of Old Testament texts that had been directly connected to Christ in the early church, and for following Jewish exegetes too closely.[83]

In his answer to the question of how the Old Testament testified to Christ, Calvin demonstrated that he was guided by the texts of the New Testament, which revealed to him the links, in his opinion, between the Law and Prophets and the gospel. According to Calvin, there was no denying that God's covenant meant nothing without Christ. Christ was, for him, the intermediary of the covenant. This tie between God and humankind could only come to pass through him.[84] This meant that Christ was present in the Old Testament in accordance with his power and grace.[85] The entire temple service, moreover, was modeled after heaven and was established upon God's command (Exod. 25:40). Calvin sought to derive the significance of the ceremonies of the Law from his reading of the Epistle to the Hebrews.[86] He also often pointed to Christ as the foundation of all that God had promised in the Old Testament. When the prophets proclaimed

78. Commentary on John 5:39 (CO 47,125).

79. Commentary on Rom. 10:4 (CO 49,196).

80. Commentary on Matt. 17:3 (CO 45,486).

81. Commentary on 2 Cor. 3:15 (CO 50,45).

82. See Commentaries on John 5:46 (CO 47,129) and Luke 24:27 (CO 45,806).

83. See Steinmetz, "Judaizing Calvin," pp. 135-45, which focuses on the criticism of Calvin in Aegidius Hunnius's *Calvinus Iudaizans* (Wittenberg, 1593) and David Paraeus's reaction to this in his *Calvinus Orthodoxus* (Neustadt, 1595).

84. See, for example, *Inst.* II,10,2 (CO 2,314), *Inst.* I,13,26 (CO 2,113), and *Inst.* II,6 (CO 2,247-52).

85. Commentaries on John 8:58 (CO 47,215-16) and 1 Pet. 1:12 (CO 55,218).

86. Commentary on Exod. 26:1 (CO 24,415).

particular promises, they often underscored this by speaking also of the savior whom God would send. This was an allusion to Christ as the foundation of God's promises.[87] Calvin, time and again, drew a connection from David and his house to Jesus Christ, who was indeed a son of David. In the end, the main goal, Calvin said, was the fulfillment of the kingdom of Jesus Christ at the Last Judgment.

Translated from German by David Dichelle, Leipzig

87. See Commentaries on Isa. 7:14 (CO 36,155-56), Isa. 9:6 (CO 36,194), and Isa. 42:1-6 (CO 37,57-64); Lecture on Jer. 23:5-6 (CO 38,406) and Jer. 33:15 (CO 39,64). Cf. Commentary on 2 Cor. 1:20 (CO 50,22-24).

Calvin's Ecclesial Theology
and Human Salvation

Christopher L. Elwood

Writing in 1552 to Thomas Cranmer (1489-1556), the archbishop of Canterbury, John Calvin counted "among the chief evils of our time" the division of Christians from one another based on rancorous debate over doctrine and practice: "the members of the church being severed, the body lies bleeding." "So much does this concern me," he averred, "that could I be of any service, I would not begrudge crossing ten seas" to serve the goal of church unity.[1]

Calvin's theology, steeped as it was in catholic traditions of reflection on God, Christ, humanity, and the church, seemed well positioned for ecumenical outreach to bring peace to a church divided. Always sensitive to the charge that Protestant leaders discerned a narrow gospel, read only from their limited perspective, Calvin consistently recurred to ancient and medieval sources in outlining what Christians rightly confess. He not only drew extensively on the theological wealth of the Latin tradition stemming from the fifth-century North African theologian Augustine (354-430), but also engaged the Greek fathers, spanning the divide that for five centuries separated the Catholic West from the Orthodox traditions of the East. Yet despite commitments that embraced the catholic breadth of the Christian past, Calvin is often regarded, with some justice, as one who promoted discord in his present. His theology helped to form communities of Christians who saw themselves as set apart from their cultures and from the

1. CO 46,313-14.

"false Christians" who were their neighbors. In some regions of Europe in the late sixteenth and early seventeenth centuries, Calvinism, the legacy of thought stemming from his reflection and practice, itself came to be equated with a violent and revolutionary politics that rent the social fabric and overturned civil order.

What are we to make of this apparent contradiction between peaceful aims and contentious outcomes? Was Calvin responsible for the divisions to which his writings gave rise? We may discover a clue in elements of Calvin's own theology — particularly in his treatment of the central role of scripture in ordering communal and individual, embodied living — and in the popular translations of his insights in the fractured political and religious world of sixteenth-century France.

Hearing the Shepherd's Voice

Calvin's writings for the church of his time concerned chiefly the quest for a truth — and thus a means of salvation — to which one might reliably adhere, a quest at the center of Reformation-era debates. In 1539, when he responded to a letter Jacopo Sadoleto (1477-1547), the bishop of Carpentras, had written to the people of Geneva, inviting them to return to the bosom of the Roman Church, Calvin addressed questions that nagged at the conscience of virtually every Protestant of his day: Had those who joined the movement for Protestant reform departed from the truth by their separation from the apostolic church? Where was truth to be found if not in this ancient body, founded on Jesus Christ's own institution and guided by the Holy Spirit, this vessel in which faith was kept pure amid the storms of error? In answer to Sadoleto's challenge, Calvin insisted that truth depended not at all on conformity with the hierarchical church and its teachings, but rather on something he considered distinct from church traditions: God's own teachings, conveyed to faithful persons through scripture. Christ said explicitly, said Calvin, "that those who are of God hear the word of God — that his sheep are those which recognize his voice as that of their shepherd." Attending to this voice meant breaking with those "who would sink and bury the word of God, so that they may make room for their own falsehoods." But such a break was not a departure from the church, properly understood. The true church treats God's word "as the touchstone by which she tests all doctrines." Far from identifying the church with an ecclesiastical hierarchy, Calvin proposed an alternative catholicism, according to which the church is "the society of all the saints, a society which, spread over the whole world and existing in all ages, yet bound together by the one doctrine and the one Spirit of Christ, cultivates and observes unity of faith and brotherly concord."[2]

In subordinating the church to God's message in scripture, Calvin avoided a narrow sectarianism. While the church's tradition was no longer normative, its most reliable contributors were worthy of attention. He eagerly cited the church fathers in support of his positions: "If the contest were to be determined by patristic authority, the tide of victory — to put it very modestly — would turn to our side."[3] The contest for the truth, however, depended on fidelity to another source, and one less amenable to institutional control. Calvin promised the liberation of Christian witness from the tyranny of church dogma, for now scripture, rather than authorized church teaching, would be "the touchstone by which the church tests all doctrines."[4]

Would the church, cut free from its institutional moorings and founded only on its faithfulness to "the one doctrine of Christ," remain, as Calvin hoped, bound together by the Spirit? There was a certain risk involved in dispensing with the alignment of authorities for which Sadoleto and various others of Calvin's opponents argued. The model of a church of unerring authority, requiring the laity's submission to its ancient consensus, provided firmer grounds for peace and unity than did Calvin's call to listen to the word of God as the voice of the shepherd. Calvin's model placed a heavy burden on the Christian's encounter with the biblical word. He trusted that this encounter would, in the right circumstances, yield authentic understanding of divine truth and an interpretation that all Christian readers and hearers would share. As it turns out, this was a naïve trust.

Preaching the Word

As a second-generation reformer, Calvin was not quite as susceptible to what David Steinmetz has called the "exegetical optimism" of the Refor-

---

2. Responsio ad Sadoleti epistolam: OS I,465.
3. Praefatio ad christianissimum regem Franciae: OS I,27.
4. Responsio ad Sadoleti epistolam: OS I,465-66.

mation's first generation of Protestants.[5] While the idea was attractive, experience had proved that direct access to the biblical text would not, by itself, lead all Christians to a common understanding of the Bible's message. Not everyone came to the text prepared to discern its authentic meaning. Bitter disagreements over what the Bible said and how it directed Christian practice occurred frequently enough that Calvin devoted most of his energy to devising means to ensure that scripture would be understood correctly. If the tools for a consistently reliable exposition of the Bible could be provided, thought Calvin, then churches could be formed around this correct, shared understanding. In other words, one needed a context to secure a productive encounter of Christians with God's message. This context, and the central feature of Calvin's project, was supplied by the preaching of the word.

In Geneva, as in many Reformed communities, going regularly to worship — or, as it was called, "attendance at sermons" — was not a matter left to individual choice. Requiring the laity not only to turn up but to pay close attention, Protestant reformers assigned to the sermon a very prominent place. Leaders of church and civil society alike sought to ensure that the benefits of preaching were shared by all the community's members.

Calvin's own view was that preaching was the chief way in which God speaks to the church and its members. At first blush, the claim sounds ridiculous. How can the words of a fallible, human preacher be equated with God's own speaking? Calvin was sufficiently well acquainted with less-than-adequate preaching to have grasped the challenge of his view. Certainly, preachers regularly fail in the preaching task. But their failure stems from inattention to their basic charge, which is to convey to hearers what God says in scripture. Preachers "ought not be adding anything new to the text, but ought to be providing a more ample exposition that would confirm our understanding of God's teachings."[6] The preacher's own speculations were to be excluded, but this did not mean that there was to be nothing contributed by the preacher. The preacher should express the text's liveliness, taking a cue from the emotional content of the message, whether the sternness of admonition and correction or the sweetness and gentleness of consolation. This was not, as Calvin saw it, so much a creative human contribution to the preaching moment as it was God's use of the preacher as God's "hands and

---

5. Steinmetz, *Luther in Context,* pp. 96-97.
6. Sermons sur le Livre de Michée: SC V,89-90.

instruments."[7] When this occurs, we experience genuine preaching, an act that is itself, in some sense, the word of God — God's own speaking. This event is not only informative; it is transformational. Through the words of the preacher God is graciously redeeming the congregation.

In this high view of preaching, Calvin supplied a crucial critical principle for those listening to the sermon: "whenever we hear anything, we have [in scripture] a basis for inquiring whether God has spoken it or not."[8] This encouragement of laypersons to pay attention and to test the preacher's veracity assumes a community of hearers who, like their preachers, are sufficiently well versed in scripture to be able to render such judgments. Calvin labored in Geneva to help build such a community through mandatory catechism classes and the teaching of basic elements of Protestant devotion, as well as through practices of church discipline designed to care pastorally for both bodies and souls. He labored also on behalf of theological education to supply ministers with the tools necessary to understand scripture rightly. Not only the founding of Geneva's Academy (in 1559) but also his theological writings — the *Institutes of the Christian Religion* and his many biblical commentaries — were key elements of this concerted effort to provide for a learned ministry that could directly and competently engage God's message conveyed in scripture.

Lifting Our Hearts on High

In his own reading and exposition of scripture, Calvin discerned a great difference between a majestic God and an originally good, but presently corrupt, creation. Many of Calvin's sermons emphasize this theme. Indeed, the prayer that characteristically closed his sermons urged the congregation to acknowledge both the immense distance between God and ourselves and the true presence of God's grace that overcomes this distance and heals human brokenness: "We bow ourselves before the majesty of our good God, in acknowledgment of our offenses, asking that He may make us so feel them that, being cast down in ourselves, we may be lifted up by the grace of our Lord, Jesus Christ."[9]

---

7. Sermons sur le Livre de Deuteronomie: CO 26,67.
8. Sermons sur le Livre de Michée: SC V,90.
9. Sermons sur le Livre d'Esaïe: SC II,297.

Underlining God's majesty and our need for grace accomplished two quite necessary things, in Calvin's view. It challenged a general human tendency to reduce God to the limits of the finite imagination, on the one hand, and, on the other, it rejected the claim that our well-being can be achieved through humanly devised means of self-improvement. These two elements came together, for Calvin, in the paradigmatic sin of idolatry. Humans, in other words, are all too eager to construct a manageable God who will provide them with avenues of salvation to suit their own desires. Idolatry was what Calvin discerned, in his own day, in the popular religious fascination with supposed presences of the divine in material things. Relics of Christ and the saints were sought out for religious benefit, as means of securing merit and paving a path back to God. "Instead of seeking Jesus Christ in his word, in the sacraments, and in spiritual gifts," complained Calvin, "the world, as is its wont, clung to his garments, vests, and swaddling clothes."[10] Devotion that centered on physical things Calvin regarded as contrary to biblical teaching. It equated the transcendent God with God's own creation and confused human religion with the spiritual worship God ordains. In his view, it amounted to a rejection of God's work of grace in Christ.

Opposing false worship required constant attention to our inclination toward idolatry, and especially the equation of God with created matter. So not only was the theme of divine transcendence and majesty a key feature of Calvin's preaching; it came to underlie all elements of worship, including the celebration of the sacraments. The sacrament of the Eucharist, or the Holy Supper as the Reformed characteristically called it, tended especially to encourage the idolatrous imagination, thought Calvin, because of the traditional and popular belief that, in the priest's celebration, Christ came to be bodily "enclosed under the corruptible elements" of the bread and the wine.[11] This was not what Jesus intended in instituting the sacrament, Calvin claimed; yet Jesus' own words of institution, "This is my body . . . this is my blood" (Matt. 26:26-28), seemed to suggest some sort of equation of Christ with the sacramental elements. How were Christians to make sense of this? Was belief in the real presence of Christ in the Eucharist consistent with scriptural teaching? Was venerating the sacrament an ex-

---

10. *Advertissement tresutile du grand proffit qui reviendroit à la chrestienté s'il se faisoit inventaire des reliques:* CO 6,409.

11. *Petit traicté de la saincte Cene:* OS I,530.

pression of authentic Christian piety or an expression of the sin of idolatry? In Calvin's own lifetime, questions such as these ran right through the center of the theological arguments that divided Christians from one another and defined distinct, and frequently mutually hostile, Christian churches.

Calvin's attempts to express a theology of Christ's presence in the Supper influenced profoundly the Reformed Protestant churches of France, the Swiss cities, the Netherlands, Scotland, and a variety of other churches that trace their lineage to Calvin's own branch of the sixteenth-century Reformation. The centerpiece of his view was his contention that in the Eucharist, as indeed in every sacramental observance, one encounters two things that must never be confused: the sign (comprising, in the case of the Eucharist, the bread and the wine) and the thing signified (Christ's body). While the sign is earthly, Christ's body has ascended to heaven. Yet God's power is such that through the gift of faith, the Holy Spirit is able to unite believers on earth with their heavenly Savior. With this interpretation, Calvin rejected the view that had dominated recent theological tradition, according to which communion between believers and Christ is effected by Christ's presence *in* the signs. In Calvin's preferred image — what we might call a transcendentist image — the faithful are raised up, by faith, to heaven, there to partake of Christ. The earthly signs, then, are not the bearers of divine presence or power; they are instruments through which God's transcendent power works upon the hearts and minds of the people. This understanding of communion was transmitted every time a Reformed congregation celebrated the sacrament, when the minister admonished all present,

> Let us raise our spirits and our hearts on high, where Jesus Christ is in the glory of the Father. . . . Let us not tarry with these earthly and corruptible elements which we see with the eye and touch with the hand, to seek him there, as if he were enclosed in the bread and the wine. For only then will our souls be disposed to be nourished and quickened by his substance when they are so lifted up above all earthly things to attain even unto heaven and to enter into the kingdom of God where he dwells.[12]

If Christ is not, in fact, "enclosed in the bread and the wine," Christians who regard the sacramental elements themselves as the media of

12. La Forme des prieres et chantz ecclesiastiques: OS II,48.

God's presence, and who honor or venerate them, are engaging in idolatry. Only by recognizing the instrumental character of the signs and seeking Christ's presence above, can they overcome this error and, through the aid of God's Spirit, open the door to an authentic participation in the means of grace Christ bequeathed to the community of the faithful.

This transcendentist and instrumental account of the sacrament, insisted Calvin, was no more or less than what scripture itself conveyed. It reflected his own convictions regarding the Bible's testimony to God's majesty, our creaturely incapacity, and our need to rely entirely on God's grace and God's own redeeming activity for salvation. Clearly, this was not the only way to read the biblical witness, as the diversity of Reformation-era positions on the Bible and the sacrament attest. But Calvin was convinced that this way of thinking about the relation of divine and human, heaven and earth, and of God's presence and power, was required by the teaching of scripture. Of course, Calvin had drawn on nonbiblical terms, using traditions of theological and philosophical reflection, especially in his construal of the sign/signified distinction. One could use these legitimately, he argued, as long as the aim and effect was to "conscientiously and faithfully serve the truth of scripture itself."[13]

Distinguishing Body and Soul

Through his vigorous arguments for his own particular reading of this sacramental core of Christian worship — conveyed both in liturgy and in numerous popular writings — Calvin gained many adherents to his view, giving shape to a distinctive theological outlook on Christian faith and life. An especially important component of that outlook concerned the question of how we are to understand the human self — and especially the relation of body and soul. On this question, the transcendentist and instrumental understanding that surfaced in Calvin's account of the Eucharist played a key role.

Calvin argued that the soul was the center of the human personality. To confuse the soul, the element of the person that bears the image of God, with the body, which does not, is "to mingle heaven and earth." The soul is "the immortal essence" of the human person, which does not die. The

13. *Inst.* I,13,3: OS III,112.

body, by contrast, dies and decays. While the body is certainly a good creation, it is nonetheless "a frail hut" for the soul. The soul is the directing agent of the body. The body, then, must be an instrument that the soul rules; when this order is not respected, when bodily urges begin to rule the self, we see the effects of humanity's inherited corruption and fallenness.[14] On human embodiment as on the sacraments, Calvin tried to put the material and tangible in its proper place. Just as the heavenly body of Christ demands priority over the "earthly and corruptible elements" in the celebration of the Supper, when one attends to who one is as a human being, the soul must be recognized as having priority over, and freedom from, the body, which is merely its earthly vehicle.

From the perspective of the history of Christian ideas, stressing a hierarchy of soul and body was hardly an innovation. Christian Platonists, including the influential Augustine, gave a similar account of the soul-body relation. The significance of Calvin's account of the self lies not in its novelty, but rather in the use to which it was put in Calvin's lifetime by a primary target audience: Reformed Christians in Calvin's native France living under government-sponsored persecution. An example of this use can be seen in the account of Jean Morel (ca. 1538-1559), a French Protestant arrested in 1558, charged with heresy, and closely interrogated before his execution. Morel, like many in his position, was urged to renounce his errors and return to the Catholic faith. His chief error, in his interrogators' eyes, was a view of the sacrament he had learned from the reformer of Geneva. The Holy Supper, he had said, consists in two things, "one heavenly, the other earthly, . . . [and] just as our body receives the earthly, that is the bread, so also our soul receives spiritually the truth, which is the flesh and blood [of Jesus Christ]."[15] Morel would not withdraw this confession, even under the threat of death. Why did he remain defiant? The reason he supplied reflected, again, the influence of Calvin: "I have hardly any more days to live. As for my soul, I have good need to care for it; for it is such a precious thing that even though our body may be the temple of the Holy Spirit, so it is that our Lord places as great a difference between the body and the soul as there is between a body and its clothing."[16]

---

14. *Inst.* I,15,2-6; OS III,174-84; Commentarii in secundam epistolam ad Corinthios (2 Cor. 5:1): CO 50,60-61.

15. Crespin, *Histoire des Martyrs,* vol. 2, p. 627.

16. Crespin, *Histoire des Martyrs,* vol. 2, p. 627.

Whether speaking of the Eucharist or reflecting on human embodiment, Morel was able to convey the basic difference between heaven and earth, Christ and bread, soul and body — in precisely the way Calvin had outlined in his own reading of scripture.

Witnessing in the Body

By the 1550s, Calvin's theology of the word of God, an attempt to allow for an authentic reading of scripture and to fashion a "society of all the saints, . . . spread over the whole world," had become an engine supporting embattled communities of Protestants resisting the "idolatry" of a state-sanctioned, Catholic religion. The power of Calvin's outlook was vividly depicted in the stories of active resistance, like those of the martyr Jean Morel, gathered from across France by Calvin's friend and colleague, the printer and author Jean Crespin (ca. 1520-1572). Crespin's tales recounted the exemplary words and deeds of the Protestants who witnessed boldly to their faith, paying with their lives for the testimony rendered. The aim of publishing the "History of the Martyrs" was, in large measure, to console and to strengthen the resolve of Calvinist communities living "under the cross" of persecution. But the martyrs' stories also served to instruct. By offering a narrative portrait of the Christian body empowered by divine grace to offer courageous resistance to unjust power, they sought to direct not just the theological reflection of Christians but their embodied practice as well.

These stories attended closely to bodies — to the martyrs' appearance, their gestures and physical attitudes, as well as to their verbal testimony to the character of bodily witness. The martyr's body and its movement radiated confidence and courage, despite the threat and the actual application of physical pain. In circumstances likely to inspire terror, Tavrin Gravelle, a young Protestant arrested in 1558, approached his execution with "a smiling face and one of good color."[17] Both he and his older companion, Nicolas Clinet, advanced boldly to the site of their final punishment with heads held high, looking constantly up, toward the sky. The pain of torture and execution caused little concern for these exemplars of faith. The martyrs, in fact, regularly refused the small mercies authorities

---

17. Crespin, *Histoire des Martyrs,* vol. 2, p. 567.

occasionally offered to relieve the suffering of execution. For example, Marguerite le Riche, executed in 1559, rejected an offer to be strangled before being put to the stake. The most striking account of voluntary bodily suffering was supplied by the young widow known as the Damoiselle de Graveron, who responded to the news that her tongue would be cut out before her execution by presenting her tongue "cheerfully" and without argument. "Since I do not pity my body," she said, "should I pity my tongue?"[18] Because she was firm in conviction and constant in witnessing to her faith, the young woman's appearance called for special comment. Her countenance never changed as she approached death with radiant face, upright stance, modeling for all who observed her the joy of preparing to meet her Savior in heaven.

From these stories, which circulated widely in France in the middle and late sixteenth century, Protestant readers and hearers absorbed an understanding of embodied living and witness for which Calvin had argued strenuously. Through these models of Christian faithfulness, one could clearly see the body subordinated to the ruling of the soul, as ought to happen in the human self rightly constituted. But the bodily component of the martyr also served as an instrument of God's grace. Calvin supplied the necessary theological reflection on this particular phenomenon. The power of the martyr's witness could not have been self-produced, he thought. The evidence for this was abundantly supplied in the numerous accounts of female martyrs. Women, Calvin insisted, were exceedingly frail — even more frail than men. Their "natural constitution" did not suit them well for bold resistance. How, then, can we make sense of the witness of women who showed exemplary courage in the face of torture? Only the supernatural power of God's grace can explain this ability: "God who works in frail vessels, knows well how to display his strength in the infirmity of his own." This was the great value of the accounts of women martyrs. Their strength was clearly not their own, not naturally derived; thus they demonstrated the truth of Paul's assertion in 1 Corinthians 1:27 that "God chose what is foolish in the world to shame the wise; God chose what is weak in the world to shame the strong."[19]

Calvin sought to encourage steadfast allegiance to the Reformed faith in France during a time of persecution, even as many — in a variety

18. Crespin, *Histoire des Martyrs,* vol. 2, p. 567.
19. CO 16,632-33.

of hostile contexts — argued that Christians could compromise with the religious culture of their surrounding environment. The suggestion that one could conform outwardly to erroneous, but obligatory, religious practices while remaining secretly faithful to scripture and its mandates for the true worship of God posed a threat to Calvin's understanding of the nature of the true church and faithful Christian witness. Calvin consistently rejected this argument, presented by persons he labeled "Nicodemites" (after Nicodemus, who would visit Christ only under the cover of darkness). The bodies of Christians, he insisted, must reflect in authentic fashion the interior condition of the soul; true worship must conform outward practice to the inward devotion of heart and mind. In his view, Christians could never compromise with idolatry. There could be no productive relation between the true church founded on scripture and the false church whose teaching and practice repudiated it.

For Calvin, then, the martyrs' witness was the perfect antidote to the call for compromise. Their refusal to conform to idolatry reflected biblical models and mandates. Like the prototypical Christian martyr, St. Stephen, they displayed a bodily radiance and majesty that indicated the presence and transfiguring power of the Holy Spirit (Acts 6:15). Like Stephen, also, they understood what rank to assign to body and what to soul. Jesus' own words — "Do not fear those who kill the body but cannot kill the soul; rather fear him who can destroy both soul and body in hell" (Matt. 10:28) — established the order clearly enough. These words also suggested to Calvin the perilous condition of sinful human beings when they appraise too highly "this shadowy life of the body." This incorrect appraisal is at the heart of the desire for compromise, the desire to preserve the body at any cost. The cost, however, is far too dear, as anyone will see who recognizes that they "have been given immortal souls, which being *under the judgment of God alone,* do not come under the authority of men."[20]

Distinguishing body and soul was then a key feature of maintaining faithful Christian witness, in Calvin's view. In order to resist the forces of violence, Christians had to attend to the conviction expressed in the liturgy of the Lord's Supper: "only then will our souls be disposed to be nourished and quickened by [Christ's] substance when they are so lifted up above all earthly things to attain even unto heaven." This metaphorical

---

20. Harmonia ex tribus Evangelistis composita (Matt. 10:28): CO 45,288-89 (emphasis added).

lifting up of the soul was, in Calvin's view, rather like Stephen's and the contemporary martyrs' gaze into the heavens (Acts 7:55-56), as though to discern Christ seated at God's right hand. There, in heaven, was the soul's true home; its home was not on earth, "where," said Calvin, "there is nothing but death before his eyes."[21]

Was this simple otherworldliness? Apparently not. Calvin did not challenge the goodness of embodied living, nor did he suggest Christians sever the social bonds that tied them to city, town, or nation. But his reflections on embodied witness — which pulled apart soul and body, heaven and earth — tended also to emphasize a critical distinction between the divine source of all life and the earthly powers that claimed temporal authority. This was a crucial development in a time when questions about who might legitimately claim political and spiritual allegiance were hotly debated. Calvin claimed that God alone rules the soul. The legitimate power of secular government extends only to bodies. What ought one to do when the temporal power allies itself with the power of the Catholic Church, as had occurred in France, and thus claims authority over the soul and its devotion to God? Earth cannot be confused with heaven; and Christians must know where their ultimate allegiance lies. Therefore, when Caesar's tribute required a denial of faith, open but nonviolent resistance was the only course — in Calvin's words, "we must suffer anything rather than turn aside from God's holy word."[22]

Seeking Peace, Finding Conflict

Calvin's insistence in 1539 that genuine Christian experience was founded on hearing the Divine Shepherd's voice was not, at the time, presented as a claim of a distinct ecclesial or political identity. He genuinely believed that careful attention to God's word in scripture would provide the basis for a united Christian community. Neither a fracture of the church nor a rending of the body politic was ever his goal. "God is not the God of division, but of peace," he asserted, and those who seek to follow God must also have peace as their goal.[23] On the other hand, he knew that asserting the

21. Commentariorum in Acta Apostolorum, liber I (Acts 7:55): CO 48,167.
22. *Inst.* IV,20,32.
23. Praefatio ad christianissimum regem Franciae: OS I,35.

authority of scripture would inevitably separate Protestants from Catholics, for whom the structure of authority was construed rather differently. Some degree of division was inevitable; but the quest for the truth in God's own speaking would not allow a tempering of the message for the goal of a false peace.

Toward the end of his life, the fissures of church and society to which Calvin's own teachings had contributed were deep and widening. Reformed and Lutheran Protestants were at theological loggerheads. Calvinists in France and elsewhere in Europe adopted the stance of a political opposition. Revolution and civil war were the seemingly inevitable consequences. Although Calvin's theology was not the only factor engineering these divisions, it played a critical role.

In some ways, the chronological suggestion is misleading. Calvin's theology did not begin with peace and end with war. Rather, the tension between concord and discord, unity and division, was apparent right at the start, evident in his earliest readings of the Bible's narratives. These readings show his inclination in both catholic and radical directions (although these were not his terms). The catholic leaning was apparent in his conviction that God spoke to humanity across a broad history, that this speaking spanned territory of great geographic and cultural diversity, that this word covered every aspect of human experience, and that God's power always ruled the forces of history. From the prophetic traditions of scripture Calvin derived a radical orientation: the present world was not as it should be, what was given in embodied living required God's transformative reordering, God's speaking addressed particular communities and called them to live into God's reformation of life. For Calvin's followers, the catholic dimension of his teaching tended to assure them that God's good aims would always prevail in history. But the radical dimension would make them impatient with human resistance to those good aims. Depending on which inclination predominated, they might either settle down in history, more or less content with the present state of affairs, or struggle against the prevailing currents, convinced that God intends more than is presently given in a broken world. Calvin's successors have reflected the tension in his own thinking with scripture.

For an age such as ours, one in desperate need of avenues for cross-confessional and interreligious understanding for the sake of peace and genuine security, the sixteenth-century outcomes of Calvin's reforming project will appear depressing. If we are searching for theological resources from the past to address present needs, surely a more irenic example would suit us better!

Perhaps. On the other hand, it may be that Calvin's persistent quest for a truth that transcends particular institutional apprehensions and his determined seeking for a faithful response to the divine leading is an example not to be overlooked. If we seek unities that may bind the human family together — or, alternatively, some common space in which differences may be examined and better understood — strategies of peacemaking that avoid the particular claims of our traditions will serve us poorly. We may find a better way in Calvin's insistence that we honestly seek, in and through the sources out of which we live, to discern together the truth that sets us all free, bringing the flourishing of life that is creation's true goal.

Election and Predestination

Christian Link

The reality of election as addressed in the Bible has been termed the "most radical theological statement" ever conceived, "the strongest of all thinkable counterstatements to the postulate of the senselessness of the world and the godlessness of humanity."[1] It explains and provides a foundation for the certainty that the ebb and flow of world history includes within it a particular history of humans with God, in deriving the question "Who is *our* God?" not from major philosophical- or worldview-related premises, but from the experience of a particular *history,* the history of Israel, in which a certainty was expressed for the first time: "And I will be your God, and you shall be my people" (Lev. 26:12). Viewed in this light, this election forms a part of God's reality, "which is a reality not apart from but in this decision," as Karl Barth (1886-1968) expressed it.[2] This was what Calvin, like no other before him, impressed upon later generations in developing his doctrine of predestination — a term that in itself took this matter to a new level.

In his *Institutes* of 1536, Calvin inquires into the foundation laid "in Christ," which Paul (1 Cor. 3:11) establishes as the basis of the Christian congregation and its doctrine: "Is it that Jesus Christ was the beginning of our salvation? Is it that he opened the way when he merited for us occasion for meriting?" The response to this is "Certainly not. But, it is that 'he [God] has chosen us in him' from eternity 'before the foundation of the

1. Ritschl, *Logik,* p. 163.
2. Barth, *Church Dogmatics,* II/2, 6.

105

world' through no merit of our own, 'but according to the purpose of divine pleasure.' . . . It is that we have been adopted unto him as sons and heirs by the Father."[3] Only through this election do we stand on the foundation that must be accountable for our faith. Only then does it become certain that our salvation "rests on a sure and solid bed, that, even if the whole fabric of the world were to fall, it itself could not tumble and fall."[4]

Calvin posed this question of election within the context of the discussion of the church, the place in which belief takes on its concrete form and in which it must prevail. One must not forget this in the course of often difficult strains of thought. When God calls people into his congregation, as Calvin follows the argumentation of the Epistle to the Ephesians (Eph. 1:3-14), he introduces "nothing but his eternal election" into the historical sphere.[5] The church — in a virtually defining description reminiscent of Augustine — is the "people of the chosen God" or, as one recent interpreter put it, "the invisible unity of those chosen in Christ."[6] In this way, the doctrine of predestination appears in its first refined form in the 1536 *Institutes* as the "deep level of Calvinist doctrine of the church." This "ecclesiological" view entered into the final major revision in 1559 as well: God's "hidden election" is the foundation of the church[7] and that which it represents for us, that is, the certainty of justification, our status as sons and daughters of God, and hope for a life in the future world — fruits that can only grow in this soil. This particular growth is, however, the great issue (and problem!) of today's visible church. Calvin decisively cleared the way forward in this regard, for Reformed Protestantism in particular. Indeed, election seeks to direct Christians to the goal of sanctification, that is, "a true visible, holy community," or the courage to take "much more energetic steps . . . than we moderns do who shrink back from what he discovered [in terms of theology]."[8] Adversely, however — and this is his se-

---

3. OS I,63. In this essay, the quotations from the *Institutes* (1536, 1559) refer to the following translations: *Institutes of the Christian Religion, 1536 Edition*, trans. F. L. Battles (Grand Rapids, 1995), and *Institutes of the Christian Religion (1559)*, trans. F. L. Battles (Philadelphia/London, 1960).

4. OS I,87.

5. OS I,87.

6. Ganoczy, *Ecclesia ministrans*, p. 147.

7. *Inst.* III,21,1 (OS IV,370,5) and IV,1,2 (OS V,4,1).

8. Barth, *Theology of John Calvin*, pp. 179-80, cf. *Inst.* III,23,12: "electionis scopus est vitae sanctimonia" (OS IV,406,26) and similar passages.

cret *cantus firmus* — election liberates us with regard to the concern that it is our task to guarantee the maintenance of the church. Just as Elijah hears in 1 Kings 19:18 — "Yet I will leave seven thousand in Israel" — Calvin establishes in the shadow of the persecution suffered by the Huguenots that God "preserves his Church even in times of darkness."[9]

And yet this certainty — which Max Weber (1864-1920) referred to as the "extreme inhumanity" of this doctrine,[10] a reference that echoes to this day — leads to a very problematic consequence. We are thus confronted with the problem of predestination, which has been linked with the question of election since the Latin Vulgate translation of the Epistle to the Romans 8:29f. I do speak here of a problem as the term "*pre*destination" threatens to move this divine decision into "prehistoric" obscurity. When one understands this term in accordance with the dogmatic mainstream referring to Ephesians 1:4 ("before the foundation of the world") as a condition before the time for all events within time, the crucial ties in the Old Testament that bind God to human history unravel. Calvin believed, in the footsteps of Paul (Rom. 9:11), that *pre-* had to be understood in this way, stating: "We call predestination God's eternal decree *(decretum),* by which he compacted with himself what he willed to become of each man. For all are not created in equal conditions *(conditio),* rather, eternal life is *fore*ordained for some, eternal damnation for others."[11]

Calvin was well aware of the horrible nature of this view. He spoke directly of a "dreadful decree,"[12] not shying from the consequences of deriving the "fall of the first man" from God's decision *(dispensatio).*[13] It would, however, be incorrect to see Calvin as the originator of these problems. Nearly all the difficulties posed to us in the final 1559 version of his doctrine in the *Institutes* could be found previously in a similar form in the writings of Augustine and Luther, with roots hearkening back to Paul. Calvin indeed reviewed his own ideas using Paul's Epistle to the Romans as a comparison, continuing this tradition forward to a virtually unerring conclusion. It is all

9. *Inst.* IV,1,2 (OS V,4,17f.).

10. Weber, *Protestant Ethic,* p. 104.

11. *Inst.* III,21,5 (OS IV,374,10-15).

12. *Inst.* III,23,7: *"decretum horribile"* with the explanation "that God foreknew what end man was to have before he created him, and consequently foreknew because he so ordained by his decree" (OS IV,401,28).

13. OS IV,402,2 with reference to Augustine, *De correptione et gratia* 10,27 (Migne PL 44,932).

the more remarkable that, as a preacher to his congregation, Calvin redirected these ideas, orienting them toward Christ, the basis of our salvation. Just as in the *Institutes,* predestination is depicted here as an *electio in Christo* in a way reflecting what election has been from the very beginning: a reason for joyous certainty. Challenged by his opponents, Calvin grappled with the problem of predestination many times. This began in his *Institutes* of 1536 within the context of the doctrine of the church, from which he surprisingly retreats nearly fully in later writings. He continued in his Commentary on the Epistle to the Romans (1539), and in a series of sermons,[14] the arguments of which were summarized in his treatise *Concerning the Eternal Predestination of God* (Consensus Genevensis, 1552)[15] and finally in the didactic summary of the 1559 *Institutes* (III,21-24). These writings feature recurring themes such as an emphatic reference to the inscrutable counsel of God, a warning not to plunge into his depths, the separation of the elected from the condemned, and the remembrance of Christ, in whom we are to look as in a mirror reflecting the secret of our election. While Calvin did not "teach" anything fundamentally different in his systematic tractates and sermons, each of these writings did reveal a particular perspective on the problem of predestination.

A Dialogue with Paul

Just as his most important dogmatic decisions were made within and in reference to his exegetic work, so too did Calvin develop his doctrine of predestination in a dialogue with Paul. The didactic renderings of his 1559 *Institutes* draw from Calvin's Commentary on the Epistle to the Romans, which appeared first in Strasbourg in 1540 and later in two comprehen-

14. Particularly the doctrinal sermon to close the Bolsec controversy: *Congrégation sur l'élection éternelle de Dieu,* 1551 (CO 8,93-118; *Congregation on Eternal Election*), and the sermon series on Gen. 25-27: Treze sermons traitans de l'Election gratuite de Dieu en Jacob, et de la Reiection en Esau (CO 58/59,31-59), and Sermons sur l'Epistre aux Ephesiens (CO 51,269-310).

15. *De aeterna Dei praedestinatione. Consensus Pastorum Geneviensis ecclesiae* (CO 8,249-366; English: *Concerning the Eternal Predestination of God* by John Calvin, trans. and with an introduction by J. K. S. Reid [Louisville, 1997]). This deals with the exceptions to human freedom of will and human abilities brought forward by the Utrecht archdeacon, Albertus Pighius.

sively revised editions in 1551 and 1556. The main terms used — *election, vocation,* and above all divine *purpose* — all derived from Paul. Calvin allowed himself to be drawn into the text of Romans and its stream of thought, and did not just search for support for his own inflexible dogmatic ideas.[16]

Just like the other reformers, Calvin consistently interpreted Romans concerning the question of justification, which he considered to be decisive *(quaestio principalis),* particularly in chapters 9 through 11, which concern the drama of Israel so important to the discussion of predestination: How is it possible that, of all people, the "original heirs and protectors of the covenant" could come out in opposition to Christ? Paul's answer, that "not all Israelites truly belong to Israel" (Rom. 9:6), brings him to the topic of God's election, which is "to regard as the source of this whole matter" (p. 9):[17] one must differentiate between physical and spiritual successors as expressed a few verses later in Romans 9:13: "I have loved Jacob but I have hated Esau." And this inscrutable decision for the younger brother indeed came about even *before* the twins were born (Rom. 9:11); as no reason for it was to materialize later in the lives of the brothers, the decision was evidently made "before all time." Calvin understands, as did Paul, that in addition to the general election, on the basis of which the entire nation of Israel remains the "inheritance and the peculiar people of God" (p. 197) — God indeed never rescinded his covenant! — there is a second "hidden" election, "which is restricted to a part of the nation only" (p. 198), and which consequently later steers our theological focus completely toward the problem of the individual.

Why does God act in this way? Calvin is more adamant about this than perhaps even the Epistle to the Romans is itself. Paul seeks to exclude any consideration of works: "Merits are of no avail here" (p. 201). Nor can one say that God has foreseen them.[18] Nobody should therefore believe that those chosen are elected because they have "in any way won for themselves the favor of God" (p. 205). These are all major tenets of the doctrine

16. Cf. Lindemann, "Erwählt vor Grundlegung der Welt," pp. 41-67.

17. The page numbers in parentheses refer to the *Commentary on The Epistles of Paul the Apostle to the Romans,* trans. Ross Mackenzie, in *Calvin's New Testament Commentaries,* vol. 8, pp. 1-328.

18. Commentary on Rom. 9:11 (200; 201). A surprising rebuke of Augustine, who states: "praedestinasse hoc est *praescisse,* quod fuerit ipse [homo] facturus" (*De dono perseverantiae* 18; Migne PL 45,1023), and of the Catholic tradition.

of justification, and Calvin summarizes his argumentation with the statement that Israel "has not obtained the true method of justification" (p. 217).[19] This was in fact God's pure grace, which becomes visible and effective through the process of election. Election — and Calvin adheres to this even in his seemingly most cutting statements — is an election in grace. Justification is thus systematically returned to the moment of election, where it has its strongest basis.[20]

This election is thus rooted in God's grace, and Calvin, following Paul (Rom. 9:11), refines this argument by introducing the term *purpose (propositum)*, which plays a crucial role in all of his major tractates. He writes of God's "eternal counsel" (p. 180), using, however, more formal lines of reasoning that provide the term *predestination* with its precise meaning and strength. This purpose indeed "depends on God's good pleasure *(beneplacitum)*, because in adopting those whom He would, God had no foreknowledge of anything outside Himself, but simply marked out those whom He had purposed to elect" (p. 181). This formal description particularly emphasizes "the will of God" (*arbitrium;* p. 208) or "His own voluntary purpose" (p. 204), that is, a full independence from all other sources, and from human thoughts of justification in particular. The word *predestine (praedestinare)* refers hence, with regard to God's freedom, to "the circumstances of the present passage" (p. 181) and "does not refer to election, but to that purpose or decree of God" (p. 181). Calvin thus differentiates between predestination and election. The term *predestination,* which is less common to the Commentary on Romans than it is to the *Institutes,* where it figures more dominantly, strongly focuses the problem on God's decision and his entitled right. Calvin, however, in contrast to Luther's nominalist view, veers away from thoughts of the limitless omnipotence of God,[21] while, on the other hand, consistently upholding the juridical concept. He thus, unlike Paul, risks making statements referring to the eternally condemned. Calvin thus concluded in his first statement on

19. He opened this discussion with three principles, the second of which is: "There is no other basis for this election than the goodness of God alone, . . . without any regard whatever to their works" (200).

20. Even within the *Institutes* (1559), the train of thought flows toward the foundations: from sanctification (III,6-10) and justification (III,11-18) to election (III,21-14).

21. In connection with the parable of the potter (Rom. 9:21), he states that Paul does not "want to claim for God any inordinate power, but the power which He should rightly be given" (210).

Romans 9:11 that God did not only elect Israel from among the peoples but also differentiates again among the *individuals* of this people by predestinating "some to salvation, and others to eternal condemnation" (p. 200).[22] Predestination, understood as a precondition for divine purpose, which cannot be differentiated but which always pursues a particular goal, is thus a double predestination *(gemina praedestinatio)*.[23] In Romans 9:17, God gave the Pharaoh this and no other role *(persona)* to play (p. 207). Here we see a remarkable similarity between predestination and providence: the condemned, Calvin states at the end of this discourse, "proceed from the secret fountain of His *providence*" (207).[24]

Calvin, in his interpretation of what Paul explicitly said, may have taken a step of great consequence; the parable of the potter (Rom. 9:20f.), which he referenced, would seem to uphold his view. The parable expresses precisely this, the vital center of his work on the matter of predestination, that is, to remind us strongly of our place before God. He therefore does not quote the parable in the version given in Jeremiah 18, which speaks of a "spoiled" vessel from which a new and better one is to be made, but the stronger version in Isaiah 45:9 instead, which focuses on the freedom of the potter, whose own right it is *(suo iure)* to decide on the purpose of his work.[25] Paul neither asked nor answered the question of why there are even "vessels unto dishonor." Calvin follows his lead when he demands that we refrain from pursuing the reason for election, this secret, which cannot come under the censure of men *(censura)*. If God does not erase these "proofs" of his vengeance and his wrath right away, what could be reprehensible in this directive? Just like Augustine before him, however, Calvin says something more. May not the destruction of these "vessels" make the extent of the divine mercy toward the elected "shine with greater clarity" as he saved them from the depths of destruction (p. 211)? People are indeed "instruments" *(instrumenta vel organa)* in God's hand, through

22. For a comparison with Paul, cf. Lindemann, "Erwählt vor Grundlegung der Welt," p. 46.

23. Calvin always avoided the idea of a simple allowance *(permissio)* with regard to the non-elected, although he joins Augustine on one occasion in speaking of a "passing by" *(praeterire)* (200).

24. Cf. *Inst.* III,23,8: "Dei providentia sic ordonante" (OS IV,402,38). Cf. Link, "Erwählungslehre," pp. 169-93.

25. Commentary on Rom. 9:21: "as the potter takes nothing from the clay, . . . so God takes nothing from man, whatever condition in which He may have created him" (210).

which he glorifies his name (p. 212). One can hardly deny that Calvin, with his lucid argumentation, brings the logic of Romans 9:11f. into focus and remains within the boundaries clearly allowed by Paul and by the author of the Epistle to the Ephesians, in particular.[26]

Two Different Types of Doctrine

Calvin clearly saw the theological difficulties that the thesis of double predestination entails, which are "explicable only, when reverent minds regard as settled, what they may suitably hold concerning election and predestination."[27] He expands this necessary knowledge through two different perspectives and thus in two different forms: first, in the form of doctrine — as in the *Institutes,* which assumes God's purpose "before the foundation of the world" and which vehemently disputes the traditional idea of the divine foreknowledge; and second, in the form of a sermon, for example, in the notable assembly of Geneva pastors (1551) which, with the proposition that election predates faith, ended one such controversy — for the time being.

One can speak of two different approaches, or even concepts,[28] which have predecessors in this dogmatic tradition. This normally begins either with the question of God who is electing, or the question of the human who is elected. In one God's freedom receives focus as a theological principle (as in the *Institutes),* and in the other it is his grace (as in the sermon). While the danger of the first lies in a reduction of election to a simple foreknowledge, the danger of the second lies in setting limitations on grace through the emphasis on free human will *(liberum arbitrium),* the independent ability to move toward this grace.

Election as Predestination

The problems with the first path were already present in Luther's polemic work, *De servo arbitrio* (*The Bondage of the Will,* 1525) directed against Erasmus. In it, Luther differentiated categorically between God preached and

---

26. Cf. Lindemann, "Erwählt vor Grundlegung der Welt," p. 67.
27. *Inst.* III,21,1 (OS IV,369,1).
28. Neuser, "Calvin als Prediger," p. 87.

God hidden[29] and attributes the question of election to the latter: it is "the secret and to be feared will of God, who, according to His own counsel *(consilium)*, ordains whom, and such as He will, to be receivers and partakers of the preached and offered mercy."[30] Indeed, this will of divine majesty, for which neither cause nor reason can be assigned, is the "rule of all things."[31] Divine foreknowledge *(praescientia)* came first, however, which meant that if "God foreknew that Judas would be a traitor, Judas became a traitor of necessity; nor was it in the power of Judas nor of any other creature to alter it, or to change that will; though he did what he did willingly, not by compulsion; for that *willing* of his was his *own* work; which God, by the motion of His Omnipotence, moved on into action, as He does everything else."[32] It is not for us to ask why God acts as he does, but to honor him for being able and willing to do so.[33] The problem with this line of argument is clear in that it moves beyond the realm in which God makes himself attainable and comes upon, as Luther well knew, an absolute theological barrier. Where one would wish to know more, God did not even define himself,[34] and there is therefore nothing to proclaim. One comes face to face with the lone majesty of a God throning "before" and "over" the world. Luther saw the secret of election as grounded in this understanding.

We do not know whether Calvin knew this work of Luther. One cannot dispute that he confronted similar problems in the *Institutes* and came to similar solutions, even if his first word — neither later questioned nor rescinded — on the matter spoke of God's revealed generosity *(liberalitas)* in Christ, his "mere good pleasure" *(merum beneplacitum)*, as the source of this election.[35] One must mention election, for it is the basis of our salvation, resting on the pillars of certainty, humility, and gratitude. Here we find the decisive support "in order to free us of all fear and render us victorious amid so many dangers, snares and mortal struggles."[36]

29. WA 18,685.

30. WA 18,684.

31. WA 18,712: *regula omnium.* This sentence is nearly identical in *Inst.* III,23,2: "For his will is, and rightly ought to be, the cause *(causa!)* of all things that are" (OS IV,395,34).

32. WA 18,715.

33. WA 18,689f.

34. WA 18,685: The well-known sentence is: "Neque enim tum verbo suo definivit sese, sed *liberum* sese reservavit super omnia." Cf. Jüngel, "Quae supra nos," pp. 220f.

35. *Inst.* III,21,1 (OS IV,369,24, 29).

36. *Inst.* III,21,1 (OS IV,369,36).

Yet, although the placement of the doctrine of election at the end of the third book of the *Institutes*, "The Mode of Obtaining the Grace of Christ," attests to its having been written in the tradition of Augustine with regard to the doctrine of grace, its dominant theme in the church tradition is evident in Ephesians 1:4 — God "chose us in Christ before the foundation of the world." Calvin forms three conclusions from this that are crucial to the profile of his doctrine: (1) If God has chosen us in Christ, we are each chosen "outside of ourselves" *(extra se)*, that is, without any consideration of merit. Since, however, clearly not all people are members of Christ, "certain ones are separated from others."[37] Election indeed entails a choice and thus separation. (2) Our election to be "holy and blameless" (Eph. 1:4b) refutes the error of deriving the choice from God's foreknowledge, as Paul very clearly declares that "all virtue appearing in man is the result of election."[38] (3) If, however, one cannot speak of divine foreknowledge, only the "divine pleasure" is then relevant, that is, the "purpose" of the divine will; and this "means the same thing as to say, that he considered nothing outside himself with which to be concerned in making his decree."[39] His decision is made without consideration for conditions and circumstances within time. It is a pretemporal, an "eternal" decree: the Consensus Genevensis of 1522 accordingly explains "that *God* begins with him*self,* when he sees fit to elect, but he will have us begin with *Christ* so that we may know that we are reckoned among his peculiar people"[40] and the *Institutes* confirm: "The elect are said to have been the Father's before he gave them his only-begotten Son."[41]

Despite the strongly emphasized reference to Christ, the *Institutes* particularly stress God's hidden choice *(election Patris).* Calvin thus returned to before the history of Jesus Christ, that is, to a choice that, just as Luther put it, resists any attempt of understanding through revelation or experience.

---

37. *Inst.* III,22,2 (OS IV,381,28).

38. OS IV, 381,33. Also cf. *Inst.* III,22,8 (OS IV,388,16-389,4), in which Calvin expressly refers to Augustine, *Retractationes* I 23,2 (Migne PL 32,621f.), and *In Johannis evangelium tractatus* 86,2 (Migne PL 35,1851). Both arguments again cover the basis of justification in election.

39. *Inst.* III,22,3 (OS IV,382,26), a nearly verbatim citation of Commentary on Rom. 8:29 (= *Commentary on the Epistle to the Romans*, p. 181).

40. *De aeterna Dei praedestinatione:* CO 8,319 (= Calvin, *Eternal Predestination,* p. 127).

41. *Inst.* III,22,7 (OS IV,387,13); also in the Consensus Genevensis: "Dei *erant* in eius corde . . . et *quia* praeordinati ernat ad vitam, Christo dati sunt" (CO 8,292).

Barth saw in this the central problem of traditional dogmatics.[42] In his summary, Calvin approaches Luther's writings very closely: "You see how [Paul] refers both to the mere pleasure of God. Therefore, if we cannot assign any reason for his bestowing mercy on his people, but just that it so pleases him, neither can we have any reason for his reprobating others but his will. When God is said to visit in mercy or harden whom he will, men are reminded that they are not to seek for any cause beyond his will."[43]

Can, however, one be solely of the view that we stand, in the end, before closed doors or before the "abyss" of a divine secret? The Reformed tradition has expanded the foundations laid by Calvin to prioritize the doctrine of divine decree above predestination, thus acknowledging God's "choosing" as a function of his general relationship with the world. A concise definition by Johannes Wolleb (1585-1629) of Basel expresses it as follows: "God's decree is the inner action of his will, in which he made his decision concerning things that are to occur within time with great freedom and certitude *(liberrime et certissime)* and from the perspective of eternity."[44] Could one not also understand this sentence to mean that God's own inner being is determined from the very beginning by his decision for the *world?* This would imply that this return to before the date of creation and before the New Testament history of Jesus Christ would have the great purpose of according their very possibility to God himself as their effective source. The actual meaning of this decree is then first revealed to us in the history of Jesus in the world. Does not the doctrine of the Trinity also differentiate between God's "internal" and "external" acts? It was, in any event, along these lines that Calvin attempted in his sermon to explain to his congregation that predestination concerns an election in Christ.

Election as Grace

Calvin considered himself to be a student of Augustine. In his view of election doctrine, Calvin placed importance in not parting "the width of a fin-

---

42. Barth, *Church Dogmatics,* II/2, esp. 63-67 and 134f.

43. *Inst.* III,22,11 (OS IV,393,27). Luther writes on this passage: "Who can resist his will? . . . When God knows something beforehand, this occurs as a necessity. The godless must . . . recognize that no freedom or free will remains for them, but that all things depend on God's *will alone*" (WA 18,717).

44. Wolleb, *Compendium,* I 3,3.

ger" from his predecessor. In doing so, he also developed, for the first time, a view that would set the tone for his sermons and for the Consensus Genevensis (1552). This was also the source of the often-cited view of Christ as the "mirror of election."[45] He is thus able to say: "I do not merely send men off to the secret election of God to await with gaping mouth salvation there. I bid them make their way directly to Christ in whom salvation is offered us, which otherwise would have lain hid in God. For whoever does not walk in the plain path of faith can make nothing of the election of God but a labyrinth of destruction."[46] And Calvin amplifies: "Let the eye of faith look fixedly in this mirror, and not try to penetrate where access is not open."[47]

For Augustine, the doctrine of election is the factual foundation of the doctrine of grace. It provides the basis for the open question of how human beings can become free of the tethers of original sin, when the very danger of this sin is that it serves to tether the sinner's will. Sinners cannot do the good that they seek and wish, and particularly not that which is decisive for Christians: they cannot have faith. Christ's work would thus never reach them and move them if grace were not to envelop them as a free and infallible power (gratia irresistibilis), providing their will with new direction. Augustine thus spoke with unsurpassable clarity of the person Jesus Christ as the "brightest light of election and grace." In his election we recognize the nature of predestination in all places and in all times: the adoption and acceptance of human beings through God's free mercy.[48]

Augustine thus laid the groundwork for the understanding that God's election is not a universal offer, but rather a particular act. From within humanity, which has become a massa perditionis, those individuals are removed who had been chosen from the beginning for salvation from general perdition. Election is thus a one-sided but clearly salvatory act. The elected receive mercy without merit, while the non-elected receive their just verdict. The idea of double predestination cannot, within this perspective, be phrased didactically. This consequence, as already established by Augustine, is, however, in fact unavoidable. This arises from the concept that those who do not come to faith remain "outside" because

45. Augustine, *De correptione et gratia* 11,330 (Migne PL 44,934f.), cited in *Inst.* III,22,1 (OS IV,380,22); *De dono perseverantiae* 24,67 (Migne PL 45,1033f.).

46. CO 8,306f. (= Calvin, *Eternal Predestination*, p. 113).

47. CO 8,254 (= Calvin, *Eternal Predestination*, p. 50). Cf. Busch, *Gotteserkenntnis*, pp. 72-74.

48. Augustine, *De praedestinatione sanctorum*, 15,30 (Migne PL 44,981f.).

they do not number among the elected, while those who lose their faith come to fall because God did not provide them with the gift of perseverance, which he did give to those he elected.[49] In Calvin's *Sermons*[50] the problems of predestination are centered on the Christology introduced by Augustine. Calvin connects election with an adoption in place of the child and recognizes its certainty in the contemporary communion with Christ. The path of God to human beings, his condescendence, is the chief source of insight (p. 717).

The systematic decision to connect "God's eternal election" with Christ's temporal act of salvation and, conversely, to clarify the meaning of salvation through election was made in Calvin's "Congrégation" sermon, which later entered into the final segment of his *Institutes*.[51] Here we can observe a change in attitude regarding the exegetic emphasis. In the sermon, for example, the "pretemporal" nature of election (Eph. 1:4) is given no importance of its own, and when the "eternal counsel" is mentioned directly, it is related to the heritage of the everlasting Abrahamic covenant, and thus, to a degree, focused on the future (pp. 705-6). This departs from causal thinking. With a remarkable difference from the *Institutes,* the question of the cause of election is replaced by the eschatological argument that steers our attention toward the future of God: in the final revelation, we will know that which remains hidden from us today (pp. 709, 710). Of importance here is not the logical consideration that election — in terms of time and meaning — predates grace, but the soteriological certainty that grace itself embodies election.

It is from this point of departure that Calvin undertakes a transition to a Christological argument: Christ is the "well-beloved" son (p. 700), in whom God exalted our human nature "in a marvellous dignity" (p. 712) that "each of us" should recognize: "God has elected me" (p. 712). In this regard, predestination is conceived consistently as a "gracious election" (*election gratuite;* p. 700). This has consequences for the question of condemnation. In contrast to the *Institutes,* double predestination for life *and*

---

49. Cf. Augustine, *De praedestinatione sanctorum,* 6,11 (Migne PL 44,968f.)

50. The page numbers in parentheses refer to the long-lost sermon "Congregation on Eternal Election" in Holtrop, *Bolsec Controversy,* pp. 695-720.

51. *Inst.* III,24,5: "First, if we seek God's fatherly mercy and kindly heart *(clementia),* we should turn our eyes to Christ. . . . Christ, then, is the mirror wherein we must, and without self-deception may, contemplate our own election" (OS IV,415,27 and 426,3). Of particular interest is Neuser's detailed analysis of this sermon: "Calvin als Prediger."

death is not taught in the sermon. The terms *praeordinatio* and its equivalent *praedeterminatio* (destination) do not in fact appear at all. Together with Augustine,[52] Calvin answers the riddle of why not everyone is saved in the end with a look to our situation as God's creation. We must admit, in considering the non-elected, that by nature, we all belong to those separated from God (p. 715). There is thus no symmetrical balance between election and condemnation. This "condemnation" is the passive manner in which God passes over certain people in his election (p. 716). In turn, the emphasis that Calvin gives to our sanctification as the goal of election becomes understandable (p. 710).

The Goal of Election

Calvin's doctrine of predestination not only looks back on the cause of "eternal" election, but looks forward with equal intensity to the goal that the "predestined" received from God (cf. the promise of "heavenly glory"; Rom. 8:30). This is a long-forgotten discovery that Jürgen Moltmann (b. 1926) returned to view with all of its ramifications.[53] As Calvin stated: "If eternal life is certain to all the elect, if no one can pluck them from Him, if no violence nor any assault can tear them from Him, if their salvation stands in the invincible power of God, what impudence for Pighius to dare to shake so fixed a certitude. . . . Thus I see myself perpetually tossed about, so that there is not a moment when I do not seem to be sinking. Nevertheless, as God sustains His elect to prevent them drowning, I am confident of standing against these innumerable storms."[54] Calvin connects the gift of perseverance with predestination. It is perseverance that maintained the Huguenots in the time of their political disempowerment after the fall of their last bastion in La Rochelle (1628).[55]

Perseverance, a theme pursued by Augustine,[56] represents the other

---

52. Augustine, *De diversis quaestionibus ad Simplicianum I* 2,16f. (Migne PL 40,120f.). Cf. Gilson, *Introduction*, p. 201f.

53. Moltmann, *Prädestination*, pp. 31-51.

54. *De aeterna Dei praedestinatione*, CO 8,321 (= Calvin, *Eternal Predestination*, p. 130).

55. Du Moulin, *Enodatio*, p. 332: the certainty that we persevere is based in the absolute decree of election.

56. Augustine, *De dono perseverantiae* 1,1; 14,34 (Migne PL 45,993f.; 1013f.).

side of predestination and corresponds with its Christological moorings: just as the story of Jesus presupposes an eternal predestinationistic context and is simultaneously the fulfillment of the history of the promise of Israel, the faith of Christians is anchored in God's election and is oriented beyond the boundaries of every possible human experience to a completion in the future life; it is "in its being *perseverantia usque ad finem*"[57] and as such is related to the eschaton. God's eternal counsel in which he shows his effective power "would be void unless the promised resurrection, which is the effect of that decree, were also certain."[58] This fundamental connection, the "actual kerygmatic point of his doctrine of predestination,"[59] makes the eschatological direction of election apparent.

Calvin is innovative in the stress he places on the practical side of this certainty, oriented more toward the life than the death of the elected. Calvin added an important third element between election and the gift of perseverance: vocation *(vocatio)*, the public and empirical testimony of God's hidden decree, connected with the potency of the Spirit.[60] This is the form and figure that the eternal election assumes in the framework of time, in and through which the divine purpose is to become reality: that God has appointed his own to bear their cross. The perseverance appointed to them with their election is the guarantee for their steadfastness in the face of attacks and suffering.[61] Indeed, all afflictions of the faithful serve only the goal of steering them to the glory of resurrection. As one exegete of an earlier generation put it: as the expression of Calvinistic piety, election becomes the testimony for the eschatological character of Calvin's theology in that perseverance is the "final and most decisive evidence for the divine election of grace."[62]

Another innovation was the emphasis with which Calvin, with reference to Romans 8:38f. and John 6:37, is adamant about the indestructibility

---

57. Translating Moltmann, *Prädestination,* p. 49.

58. Commentary on Rom. 8:23 (= *Commentary on the Epistle to the Romans,* p. 175). Calvin speaks of an inheritance that is "incorruptible and eternal, and such as has been manifested in Christ" (*Commentary on the Epistle to the Romans,* p. 171).

59. Translating Moltmann, *Prädestination,* p. 34.

60. Cf. Commentary on Rom. 8:30 (= *Commentary on the Epistle to the Romans,* p. 182), similar to *Inst.* III,24,1 (OS IV,410,12).

61. Cf. Commentary on Rom. 8:30 (= *Commentary on the Epistle to the Romans,* p. 182).

62. Translating Otten, *Anschauung,* p. 65.

of the faith of the elected, once it has been awakened by vocation, which looks by its very nature "to a future immortality after this life is over"[63] and is not, as taught in scholasticism, limited to a *punctum temporis* (point of time). Perseverance is not a human ability but a gift of God and is therefore for all time *(perseveratia finalis)*. This is preservation in time, as the first *Institutes* stressed with the remarkable statement that "there was no time from the creation of the world when the Lord did not have his church upon earth, also that there will be no time, even to the end of the age, when he will not have it, even as he himself promises."[64] The great exultation of Paul (Rom. 8:38f.) must have its reason "in this gift of perseverance." The certainty of perseverance derives from the steadfast constancy with which God fulfills his promises and from the strength *(firmitudo)* of Christ, who does not allow the faithful to slip from his hand.

One must notice that Calvin, in the explanation of this main statement of his predestination doctrine, no longer uses the eternal decree as his main argument but, as in the sermon, nearly exclusively uses reference to Christ, and God's word and promises. The Christological cognitive ground is in fact borne out here as an existential ground. With a look to the inner-historical path lying ahead for the faithful, there is no division between a pretemporal divine decision and worldly life and action. Within time, they approach the future life and experience the *donum perseverantiae*. Calvin was only able to justify and realize the eschatological orientation of the doctrine of predestination through the mediation of the Spirit, who does not allow the faithful to lose view of the goal of their path. Those who would wish to separate predestination from its historical development and the fulfillment of election would have erased its very meaning. "We cannot be sufficiently grateful to Calvin for presenting the statement of *perseverantia* in this manner," as even Barth, the strongest critic of the doctrine of election, expressed it. "The full Gospel can shine out only with this doctrine."[65]

Was this perhaps the final word on the matter? Wilhelm Niesel (1903-1988) sought to understand Calvin fully in this light. He summarized the force of these ideas in that "Christ makes himself into the author of election *(author electionis)*."[66] The shadow of double predestination, however,

---

63. *Inst.* III,2,40 (OS IV,50,27).

64. OS I,87. Cf. the development of this promise as geared toward the individual in *Inst.* III,24,6 (OS IV,417,23–418,15).

65. Barth, *Church Dogmatics*, II/2, 332 and 333.

66. Translating Niesel, *Theologie*, p. 166, with regard to *Inst.* III,22,7 (OS IV,387,36).

continues to loom over the promise of perseverance, which, according to Calvin, "does not happen to all."[67] Does he not, however, have the Gospel of John on his side, wherein Christ does not pray "for the world but for those whom thou hast given me"?[68] Must we not take seriously the final public word of proclamation made by Jesus according to Matthew, in which he speaks of a double outcome of final judgment (Matt. 25:46)?

Eberhard Busch (b. 1937) pointed out how Calvin clearly referred to this problem in his last work, his Commentary on Ezekiel. How can God want both the blessedness of all (Ezek. 18:23, 32) and a separation of the elected from the condemned?[69] How can one then not continue to deny the possibility of God's conflicting nature? The problem of predestination comes to a head in these questions, which cannot be answered by reason alone, and one can sense in Calvin's final lectures before his death that neither he — nor likely anyone — can master this "contradiction." The goal of prophetic proclamation *(coelestis doctrina)* is unambiguous: "everyone should be called to salvation without preference." God receives no joy in the death of those who die but if we were to penetrate into his hidden counsel, things *(ratio)* would seem different.[70] We must therefore be content to see things now "as in a mirror or a riddle" (1 Cor. 13:12).[71] It speaks well of Calvin that he resisted the temptation to find a solution or an understandable intellectual, rational means to diffuse this dilemma. He observes this mirror where he was lit by the light of the "heavenly decree" *(coeleste decretum),* which grew bright in the person of the mediator Jesus Christ, who is to become our "Immanuel," and thus Christ is "the mirror wherein we must, and without self-deception may, contemplate our own election."[72] This mirror indeed becomes the manifestation of God's faithfulness. And is that not a basis with which those who have recognized the certainty of their election can share the promise of God's faithfulness with those who have yet to do so?

Translated from German by David Dichelle, Leipzig

---

67. *Inst.* III,24,6 (OS IV,417,23).
68. John 17:9 cited in *Inst.* III,22,7 (OS IV,387,22)
69. CO 40,446. Cf. Busch, *Gotteserkenntnis,* p. 75.
70. CO 40,459.
71. CO 40,446.
72. *Inst.* II,12,1 (OS III,437,6,18) and *Inst.* III,24,5 (OS IV,416,3).

Mutual Connectedness as a Gift and a Task: On John Calvin's Understanding of the Church

Eva-Maria Faber

"How unworthy it is to wrest from Christ His place of honor as sole Head of the church, sole Teacher, sole Master; or to take away any part of that honor from Him and transfer it to men."[1] It cannot go unnoticed that the ecclesiology of the reformer John Calvin had a critical dimension to it.[2] Calvin shed light, with his great theological focus, on the origins of the church in divine acts of salvation: as the church's fundaments, beyond the reach of humankind, lay in divine election,[3] the elected were connected to Jesus Christ as the head of the church and thus grew together as one body.[4] This theological view of the church required a critical view of everything that could obscure the reality of the church granted to us by God.

Despite his theological "reduction" to the inner reality of the church,

---

1. CO 49,316f. (Commentary on 1 Cor. 1:13). For related quotes from Calvin's commentaries on the Epistles to the Corinthians, refer to the corresponding translations in *Calvin's New Testament Commentaries*, ed. D. W. Torrance and T. F. Torrance (Grand Rapids, 1961-74).

2. Cf. all of Chapter 2 of Book IV of the *Institutes* on a comparison of the false and the true church as in similar passages such as in n. 1: *Inst.* IV,6,3-9. All quotations from the *Institutes* (1536, 1559) refer to these translations: *Institutes of the Christian Religion, 1536 Edition*, trans. F. L. Battles (Grand Rapids, 1995) and *Institutes of the Christian Religion (1559)*, trans. F. L. Battles (Philadelphia/London, 1960).

3. Cf. *Inst.* IV,1,2. According to the Geneva Catechism of 1545, the church is the "body and society of believers whom God has predestined to eternal life": CO 6,40. All related quotes refer to Calvin's *Tracts and Treatises,* vol. 2.

4. Cf. *Inst.* IV,1,2 (already similar in 1536).

to be found within faith, Calvin did focus much of his attention on the external development of the church. "Calvin could only conceive the Church as 'bien ordonee et reiglee.'"[5] The longer he himself was responsible for church development, the more questions of church order and the actual unity of the church grew in importance to him.

One indication of this was the increase in ecclesiological reflection throughout the development of Calvin's *Institutes*.[6] While the first version of 1536 included, apart from a few marginal notes in other contexts, only a short piece on the church within the context of the interpretation of the creed, he began later to treat the subject in greater depth, especially beginning in 1543, when it formed the longest chapter on the creed. By 1559, the fourth book on "the external means or aids by which God invites us into the society of Christ and holds us therein" took up 374 columns of the second volume of the Corpus Reformatorum. It is remarkable that some of the phrasings used in the short ecclesiological texts of the first edition of the *Institutes* from 1536 remained nearly unchanged through the final edition of 1559. This continuity coincided with developments that are easily recognized as being the consequence of Calvin's reformation activities in Geneva, and, in particular, shifts in emphasis from the invisible to the visible church and its concrete structures.

It is thus incorrect to accuse Calvin of paying little heed to the church as a matter for theological reflection and one-sidedly pursuing a purely practical program for the church instead.[7] The combination of acute theological concentration and a practical interest in the life of the church is indeed more characteristic of Calvin's ecclesiology, driven by a dedication to the authentic face of the church. For the church to be able to be true to its own being, its being must be recognizable in church life. It is for this reason that Calvin evolves into a "churchman" and the controversy concerning his work as a reformer is mostly (for example, more than for Martin Luther) controversy concerning his connection to the church. In his reply to Cardinal Sadolet, he vehemently fought the accusation that he endangered church unity. Once called to divine judgment by the cardinal's charge, Calvin submitted himself to this judgment, calling upon the divine

---

5. Translating Becht, *Pium consensum tueri,* p. 364, with quote from *Articles concernant l'organisation de l'église et du culte à Genève,* 1537: OS 1,369.

6. Cf. Ganoczy, *Ecclesia ministrans,* pp. 140-75.

7. Cf. Bouwsma, *Calvin,* p. 214.

judge as the witness to the truth and honesty of his path "who, by the mere brightness of his countenance, will disclose whatever lurks in darkness, lay open all the secrets of the human heart."[8] "Mine, however, was a unity of the Church, which should begin with thee and end in thee. For as oft as thou didst recommend to us peace and concord, thou, at the same time, didst show that thou wert the only bond for preserving it."[9] In following Calvin's pointed allusion to 1 Corinthians 4:5, one is reminded of Paul's "self-justification" in relation to the Corinthians.[10]

This sort of parallel is not the only reason to view Calvin's commentaries on the Epistles to the Corinthians as a promising opening into his understanding of the church. His treatment of the conflict within the Corinthian congregation shows us how Calvin could reconcile points of criticism with a positive view of the church. The endangerment of the church through adverse conditions furnished him with more reason to recall — as a previous given and as a future task — the positive nature of the church. The allusion to the situation provided the discourse in the commentaries on the Epistles to the Corinthians with a particular appeal, while providing insight into Calvin's efforts toward a church reformed in accordance with God's word. The commentaries, published in 1546 and 1548, came several years after his earliest commentaries on the Epistle to the Romans.[11] At the time, Calvin had already been active for many years in his service to the Geneva church, and had been on the receiving end of resistance from within the congregation, leading even to his expulsion; he was able, after his return in 1541, however, to achieve even more in terms of forming the congregation. As mentioned above, the 1539 and 1543 editions of the *Institutes* already included major statements of ecclesiology. Many of these can also be seen again in the commentaries on the Epistles to the Corinthians in similar form. This constitutes, as it must, a theological foundation for the church, in the direct context, however, of certain

---

8. CO 5,407 (Reply to Cardinal Sadolet). All related quotes refer to Calvin's *Tracts and Treatises*, vol. 1.

9. CO 5,409 (Reply to Cardinal Sadolet).

10. The allusion to 1 Cor. 4:5 is not indicated in his reply to Cardinal Sadolet; there is also no sign of Calvin styling his writings to follow Paul. In contrast, however, it does not seem that Calvin includes his own experience in his commentary on the relevant passages of the Epistle to the Corinthians.

11. The Commentary on 2 Corinthians was completed in 1546, but did not appear until 1548. Cf. Feld, *Einleitung*, pp. xi-xiii.

situations in which believers either act or do not act in accordance with these roots. One major topic of the Epistles to the Corinthians is the unity of the church as well as solidarity among the faithful. Lastly, and this can only be treated briefly here, the Epistles to the Corinthians provide Calvin with impetus for numerous statements on the significance of the ministry and church office.

The Church's Anchorage in Grace

Dangers to the Life of the Church

The first thing to be recognized empirically is not always the most salient or the fundamental aspect of a reality. This is equally valid for the church. The Protestant tradition thus speaks of the invisible church, just as Catholic ecclesiology speaks of the mystery of the church. People of all confessions experience that what they see does not directly reflect the actual being of the church, which can be perceived through faith. There is indeed much that one can perceive that even contradicts the meaning of the church. The Epistles to the Corinthians instruct us not to deny this but to face the challenges posed by the problems and errors of church life.

The quote from Calvin's Commentary on 1 Corinthians at the beginning of this essay includes turns of phrase that can be found elsewhere in his works as the expression of critical distance in his understanding of the church. The commentaries on the Epistles to the Corinthians also feature other specific points of emphasis, including the critical treatment of erroneous church developments. To Calvin's critical mind, the church is, first and foremost, a positive topic. He therefore does not begin his ecclesiological writings with polemic statements. This contrasts with the commentaries under discussion; Calvin begins the introduction to the Commentary on 1 Corinthians with a discussion of errant developments in the Corinthian congregation. This inspired and justifies the placement of the opening quote and the diagnosis of dangers to church life in this essay. It was the goal of Calvin's teachings and work not to suppress these dangers but to strive to reach the very core of the church's being, despite all difficulties.

Calvin's efforts to outline the unique quality of the difficulties are characteristic of the critical side of the commentaries on the Epistles to the

Corinthians. In Calvin's view, it was less false teachings than it was false attitudes that led to errant developments in Corinth. Rival apostles appeared who, in their quest for fame, supplanted Paul's simple message with their own vain words: the believers were seduced by ostentation and show (*ostentatio,*[12] *pompa*[13]). Calvin speaks repeatedly of ambition (*ambitio*[14]) as the "fountain of all evil," leading to divisions in the congregation, tied together with arrogance (*fastus*[15]) and jealousy (*invidia*[16]).

Not only was the success of interpersonal community at stake in this regard, but a preacher's lack of selflessness could indeed serve to skew Christ's message. The gospel, which is characterized in its essence by simplicity *(simplicitas),* is remodeled into a human, worldly philosophy.[17] At the same time — and the opening quote, which apparently also reflects Calvin's criticism of the Roman church, is relevant in this regard — those driven by ambition could win disciples not for Christ but for themselves instead.[18]

Theological Outline: The Origins of the Church in God's Actions

In response to the temptation to build the church on a gospel that is embellished splendidly — but also hollowed out — by human addition, Calvin returned it to its true identity. He linked ecclesiology and the doctrine of election in the commentaries on the Epistles to the Corinthians as well. Church members were referred to repeatedly as the "elected." Calvin saw Paul's reminder of God's faithfulness in 1 Corinthians 1:9 as testimony to the certainty of election. This is where the central concern of Calvin's doc-

12. Cf. CO 49,297,302 (Introduction to 1 Corinthians); CO 49,496,529 (Commentary on 1 Cor. 12:1; 14:27).

13. Cf. CO 49,299 (Introduction to 1 Corinthians); CO 49,496 (Commentary on 1 Cor. 12:1).

14. CO 49,348 (Commentary on 1 Cor. 3:3). Cf. also, for example, CO 49,297 (Introduction to 1 Corinthians); CO 49,316 (Commentary on 1 Cor. 1:12); CO 49,480,503 (Commentary on 1 Cor. 11:18; 12:15); COR 2,15,47,207 (Commentary on 2 Cor. 2:17; 12:20).

15. Cf. CO 49,480 (Commentary on 1 Cor. 11:18).

16. Cf. CO 49,503 (Commentary on 1 Cor. 12:15).

17. CO 49,298f. (Introduction to 1 Corinthians) speaks repeatedly of the transformation of the gospel into a *philosophia humana* or *mundana.*

18. Cf. CO 49,316 (Commentary on 1 Cor. 1:12).

trine of election comes into play: the reference to eternal election does not serve to reduce but to strengthen certainty regarding the salvation of the faithful. Calvin saw God's acceptance of the Corinthians, despite all their failings, to be emphasized in God's faithfulness, as interpreted from the point of view of election. This was also underscored by membership in the visible church, though hardly identical with election. Calvin saw calling or vocation *(vocatio),* which he attached to concrete historical forms of being a Christian, as evidence for election *(electio).* In this view, those individuals are called for whom the word takes root and brings forth fruit, who recognize Christ, and who have begun the right path of salvation. Those called into this communion with Christ can view themselves as part of the body of Christ and can rest assured of their salvation.[19] In contrast with the *Institutes,* in which Calvin understood the eternal election as the *fundamentum* of the church, Calvin described Christ, in his Commentary on 1 Corinthians, as the fundament of the church, the ground upon which the house of the church must stand.[20] Calvin connected a clear view of the church's mooring in God's acts of grace with the concept of Christ's body, which appeared in the commentary not only with regard to 1 Corinthians 12 but also in other passages, particularly in connection with the church as a whole. This was theologically significant for Calvin's ecclesiology, as it established the dependence of the body of the church and its unity (which was shaken in Corinth) on their connection to Jesus Christ. It is not the links between the faithful themselves that constitute the body of Christ but their participation in Jesus Christ as described in terms of the Lord's Supper in 1 Corinthians 10: "It is true, that believers are bound together by the blood of Christ, so that they become one Body. It is also true that a unity of that kind is properly called a *koinonia* or communion. I would also say the same thing about the bread. . . . [W]e 'are all made one body, because we share the same bread together'. But, I would ask, what is the source of that *koinonia* or communion, which exists among us, but the fact that we are united to Christ so that 'we are flesh of his flesh, and bone of his bones'? For it is necessary for us to be incorporated, as it were, into Christ in order to be united to each other."[21]

19. Cf. CO 49,312f. (Commentary on 1 Cor 1:9).
20. CO 49,353 (Commentary on 1 Cor. 3:11); cf. CO 49,300 (Introduction to 1 Corinthians).
21. CO 49,464 (Commentary on 1 Cor. 10:16).

In the commentaries on the Epistles to the Corinthians, Calvin often associated the theme of the body with the (deutero-Pauline) view of Christ as the head, to which the entire church must belong and subordinate itself.[22] This closes the circle of thinking with a critical culmination in the theological examination of the church: since Christ is the head of the church, only he may rule, and only he has the authority to teach in the church. Only he is lord and master. Nothing may reduce his glory.[23]

Church between Being and Becoming

The necessity of coming out against errant forms of church life, with a view to theological reality, points to something of concern to Calvin independent of all such critical expositions. With the decisive founding of the church by God's act of grace, we do not lose sight of the fact that believers must responsibly adopt, fulfill, and work to shape the reality of the church that is brought about by God. The church's *being,* God's gift by grace alone, relies on a *becoming* that depends on humankind. This becomes most evident in the concept of the body of Christ. It is beyond question that the church's position as the body of Christ comes thanks to the gift of communion with Christ. According to Calvin, however, growth together into one body is a process that is still under way and still needs to become concrete reality. This is why he stated that the church not only *is* the body of Christ but must also *coalesce* through the believers' interaction with each other.[24] One must uphold and cultivate the communion founded in the engraftment into the body of Christ by baptism.[25]

The concept of vocation and calling also extends further: according to 1 Corinthians 1:2, Christians are called to sanctification. Calvin considered two possible interpretations: sanctification as a divine gift of grace; or sanctification as the goal of one's calling, which needs to be fulfilled by each individual. Calvin moved beyond this dichotomy, as both corre-

---

22. In CO 49,316 (Commentary on 1 Cor. 1:13; cf. the citation in n. 1). The connected concern becomes clear: "Solus enim Christus regnare in ecclesia debet." Cf. very similarly the section that begins *Inst.* IV,3,1, concluding in a quote from Eph. 4:8-16.

23. Cf. CO 49,316 (Commentary on 1 Cor. 1:12); COR 2,15,34 (Commentary on 2 Cor. 1:24).

24. Cf. CO 49,302 (Introduction to 1 Corinthians). Cf. *Inst.* IV,1,2.

25. CO 49,501 (Commentary on 1 Cor. 12:13).

sponded at a deeper level.[26] It is "of the very nature of God's promises that they summon us to sanctification."[27]

If, however, being part of the body of Christ is to be ratified through the interconnectedness of the members of the church, if one must fulfill one's calling in holiness, one may begin to harbor doubts about the place of the church. In light of the contraposition between the being and becoming of the church, which clearly converges with the contraposition between the visible and invisible church — which is not treated in the commentaries discussed here — one must ask how one can establish that real, existing churches are indeed of church-nature.

The Marks of the Church

In the *Institutes,* Calvin mentioned two marks or tokens *(notae, symbola)* through which the church, hidden in its true being, could be recognized: "Yet where we see the Word of God purely preached and heard, where we see the sacraments administered according to the Christ's institution, there, there is not to be doubted, the church of God exists."[28] This remained true, as Calvin maintained in contrast to the radical reformers, even if the churches were marred by imperfections or disgraceful conditions.[29]

It was indeed this last matter that served as a driving force in Calvin's commentaries on the Epistles to the Corinthians; his treatment of the marks of the church was not triggered by a fundamental reflection on the relationship between the visible and invisible church but the placement of the church within a situation of disgrace. This did not indeed prevent Paul from using the term of honor *church of God* for the Corinthian congregation. Calvin stressed how little this designation in 1 Corinthians 1:2 was to be taken for granted, instead emphasizing all the more strongly the identification of the church based on its symbols or tokens. Signs of the true church *(verae ecclesiae signa)* were indeed to be recognized in the Corinth church; Paul was able to recognize the congregation there as such because "he saw among them the teaching of the Gospel *(doctrina evangelii),* bap-

---

26. Cf. CO 49,308 (Commentary on 1 Cor. 1:2).

27. COR 2,15,119 (Commentary on 2 Cor. 7:1); cf. all of COR 2,15,113-20 (Commentary on 2 Cor. 6:11-7:1) and CO 49,384 (Commentary on 1 Cor. 5:9).

28. *Inst.* IV,1,9 (Text of 1536); cf. *Inst.* IV,1,10.

29. Cf. *Inst.* IV,1,14f.

tism and the Lord's Supper, the marks by which the Church ought to be determined *(quibus symbolis censeri debet ecclesia)*."[30] Similarly, Calvin established at the beginning of 2 Corinthians that the moral failures of individuals cannot prevent one from recognizing the church as such as long as it maintained the true signs of the religion *(veras religionis tesseras)* — without, however, specifying the actual nature of these signs.[31] Calvin did not speak here, as he otherwise often did, in the twofold terms of preaching *and hearing* the gospel. The end of his interpretation of 1 Corinthians 1:2 did, however, include an alternative manner of justifying the recognition of the church in the Corinthian congregation despite the widespread failures there. Without using the terms *signa, symbola,* or *tessera,* he introduced ways in which the congregation could be recognized as the church. The Corinthians "held on to the fundamental teaching — the One God was worshipped by them and was invoked in the name of Christ — they rested their confidence of salvation in Christ, and they had a ministry that was not wholly corrupt. For those reasons the Church still continued to exist among them. Hence wherever the worship of God is unimpaired, and that fundamental teaching, of which I have spoken, persists, there, we may without difficulty decide, the Church exists."[32] These considerations — except for the allusion to the ministry — did not involve the realm of preaching and the administration of the sacraments (that is, imparting salvation) but more so the level of the acceptance and practice of faith. This view corresponds with Calvin's aim of ensuring the proper worship of God because "there is nothing more perilous to our salvation than a preposterous and perverse worship of God."[33]

Between the Quest for the Pure Church and the Concern for the Sanctity of the Church

Calvin presents the recognition of the church-nature of one problematic congregation as a model, and in doing so rejects the search for a pure

30. CO 49,307 (Commentary on 1 Cor. 1:2).

31. COR 2,15,10 (Commentary on 2 Cor. 1:1). The term *tessera* can also be found in *Inst.* IV,2,1.

32. CO 49,307 (Commentary on 1 Cor. 1:2). The fundamental doctrine here refers to the view of faith implied in these considerations. Cf. *Inst.* IV,1,12.

33. CO 5,392 (Reply to Cardinal Sadolet).

church. The perfect church is not to be found on earth, and whoever seeks this church ends up alone unto themselves. "We should give close attention to this verse, however, lest we should expect in this world a Church without spot or wrinkle, or immediately withhold this title from any gathering whatever, in which everything does not satisfy our standards. For it is a dangerous temptation to think there is no Church where perfect purity is lacking. The point is that anyone who is obsessed by that idea, must cut himself off from everybody else, and appear to himself to be the only saint in the world, or he must set up a sect of his own along with hypocrites."[34]

The *Institutes* of 1539 already warned of the temptation to seek out the pure church, as part of a debate with the left wing of the Reformation. Calvin pointed in this context to the parable of the net (Matt. 13:47-50) and the parable of the tares among the wheat (Matt. 13:24-30) as well as to Paul's attitude to the Corinthians. In 1543, Calvin expanded on his reference to 1 Corinthians 1:2, originally provided in 1539, examining it in interplay with the necessity, introduced in 1 Corinthians 5, of removing flagrant sinners from the congregation: this did not, conversely, grant individuals the right to abandon the church due to the existence of these sinners.[35]

Calvin's commentary on 1 Corinthians 5 did not establish a connection between church discipline and a verdict against a retreat into a pure church. The necessity of church discipline was, however, stressed and founded in the bonds between members of the church. This meant that the wrong turns of a single individual affected all members of the church. The entire congregation therefore had to repent for the sins of individuals, and in some cases the congregation would need to take action against persons who had done wrong, even to the point of excluding them from the congregation. As Calvin, for example, underscored with regard to the example of Paul, this should not be for a single individual to decide, in order to avoid tyranny.[36] Calvin gladly entertained the topic of relativization in Paul's text (1 Cor. 5:5), as the temporal punishment opened the door for eternal salvation.[37] Moreover, Calvin was of the view that this exclusion should only affect the Eucharistic communion, but not participation in

---

34. CO 49,307 (Commentary on 1 Cor. 1:2).

35. Cf. *Inst.* IV,1,13-16.

36. Cf. CO 49,378-80 (Commentary on 1 Cor. 5:2-4). The necessity of excommunication is already upheld in the first edition of the *Institutes* of 1536 with reference to 1 Cor. 5: cf. OS 1,89f.

37. As also in the *Institutes* of 1536: OS 1,90f.; cf. *Inst.* IV,12,5.

life's necessities, as Calvin stresses in contrast to the more radical methods of the Roman Church. Those excluded should not be made into enemies but would instead remain brothers.[38]

Calvin's commentary on 2 Corinthians 2:6-11 followed this line of thought. He linked this passage (in contrast with present-day exegesis) with the case depicted in 1 Corinthians 5, and did so to call for clemency following a previous call for stringency. In Calvin's view, this involved a basic statement on upholding patience and clemency in church discipline (*qua aequitate et clementia temperanda sit disciplina Ecclesiae*).[39]

Unity of the Church: Received as a Gift, Fulfilled in Church Life

In the Corinth congregation, withdrawal was a temptation less connected to aspirations for a pure church than it was tied to a struggle between different factions. As this is one of the central themes of the epistle itself, it is not surprising that Calvin focused on the unity of the church in his commentaries.

Harmony in Concrete Bonds and Freedom

Calvin viewed unity as being of central importance to the church, a unity that was not a human creation but that evolved thanks to the spirit of Christ.[40] And yet — with a particular view to the factiousness and division in Corinth — unity remained something for which the members of the church bore responsibility. Calvin realistically understood that matters of faith, while they brought people together, could also bring about strife all the more rapidly.[41] He underscored how much was at stake when it came to unity. Paul's question of whether this would then divide Christ reflected to the Corinthians the consequences of what they were doing: in dividing themselves into different bodies, they separated themselves from him as

---

38. CO 49,386 (Commentary on 1 Cor. 5:11).

39. COR 2,15,39 (Commentary on 2 Cor. 2:6). Cf. *Inst.* IV,1,29 (1539) with reference to 2 Cor. 2:7.

40. Cf. CO 49,314 (Commentary on 1 Cor. 1:10).

41. Cf. CO 49,315 (Commentary on 1 Cor. 1:12).

well; once divided, they were to understand that they were then made foreign to Christ.[42]

For Calvin, the unity of the church was not an abstract concept or a primarily theoretical idea for reflection, but a living reality. For precisely this reason, he was interested to know exactly how unity could come about and what it actually meant. Options came into play that would pose a permanent challenge to Roman Catholic ideas of unity, but that would also prove uncomfortable for liberal Reformed interpretative traditions.

Paul established a threefold formula for unity (1 Cor. 1:10): the Corinthians were to be in agreement, suffer no divisions, and be "united in the same mind and the same purpose." Calvin reordered these three elements. Logically speaking, the elimination of division should come first. This would lead to an inner harmony *(concordia)* "of one heart and one soul" (Acts 4:32). Calvin was strongly convinced of the significance of this consensus, upon which the "safety of the Church rests and depends."[43] Beyond unity in doctrine, Calvin foresaw a consensus in thought and volition *(mentibus et voluntatibus)* or in aspiration and volition *(in studiis et voluntatibus)*. This unity is anchored in the action of the Spirit.

According to Calvin, speaking with one voice logically came in third. This does not, however, mean that agreement was any less important to him; it was indeed particularly desirable as the fruit of Christian harmony *(apprime optabile ut fructus christianae concordiae)*. "When Paul tells them to speak the same thing, which is the fruit of unity, he is bringing out even more clearly how complete *(absolutus)* the agreement *(consensus)* ought to be, viz. that not even in words should any diversity appear. This is certainly difficult to do, but all the same it is necessary among Christians, from whom there is asked not only one faith, but also one confession."[44] Did Calvin assign more importance to words of agreement here than is the case in other contexts[45] — although his conflicts with Petrus Caroli (ca. 1480–after 1545) had already ceased before he wrote the commentaries on the Epistles to the Corinthians?

The expression of faith, its conveyance to the external world, was for Calvin a concern that corresponded perfectly with his activity as a re-

---

42. Cf. CO 49,316 (Commentary on 1 Cor. 1:13).

43. "Hoc etiam consensu stat et subnixa est salus ecclesiae": CO 49,314 (Commentary on 1 Cor. 1:10).

44. CO 49,314 (Commentary on 1 Cor. 1:10).

45. Cf., for example, *Inst.* IV,1,12.

former. The faith within had to find a means of expression. Calvin supported this in contrast with the "Pseudo-Nicodemites," that is, reform-oriented Christians who did not openly support the Reformation, or who even continued to participate in condemned Catholic rites, and the Sacrifice of the Mass in particular, thus burying their faith within while boasting of wisdom, all without uttering a single word of confession their entire lives. To this Calvin said that "believers ought to be brave and undaunted in confessing what they have believed in their heart."[46]

This was linked with a well-developed sense for the social dimension of the actual practice of faith. Calvin wrote that nothing was as effective in binding believers together and that nothing maintained peace as much as a religious consensus (*religionis consensio*). *Religio* in this context, with great certainty, refers to the outward manifestation of faith.[47] Calvin placed particular responsibility with those who proclaimed the gospel: they are linked together, serve one Lord, and work toward a common goal. This unity of purpose permitted no individual withdrawal from this common path.[48]

This quest for unity in the outward manifestation of the church, however, does not cast doubt on Calvin's differentiation between necessary forms of manifestation and those left to one's free choice. First Corinthians 14:40 served Calvin as an important reminder of the difference between "tyrannical edicts of the Pope, which crush the consciences of men in a detestable form of slavery, and the godly laws of the Church, which preserve its discipline and order."[49] God granted us liberty with regard to external rites, but not "unbridled liberty." With regard to the call to collect for Jerusalem as well, Calvin stressed this freedom, as Paul did not give us orders; God only "bids us be guided by the rule of love."[50]

It is characteristic of Calvin, as well as the Reformed tradition that he founded, that they apply the relative authority of ordinances to the indi-

---

46. COR 2,15,81 (Commentary on 2 Cor. 4:13).

47. Cf. CO 49,315 (Commentary on 1 Cor. 1:12). *Inst.* IV,1,9 views the universal church (*ecclesia universalis*) to be tied together through religious practice (*eiusdem religionis vinculo colligata esse*). On the meaning of *religio*, cf. Opitz, "Gebrauch." Becht, *Pium consensum tueri*, pp. 406-19, treats the agreement in the worship of God, which was of such importance to Calvin.

48. Cf. CO 49,351 (Commentary on 1 Cor. 3:8).

49. Cf. CO 49,535f. (Commentary on 1 Cor. 14:40).

50. COR 2,15,138 (Commentary on 2 Cor. 8:8).

vidual churches. These ordinances are by no means arbitrary within each local church, but each church should have the particular ordinances best suited to it.[51]

How did Calvin reconcile an externally maintained harmony, on the one hand, and room for liberty, on the other? His interpretation of 1 Corinthians 11:19 ("there have to be factions [*haereses*] among you") may shed some light on this. Calvin placed the roots of these divisions not in differences of doctrine but in inner attitudes, just as he saw that it was not errant doctrine but false attitudes that accounted for the problems in Corinth. As an exegete, he modified the definition of a schism that he previously knew — and did not in fact entirely reject — to an "alienation of spirits," and he defined heresy as a disagreement with doctrine. With a view to Paul, schisms are to be found "where there are secret animosities, with not a sign of that agreement which ought to be among believers." This leads to the spread of disagreement in which all maintain their own ways and find fault with the concerns of others, while sliding into heresy when "evil goes so fast and so far that hostility breaks out into the open, and men are quite deliberate about dividing themselves up into conflicting groups."[52]

As important as it is to find unity in the major points of doctrine and structures of the church, and agreement as to what constitutes these points, Calvin's intuition was all the more accurate that the roots of division lie in a lack of mutual goodwill and a lack of concern for the concerns of others.

Bonds of Mutual Exchange

The reality and responsibility of unity, and thus the dichotomy of the being and becoming of the church, become manifest in one topic brought into focus in 1 Corinthians, a topic that is indeed characteristic of the concerns that moved Calvin. The church lives and is unified through the multifaceted spiritual gifts that are to be used in the construction of the church. These gifts are an important theme in 1 Corinthians that moves Calvin to make subtle distinctions in the use of the term *grace*. This not only refers to God's disposition of grace but also to the gifts of grace

51. Cf. CO 49,473 (Commentary on 1 Cor. 11:2).
52. Cf. CO 49,481 (Commentary on 1 Cor. 11:19).

granted by God. The gifts can be viewed as belonging to the church as a whole as they were indeed granted for the purpose of its construction.[53] They thus form ties that boost the unity of the church. Time and again, Calvin maintained that God, to a certain didactic purpose, distributes different gifts, granting each individual only a certain degree of talent or strength, so that all believers are made to rely on each other.[54] Nobody is so well endowed that he or she can suffice alone without needing others, or put more precisely, no single individual receives everything from God, so that nobody can withdraw from the community, and so that no individual can form the entire body. The body can become perfect and complete only when each member plays his or her part.[55]

The variation of gifts serves to build unity in this manner, and must therefore be maintained: the "gifts are not distributed to believers in such variety, in order that they may be kept in isolation from each other; but there is a unity in difference."[56] This is the case, for one reason, because the gifts derive from the same source — the one God and his Spirit. For another, the gifts all have the same goal and are suited to harmonize with each other. The members of the body differ in their abilities and tasks so that they may come together in a common connection.[57] Calvin saw a symphony as a suitable metaphor for this: "The harmony of the Church lies in the fact that it is, so to speak, a unity of many parts; in other words, when the different gifts are all directed to one and the same end, just as in music different parts are adjusted to each other and combined so well that they produce one harmonious piece. It is only right, therefore, that gifts should be distinguished from each other just as much as offices, and that they should, nevertheless, be all combined in a unity."[58]

Calvin interpreted this variety of gifts in two ways. First, he referred

---

53. Cf. CO 49,310 (Commentary on 1 Cor. 1:4). Calvin summarized in brief what Paul taught to be the purpose of three gifts: "hoc est, in fratrum aedificationem": CO 49,496 (Commentary on 1 Cor. 12:1).

54. Cf. for all Christians: CO 49,367 (Commentary on 1 Cor. 4:7); in reference to ministers: CO 49,349 (Commentary on 1 Cor. 3:5).

55. Cf. CO 49,500 (Commentary on 1 Cor. 12:11); CO 49,507 (Commentary on 1 Cor. 12:29).

56. CO 49,498 (Commentary on 1 Cor. 12:4).

57. Cf. CO 49,504 (Commentary on 1 Cor. 12:20).

58. CO 49,497 (Commentary on 1 Cor. 12:4). Also CO 49,503 (Commentary on 1 Cor. 12:19) and COR 2,15,143 (Commentary on 2 Cor. 8:14) honored the *symmetria*, which were granted through the distribution of gifts (in 2 Cor. 8:14 this refers to material goods).

to Paul's discussion of the body in Romans 12, which he mentions in the Epistles to the Corinthians as well. This involves an admonition to be modest: nobody should seek to rescind the differences that God put in place and to cross boundaries instead of being content with one's own gifts and position. This more "conservative" directive to make do with one's own position and gifts was geared toward maintaining order. Calvin saw this point made in 1 Corinthians 12:15-27 as well: dissatisfaction with one's position in life is equated with a battle with God.[59]

The messages conveyed in 1 Corinthians 12:1-14, by contrast, do not focus on personal modesty, in Calvin's view, but on personal efforts. Believers are urged to use their special gifts for the benefit of all. These gifts are not endowed upon individuals for their own use but for the mutual support of one other.[60] Herein, in particular, lies the responsibility of believers: to use their gifts appropriately. The gifts are not granted for their own sake, as Calvin stressed with regard to 2 Corinthians 1:4, but are extended in order for the receiver (in this case, the apostles) to have greater opportunity *(facultas)* to help others.[61] This also holds, in the sense of 1 Corinthians 8, for maintaining the right amount of knowledge in a desire to edify one's fellows,[62] connected — in accordance with Paul's example — with limiting liberty for the sake of love.[63] God grants his gifts so that believers can follow his example and can be generous to others.[64] They should encourage each other to do so.[65]

This topic is so important to Calvin that he decided, not likely by chance, to close his commentary on 2 Corinthians with it. In the closing verse of the epistle, Paul seems to allude "to the variety of the Spirit's gifts, which he mentions elsewhere, since God does not give the Spirit to a man as an isolated individual but distributes to each according to the measure of grace, so that the members of the church may share their gifts with one another and so cherish their unity."[66]

---

59. Cf. CO 49,497f.,501, 503-5 (Commentary on 1 Cor. 12:4, 12, 15-27).

60. Cf. CO 49,501 (Commentary on 1 Cor. 12:12); cf. CO 49,498 (Commentary on 1 Cor. 12:4).

61. Cf. COR 2,15,11 (Commentary on 2 Cor. 1:4).

62. Cf. CO 49,428 (Commentary on 1 Cor. 8:1).

63. Cf. CO 49,433 (Commentary on 1 Cor. 8:8).

64. Cf. COR 2,15,11 (Commentary on 2 Cor. 1:4).

65. Cf. COR 2,15,141 (Commentary on 2 Cor. 8:13).

66. COR 2,15,218 (Commentary on 2 Cor. 13:13).

The exchange among believers is a concern that appears earlier in the first 1536 version of the *Institutes* in the interpretation of the creedal phrase "communion of saints" with reference to 1 Corinthians 12. In this sort of social order, the saints are "united in the fellowship of Christ" so that they may communicate to each other "all the blessings which God bestows upon them."[67] Calvin's way of closely connecting the task with the gift becomes apparent in a turn of phrase that he used repeatedly: when believers are "persuaded that God is the common Father of them all, and Christ their common head, they cannot but be united together in brotherly love, and mutually impart their blessings to each other."[68]

Calvin raised the believers' responsibility for each other above any exclusively individual path to salvation. It was, to be certain, justified and necessary to be concerned about oneself and one's own salvation. Calvin even emphasized this when it came to replacing one's hasty judgment of others with self-examination.[69] Concerns for one's one salvation are, however, limited by concerns for others.[70] Calvin interpreted this in different ways in his commentary on 1 Corinthians 8f. Knowledge that is not useful for others is empty knowledge; it leads to nothing if each individual only pursues his or her own advantage above that of others.[71] This was not only inspired by the relevant (and unambiguous) passages of 1 Corinthians, but also reflects a core concern held by Calvin, as illustrated by an eloquent passage from his reply to Cardinal Sadolet: "It certainly is the part of a Christian man to ascend higher than merely to seek and secure the salvation of his own soul."[72]

According to Calvin, the exchange between the members of the church body not only included the implementation of gifts received, but also extended to prayers of intercession.[73] This community and these bonds were indeed more profound than could be seen at the visible level; Calvin saw a "secret communion that the members of Christ have with each other."[74]

---

67. Cf. OS 1,91, a passage that returns in similar form in 1559 in *Inst.* IV,1,3. Cf. Geneva Catechism of 1545: CO 6,40.

68. *Inst.* IV,1,3.

69. Cf. *Inst.* IV,1,15.

70. Cf. CO 49,301 (Introduction to 1 Corinthians).

71. Cf. CO 49,429,432,435 (Commentary on 1 Cor. 8:1, 7, 11).

72. CO 5,391f. (Reply to Cardinal Sadolet).

73. Cf. COR 2,15,18 (Commentary on 2 Cor. 1:10).

74. COR 2,15,81 (Commentary on 2 Cor. 4:15).

Relations between Congregations

How Calvin viewed the reach of church community can also be seen in his treatment of the Corinthian congregation in the context of the church as a whole. While the difficulties in Corinth were primarily internal in nature, Calvin sought their solution in an external opening of the congregation. Calvin noted, for example, that Paul's scope went beyond the individual congregation in the introduction to 1 Corinthians (1 Cor. 1:2). In order to deflate criticism, he made himself a public figure[75] just as the apostles were duty-bound to the entire church. Calvin applied this to the ministers of his time: "So in our day it is indeed our duty *(officium)* to serve the whole Church and care for the whole Body."[76] All these exhortations were thus equally valid for relations across congregations.[77] At the same time, in Calvin's eyes, the Corinthians were criticized by Paul as the result of their arrogant withdrawal: "So Paul inquires if they are the only, indeed, if they are the first and the last, Christians in the world. He asks: 'Do you mean to say that it was from you that the Word of God went forth? In other words, did it originate with you? Did it come to an end with you? That is, will it not be spread any further?' . . . But this teaching is of a general nature, for no church ought to be turned in on itself, to the neglect of others. But, on the contrary, all of them should be extending the right hand to each other, to promote their fellowship with each other; and as the concern for unity demands, they should be adjusting themselves to one another."[78]

Despite this call for a readiness to adapt oneself to other churches, Calvin continued to uphold the freedom of each church to take on an external order that is appropriate and useful, as the Lord provided no specifics in this regard.[79] Calvin also joined Paul in his call for one church to serve as a model for others, originally with a view to the collection for Jerusalem. The example of the other Christian congregation was to serve as an opposing force to the accustomed human tendency not to deny one's own needs and help others.[80]

75. Cf. CO 49,309 (Commentary on 1 Cor. 1:2).
76. COR 2,15,43 (Commentary on 2 Cor. 2:12).
77. Cf. CO 49,414 (Commentary on 1 Cor. 7:17).
78. CO 49,533 (Commentary on 1 Cor. 14:36).
79. Cf. CO 49,473 (Commentary on 1 Cor. 11:2).
80. Cf. CO 49,566 (Commentary on 1 Cor. 16:1). For the example of other congregations, cf. COR 2,15,134 (Commentary on 2 Cor. 8:1).

In the commentaries on the Epistles to the Corinthians, Calvin almost always uses the term *ecclesia* for individual churches, and often in its plural form.[81] He, however, also uses the term *ecclesia* for that which he refers to in the *Institutes* as the *ecclesia universalis*. This *ecclesia* exists in different locations, corresponding to the single truth of divine doctrine at least in essential teachings, and is connected to religious practice *(religio)*.[82] Interestingly, this is often depicted in the commentaries by the body of Christ, a theme that Calvin, in contrast with 1 Corinthians 12, did not apply primarily to individual churches, but rather in passages that refer to the context of the (entire) church.[83] The Geneva Catechism of 1545 underscores this in an explanation of what "catholic" refers to with regard to the church: "As all believers have one head, so they must all be united into one body, that the Church diffused over the whole world may be one — not more."[84]

Service in the Church

The Significance of the Ministry in the Church

As mentioned above, Calvin saw the existence of the ministry (which was not entirely undermined in Corinth) as one of the reasons why the Corinth congregation could in fact be mentioned. This observation indeed illustrates the value of the ministry as presented in Calvin's ecclesiology. The section of the *Institutes* that upheld the high value of these elements — sermons and the administration of the sacraments — featured a similar convergence of church office and the listing of these "signs and badges" of the church. The removal of these elements would hence destroy the purpose of the church. For centuries, however, this had, in Calvin's view, indeed occurred through the erosion of the sermon. Somewhat surprisingly, Calvin does not criticize the false practice of the sacraments, but rather fo-

---

81. Cf. *Inst.* IV,1,9.

82. Cf. *Inst.* IV,1,9-12. *Inst.* IV,2,5: Calvin considers agreement in "sound doctrine and brotherly charity" to be the bonds of the church.

83. Cf. in addition to CO 49,501-5 (Commentary on 1 Cor. 12:12-27), for example, COR 2,15,19,43,66,130,143 (Commentary on 2 Cor. 1:11; 2:12; 3:18; 7:11; 8:14); cf. citation in n. 76.

84. CO 6,39f. (Geneva Catechism of 1545).

cuses on the looming elimination of the ministry, as this would threaten the edification of the church.[85] He thus saw the existence of this office as being closely connected with that of these two signs of the church.

Irrespective of — or more accurately, because of — the significance of church offices, one must look into correct ministerial practice. The Epistles to the Corinthians provide sufficient cause for this. Helmut Feld refers to the Commentary on 2 Corinthians as something like the "*Magna Charta* of the Church *ministerium*."[86] It is thus important to reject the self-aggrandizement of false apostles, while also upholding Paul's authentic claims of authority. This is reflected in Calvin's interpretation of the Epistles to the Corinthians: just as he warned not to obscure the instrumental character of the servants in ministerial office and to transpose the glory of Christ onto them, he also insisted that the ministers must not be separated from Christ as if the office of proclamation were created in vain.[87] Calvin praised the middle path *(temperamentum)*, which Paul places between the overelevation of pastors, at the expense of the glory of Christ, and an equally impermissible contempt for them.[88] This also illustrates Calvin's own efforts toward an integrative view of conduct in office, in which divine and human aspects intermesh and in which neither can be isolated.

Describing this middle path would go beyond the scope of this essay. Let it suffice to allude to an image that inspired Calvin, comparing the congregation with God's planting field. He explained that the work of a planter was all for naught if God did not grant the gift of growth to the seed through his blessings. For Calvin, this simile does not, however, allude merely to the relative meaning of the sermon and the preachers' human efforts that go into it, but indeed to its very necessity: "Therefore the person who is sure that he can come to faith by disregarding this means, acts just as if the farmer, giving up the plough, neglecting sowing and leaving all cultivation, were to open their mouths and expect food to fall into them from heaven."[89]

---

85. Cf. *Inst.* IV,1,11.

86. Feld, *Einleitung*, p. xxxii.

87. Cf. CO 49,351 (Commentary on 1 Cor. 3:7). Similarly: CO 49,438 (Commentary on 1 Cor. 9:1); COR 2,15,55,74,107 (Commentary on 2 Cor. 3:6; 4:5; 6:1).

88. The term *temperamentum* is found in CO 49,351,362 (Commentary on 1 Cor. 3:7; 4:1).

89. CO 49,350 (Commentary on 1 Cor. 3:6).

Ministers, the Demands of Their Vocation,
and Their Conduct in Good Faith

Calvin used the struggles among the different ministers in Corinth as a basis for a discussion on the appropriate view of ministry. He explained that not all those who claimed to speak in the name of Christ did this in truth, and that they could not be exempt from scrutiny.[90] Apart from the aforementioned flaws of manner such as ambition and thirst for glory, Calvin introduced three terms that express attitudes he saw as improper for pastors to adopt with regard to their congregations: excessive insolence, unfaithfulness in teaching, and avarice.[91]

Calvin named two formal conditions that needed to be fulfilled by ministers for them to be viewed in a positive manner, though he also mentioned criteria based on content. First, he stipulated that ministers absolutely needed to be called to office by God, as he repeatedly insisted. One could not simply decide on one's own to enter into office. Calvin differentiated between a calling by God and a calling by the church.[92] Second, he called upon teachers and preachers within the church to be faithful in the discharge of their duties. "Since no-one can by right arrogate to himself the description and the office of minister unless he is called, so it is not enough that a person be called, if he does not also give satisfaction in carrying out his work."[93] In sum, it was not enough to hold a title if the truth were not also present and if those who claimed apostleship did not prove this in their actions.[94] Competence in one's office thus is a constitutive part of the legitimacy of the office. Calvin stressed the binding character of the minister's role: "For he is dedicated to the Lord and to the Church, and held fast by a sacred bond, which it would be sinful for him to break."[95]

With regard to ministerial success, other concerns came into account, including the edification of believers *(aedificatio fidelium)* and the

---

90. Cf. CO 49,361 (Commentary on 1 Cor. 3:22); COR 2,15,210 (Commentary on 2 Cor. 13:3).

91. Cf. COR 2,15,121 (Commentary on 2 Cor. 7:2).

92. Cf. CO 49,305f. (Commentary on 1 Cor. 1:1) with allusion to *Inst.* IV,3,11 (1543).

93. CO 49,305 (Commentary on 1 Cor. 1:1); cf. CO 49,362 (Commentary on 1 Cor. 4:2). Also *Inst.* IV,3,10, in which Calvin specifically alludes to Paul's justification of his apostolic office with regard to his calling and his faithfulness in conducting his office.

94. Cf. COR 2,15,10 (Commentary on 2 Cor. 1:1).

95. CO 49,445 (Commentary on 1 Cor. 9:16).

health of the church.[96] Calvin focused even more closely on criteria of content with regard to the controversy between Paul and the Corinthians and Paul's claim to be proclaiming the gospel in an authentic way. As this showed, even a minister, such as Paul, who executed his office with the proper attitude, could be contested. The Corinthians, as Calvin commented, had not yet returned to the sound mind necessary "to form a just and fair opinion *(iusta trutina et aequa)*" of his fidelity.[97] In his Commentary on 2 Corinthians, Calvin seized the chance to return to this problem. The Corinthians did not thus have the ability to differentiate between true and false ministers (servants) since they were taken by boasting. In 2 Corinthians 5:18, by contrast, Paul stated what was needed in apostolic office: the doctrine of justification was the final criterion inasmuch as the goal of the entire gospel was to impart peace through the reconciliation with God through Jesus Christ, and to grant a good conscience. The servants were thus to convey this message and to assure the faithful of God's fatherly love. "Thus when a duly ordained minister *(minister rite ordinatus)* declares from the Gospel, that God has been made propitious to us, he should be heard as God's ambassador, carrying out a public duty as God's representative, and endowed with rightful authority to make this declaration to us."[98] Similarly, Calvin fashioned 2 Corinthians 1:19 (on the "yes" turned reality in Christ) into a criterion for the authentic performance of ministerial office: Christ could be recognized only in ministers "in whom can be seen this unvariable and perpetual 'yea' which Paul here declares to be characteristic of Him."[99] Time and again, Calvin saw charity and clemency as an appropriate ministerial attitude; pastors were to weep themselves instead of bringing others to do so.[100]

Outlook

To this day, one must be impressed by the concentration with which Calvin retraced the life of the church to its roots in the acts of the triune God

96. So COR 2,15,166 (Commentary on 2 Cor. 10:8); CO 49,300 (Introduction to 1 Corinthians).

97. COR 2,15,23 (Commentary on 2 Cor. 1:13).

98. COR 2,15,101 (Commentary on 2 Cor. 5:18) with context.

99. COR 2,15,29 (Commentary on 2 Cor. 1:19).

100. Cf. COR 2,15,37,39,164,206f.,209 (Commentary on 2 Cor. 2:4, 6; 10:6; 12:20; 13:2).

and held it up to these standards. Beyond all "definable" forms of imparting grace, he saw God's action, such as the gifts he grants, as extending far into the realm of the visible communion of believers. Just as Calvin rejected false claims of divine authority in the human aspects of the church, he also held the church to the standard of following the calling of God's grace in all forms of its living expression.

Reformed Christians and Catholics have different understandings of the degree to which the visible structures of the church are the result of an inaccessible gift of God, and the degree to which they reflect this gift — despite the sinfulness of all humankind. And yet, a look at John Calvin's work can remind both groups that their common goal can only be to form the life of the church in line with their conscience and in accordance with God's gifts and will. One of the most significant steps in an ecumenical dialogue must be to recognize each other by overcoming "schismatic" thinking and to be motivated by these concerns in forming the life of the church. This can serve as a driving force in the process of purification, in a willingness to repent, and in a heedfulness in living up to God's gift and not reducing his glory in the church.

Translated from German by David Dichelle, Leipzig

Calvin's Ethics

Eric Fuchs

Calvin's teaching on ethics responds to two needs: not to play down the drama of human existence, subject to sin and death, and to explain all the moral consequences of faith, including the regeneration of human responsibility. By losing the knowledge of God, man loses himself and can only trap himself in his own illusions and pretensions: "that part in which the excellence and nobility of the soul especially shine has not only been wounded, but so corrupted, that it needs to be healed and put to a new order as well" (*Inst.* II,1,9).

At the Foundation of Moral Responsibility: God's Providence

Man is not lacking in "dignity" — but only faith, the fruit of the grace of God, can give him his true value. If God himself, through his word contained in holy scripture, does not reveal man's true vocation to him, he strays into incertitude — or worse, into the illusion of knowledge that is idolatrous. Any remaining "sense of religion" in natural man is sterilized by sin. Nevertheless, he is tormented by the question of good and evil and there are still some gleaming sparks that "show him to be a rational being,

All quotations from the *Institutes* (1559) refer to *Institutes of the Christian Religion (1559)*, trans. F. L. Battles (Philadelphia/London, 1960).

differing from the brute beasts, because he is endowed with understanding" (*Inst.* II,2,12); his natural gifts, corrupted in their use, are not abolished. With regard to the social and political order, the "manual and liberal arts," human intelligence is capable of usefully working toward the establishment of a reasonable order. There are therefore natural human ethics resulting from the providence of God, who does not abandon his creation.

Believing in a Creator God is to believe that he takes care of his creation, "that he sustains, nourishes, and cares for everything he has made, even to the least sparrow" (*Inst.* I,16,1). The world is not the result of chance, but an expression of will and sense; it has a fundamentally positive nature. Divine protection raises it from the absurd and nonsensical, right from the heart of suffering and death. "Not only heaven and earth and inanimate creatures, but also the plans and intentions of men, are so governed by his providence that they are borne by it straight to their appointed end" (*Inst.* I,16,8).

Tested by circumstances of life that so often seem to contradict it, faith in divine providence is based on the assurance of God's justice: "We must be resolute, persuaded that God does not make our world like this by playing with us as if with a ball. . . . [W]e know that God's power is not tyrannical or disordered, but that it is inseparably linked to his justice, and he does everything fairly" (seventy-fifth sermon on the Book of Job). We know that God acts with justice, but the secrets of how he does that remain hidden from us.

This faith in God's justice and providence, far from leading to an idle fatalism, is to Calvin a powerful call to ethical responsibility: "For he who has set the limits of our life has at the same time entrusted to us its care; he has provided means and helps to preserve it" (*Inst.* I,17,4). The "means" in question is with our reason, the ability to discern in reality the call of God's wisdom, but coupled with a modesty that should rein in our pretensions, because ultimate knowledge belongs only to God. That is why it is necessary to "employ" the human aid at our disposal and that man "will neither cease to take counsel, nor be sluggish in beseeching the assistance of those whom he sees to have the means to help him" (*Inst.* I,17,9). In fact, other people can also be instruments of providence, distributors of God's kindness.

Providence is the foundation of ethics, because it guarantees that there is a promise attached to human existence; ethics are therefore understood as man's response, whether conscious or unconscious, to this promise.

Why does faith in providence guarantee hope? Because it no longer depends on how we feel when we face the changing circumstances of life, but instead on the assurance that God does not abandon his children, that he guides them where he wants them to be, in accordance with his justice. If "all things work together for good for those who love God," as Paul says (Rom. 8:28), believers can always say that their existence is positive, whatever the circumstances.

Therefore, with this guarantee, man can act on his intelligence and his will and reasonably endeavor to become a partner in the active grace of God. This is Calvin's ethical program: to behave with full responsibility as if everything depends on you, while knowing that ultimately everything depends on God and his providence.

Ethics exists because divine providence exists. Left to itself, that is to say, merely with natural reasoning, morality goes nowhere. It is deluded about man's ability to know good. Men fail when they believe "that virtues and vices are in our power" and that human reason "is a sufficient guide for right conduct" (*Inst.* II,2,3). Sin anesthetizes this moral potentiality, turning it away from its purpose and using it for human egotism and pride. "Because of the bondage of sin by which the will is held bound, it cannot move toward good, much less apply itself thereto" (*Inst.* II,3,5).

Therefore, while natural morality maintains a semblance of order, it also shows its inability to bring man to a complete assumption of his responsibility. Only the word of God can shed light on this.

The Standard of Ethical Responsibility: God's Law

According to the teaching of scripture, and throughout the whole of scripture including the Old Testament, God's will is expressed in three areas: the area of the worship before God, that of common social and political life, and that of the basic moral standard.

Recalling that the teaching of the Old Testament is an image of what Christ's work will fully realize, we must understand that the Old Testament laws regarding religious life and worship — for example, the need for sacrifices — have been accomplished and therefore abolished by Christ, who revealed their spiritual meaning through his death. The political laws given to Israel should be interpreted as an image, an example, a practical application of the ethical standard that should govern political life, namely justice. These political laws show how the standard of justice has taken concrete forms; their value is more methodological than substantial. All these laws are historical examples of basic moral law that perfectly reflect divine will, as expressed by "two heads, one of which simply commands us to worship God with pure faith and piety; the other to embrace men with sincere affection" (*Inst.* IV,20,15).

Thus clarified by scripture, ethics is given three functions: to break down any pretension of moral self-satisfaction, to provide the minimum guidelines to enable common life, and to encourage obedience in believers and guide them on the path of sanctification.

Calvin describes the first function of the Law: "While it shows God's righteousness, that is, the righteousness alone acceptable to God, it warns, informs, convicts, and lastly condemns, every man of his own unrighteousness. For man, blinded and drunk with self-love, must be compelled to know and to confess his own feebleness and impurity. If man is not clearly convinced of his own vanity, he is puffed up with insane confidence in his own mental powers, and can never be induced to recognize their slenderness as long as he measures them by a measure of his own choice. But as soon as he begins to compare his powers with the difficulty of the law, he has something to diminish his bravado" (*Inst.* II,7,6). The Law therefore acts as a judgment and a revelation of our natural incapability. At the same time it is an invitation to appeal for the merciful closeness of the Savior, to admit our need to find justification not in ourselves but in Christ.

The Law can in some way convince man of his inability to meet these standards, which he nonetheless recognizes as legitimate — not to drive him to despair but so that he will open himself up to the kindness of those to whom the Law gives it, first God and then all the others through whom he calls and approaches. Like Paul, Calvin is determined to highlight the ambiguity of ethics: a means for human pride to manifest itself and a revelation of the inability of human will to obey, which leads him to call on the grace of God. Paul teaches that "'God has shut up all man in unbelief,' not that he might destroy all, . . . but 'that he may have mercy upon all' (Rom. 11:32). This means that, dismissing the stupid opinion of their own strength, they come to realize that they stand and are upheld by God's hand alone" (*Inst.* II,7,8).

This Law, which reveals our inability to obey the ethical standards, also provides the means to prevent that inability and pride from degenerating into social violence. This is the second function of the Law, which legitimizes judicial constraint and sanctions for those who refuse to respect the civil law that is so important for common life. "But this constrained and forced righteousness is necessary for the public community of men, for whose tranquillity the Lord herein provided when he took care that everything be not tumultuously confounded. This would happen if everything were permitted to all men" (*Inst.* II,7,10). This again is an act of providence, restraining with the bridle of the Law those who remain dominated by the flesh, which in some way guarantees social peace (*Inst.* II,7,11). Calvin develops this point and gives it its full importance in Book IV of the *Institutes.* There he says that political order is not only characterized by the right to punish, but also by the willingness "so long as we live among men . . . to adjust our life to the society of men, to form our social behavior to civil righteousness, to reconcile us with one another, and to promote general peace and tranquillity" (*Inst.* IV,20,2).

This positive nature of the Law is shown plainly in the third use, "being also the principal use" — that is, to encourage the obedience of believers and to provide them with a written reference. The Holy Spirit acts in the hearts of believers to assure them of their righteousness before God; obeying the Law does not save, but it demonstrates the seriousness with which, in faith, the believer is assuming his or her spiritual and moral responsibility. The Law stimulates us to take the path of sanctification resolutely. It is therefore the whole of scripture, both Old and New Testaments, that feeds the ethical consciousness of the believer. The Law recognized in this manner offers a positive lesson: meditating on it lets those who give themselves over to it into the secret of God's will. In order to underline that there is no legalism in his proposition, Calvin clarifies that when we are in the grace of God "the Law is not now acting toward us as a rigorous enforcement officer who is not satisfied unless the requirements are met. But in this perfection to which it exhorts us, the law points out the goal toward which throughout life we are to strive. In this the law is no less profitable than consistent with our duty. If we fail not in this struggle, it is well" (*Inst.* II,7,13). Calvin's educational and pastoral concern is evident here: the Law understood in the light of the gospel no longer condemns or oppresses; it stimulates, lighting the path and showing the goal to aim for.

Therefore, the Law, the whole of scripture, should be read in the light of the gospel, that is to say, the loving and forgiving grace of God. It is the person of Christ who reveals its meaning. For those who know and recognize a figure of Christ, his promises and his call to follow him, the Law is a gift of God's love. Calvin firmly defends two affirmations: Law without grace results in guilt and death, but understood in the light of the gospel it becomes rich with the promise to make our works acceptable before God. "When the promises of the gospel are substituted, which proclaim the free forgiveness of sins, these not only make us acceptable to God but also render our works pleasing to him. And not only does the Lord adjust them pleasing; he also extends to them the blessings which under the covenant were owed to the observance of his law" (*Inst.* III,17,3). Salvation is obtained through faith alone, but that is not without works.

We understand that God's Law goes beyond any text; it is not a rule; it incites the freedom and the will of the believer's consciousness while also reminding him or her that freedom and will can produce no good thing without the grace of God. Through the ethical standard, man is led to repentance and faith (first use), social and political life is legitimized and limited (second use), and the believer can find the path of active and meaningful obedience (third use).

The latter point is particularly interesting. As the quality of the tree is known by the quality of its fruit, the truth of faith is known by the quality of the works it produces. As stated in the Heidelberg Catechism, the most famous Reformed catechism, the response to the question "Why must we do good works?" is not only to show our gratitude to God but also "that every one may be assured in himself of his faith, by the fruits thereof; and that, by our godly conversation others may be gained to Christ" (question 86). Protestant morality has evidently been marked by this tension between a strong affirmation of obedience to the moral standard and a no-less-strong affirmation of free salvation by faith. Only God can bring us to him by his grace, and our obedience to his will as explained in the Law shows that we are his children. Calvin's morality is therefore situated between these two poles: suspicion of that which comes naturally to man and confidence in the capacity of human freedom enriched by the gospel.

The Places for Ethical Responsibility

The first place where our responsibility should come into play is in ourselves. We should participate in God's work in us through a process of personal reform that Calvin calls penitence. This term implies first fighting the forces of death that constantly undermine us, having a critical demand on ourselves, which can and should extend to an abhorrence of self. This is undoubtedly a foretaste of a Puritanism that is always poised to crush man under the weight of guilt and that believes that man should be humbled in order to better praise God. But we must not forget that penitence also describes our participation in the life and death of Jesus Christ in order "to restore in us the image of God that had been disfigured and all but obliterated through Adam's transgression" (*Inst.* III,3,9). That is why the pages about penitence are the prelude to the long section that Calvin dedicates to Christian life, to the work of sanctification whose fundamental aim is "to frame one's life aright" according to the teachings of scripture.

Chapters VI–X of Book III of the *Institutes* are the ones that describe "the life of a Christian man." They have a great resonance, to the point that they have been published separately as *Most Excellent Treatise on the Christian Life* (original title: *Traicté très excellent de la vie chrestienne*). This passage of the *Institutes* is probably the most accomplished expression of Calvin's ethics. Our lives must aim toward perfection, but, Calvin adds, we should not lose heart when we only feebly reach this goal, "for even though attainment may not correspond to desire, when today outstrips yesterday the effort is not lost" (*Inst.* III,6,5); we must therefore make an effort to act in goodness "until we attain to goodness itself" (*Inst.* III,6,5). The gospel acts as a powerful moral ferment of will, as its strength is that it is not only an external exhortation calling on mere reason: "For it is a doctrine not of the tongue but of the life. It is not apprehended by the understanding and memory alone, as other disciplines are, but it is received only when it possesses the whole soul, and finds a seat and resting place in the inmost affections of the heart" (*Inst.* III,6,4).

Consequently, Calvin characterizes Christian life by three traits: asceticism, hope, and responsibility. Asceticism is not an end in itself, but rather a matter of not letting oneself be dominated by a boundless desire "to covet wealth and honours, to strive for authority, to heap up riches, to gather together all those follies which seem to make for magnificence and pomp" (*Inst.* III,7,8). The only Christian response to this restlessness is to have confidence in divine providence; free from any concern we may have, we can answer the call to love our neighbor: "Now he who merely performs all the duties of love, does not fulfil them, even though he overlooks none; but he, rather, fulfils them who does this from a sincere feeling of love" (*Inst.* III,7,7).

The second aspect of the Christian life is that it is marked by hope. A peaceful acceptance of the difficulties that life presents is made possible by the assurance of the expected riches in the future life. This should not lead us to hate our present life but to discern within it the signs of God's goodness. "For before he shows us openly the inheritance of eternal glory, God wills by lesser proofs to show himself to be our Father. These are the benefits that are daily conferred on us by him" (*Inst.* III,9,3).

The third mark of the Christian life is responsibility for the proper use of goods. Here in the final chapter of his "treatise on the Christian life," Calvin slightly adjusts his previous statements on asceticism and renunciation by saying that "by such elementary instruction, Scripture at the same time duly informs us what is the right use of earthly benefits — a matter not to be neglected in the ordering of our life. For if we are to live, we have also to use those helps necessary for living. And we also cannot avoid those things which seem to serve delight more than necessity. Therefore we must hold to a measure so as to use them with a clear conscience, whether for necessity or for delight" (*Inst.* III,10,1).

Use things in moderation so that we can find pleasure in them in good conscience. Not being a slave to the things we desire does not mean refusing all pleasures. It is part of God's gift to us in creation. "In grasses, trees, and fruits, apart from their various uses, there is a beauty of appearance and pleasantness of odour. . . . Has the Lord clothed the flowers with the great beauty that greets our eyes, the sweetness of smell that is wafted upon our nostrils, and yet will it be unlawful for our eyes to be affected by that beauty or our sense of smell by the sweetness of that odour?" (*Inst.* III,10,2). Can you say now that Calvin was an enemy of pleasure and that he condemned Protestantism to being a dreary form of Christianity? "Away, then, with that inhuman philosophy which, while conceding only a necessary use of creatures, not only malignantly deprives us of the lawful fruit of God's beneficence but cannot be practiced unless it robs a man of all his senses and degrades him to a block" (*Inst.* III,10,3). These few pages provide a (very) brief treatise on Protestant aesthetics that in turn formed the basis of what could be the early principles of Christian ecology.

While ethical responsibility first concerns the person called to sanctification, it does not ignore the fact that the requirement for justice also concerns society and its political structure. Yet this is threatened both by those who would give it over to the arbitrariness of princes who forget that their power is not absolute, and by those who would establish God's kingdom down here by political means. The gospel is not a political manifesto, but God's Law as an authority on ethics does concern politics. The state needs the church in order to be reminded of its function and duty; "to adjust our life to the society of men, to form our social behavior to civil righteousness, to reconcile us with one another, and to promote general peace and tranquillity"; in turn, the church needs the state "to cherish and protect the outward worship of God, to defend sound doctrine of piety and the position of the church" (*Inst.* IV,20,2).

Specifically, in Geneva, this interaction between church and state became a powerful driving force for social transformation. There, the reform was also social and political. Influenced by Calvin's preaching, new laws were passed organizing the management of funds for public aid, and public teaching was made compulsory. In that regard two of his creations should be mentioned: the diaconate and the organization of the general hospital. The diaconate is one of the four church offices founded by the Ordinances of 1541 *(Ordonnances ecclésiastique),* along with pastor, doctor, and elder. The deacons are responsible for administering the goods entrusted to the church intended for community support and taking care of the sick. We can see that the social work was part of the church's ministry and it was their responsibility to ensure that the political authorities did not neglect that responsibility. That was why those same *Ecclesiastical Ordinances* also organized in great detail the work of the hospital, which was a show of social solidarity. The best way of combating begging and immorality is to target the economic and moral causes, enabling everybody to find work and receive an education.

This diaconal activity is one expression of Calvin's thinking on political ethics. He believed politics to be one of the most distinguished expressions of God's providence, but in view of sin, there should be a constant guard against power becoming tyrannical and arbitrary. It should be reminded of its limit, which is the ethical standard of justice, which God's Law guarantees and which expresses the meaning of freedom. The "natural instinct to foster and preserve society" that man receives from his social nature ("man is by nature a social animal") should be structured by an ethical concern for justice (*Inst.* II,2,13).

With regard to economics, this understanding of responsibility leads to a new appreciation of work and money. Work becomes noble because God works himself; he is the Creator who continues to care for his creation. So that work does not become a tyrannical master, we should understand how to rest, as God rested; that is the meaning of the "day of rest" when man takes note that everything comes from God. By his work, man continues God's work, which is why "men were created to employ themselves in some work, and not to lie down in inactivity and idleness" (Commentary on Gen. 2:15). Work is part of the human vocation; there is no place in this regard for idleness, unemployment, or begging. The image of the poor changes: rather than being living symbols of Christ to be honored through charity, instead they are a sign of a personal or social failing that is to be corrected, by helping them out of their state by providing work and a means of subsistence. This strong validation of work would become a mark of Protestantism and one that Calvin linked to vocation. By answering the call to use our abilities to serve the whole community, work does not aim to accumulate wealth but to honor God, in the care that we take over it and in serving our neighbor. It should be noted that, in justifying the enrichment of society and of individuals and even calling it a sign of divine blessing, this moral validation of work had very significant economic consequences.

Thus we can see the dynamism of this code of ethics, which is both respectful of divine providence and keen to engage moral responsibility. Nobody should boast of their successes; we should take them as opportunities to use our riches for the service of those to whom providence has not been so generous. If a Protestant merchant, craftsman, or banker does well, they owe it in part to their competence and in part to God's kind providence, without which their efforts would be in vain. They should therefore make sure to use part of their gains for the service of others, in the form of gifts or investments. Calvin shows modernism here particularly when he discusses the issue of lending with interest. He understood that the moral tradition that the church had thus far upheld forbidding those loans, because the money could not produce fruit by itself and because it could not be said to be paid back without injustice, was undoubtedly legitimate with regard to loans for consumption but disastrous for loans enabling others to work and permitting the production of additional goods. Authorizing that type of loan would encourage social and economic development; it was consistent with ethical responsibility. A just rate had then to be set to efficiently combat the social scourge of depreciation. The authorities would monitor it. In Geneva, the rate was fixed at 5 percent in 1538 and at 6.66 percent soon afterward, which was a relatively low rate at the time. This is an interesting example of how Calvin interpreted the requirements of God's Law while taking the economic situation and its social effects seriously.

Another aspect of Calvin's teaching on ethics that also had a certain influence on conventions is that concerning marriage, sexuality, and family. Arguing against both the obligation of celibacy for clergymen, which "has introduced a fearful sink of iniquity, and plunged many souls into the gulf of despair," and the prohibition of divorce — "if a woman is not loved by her husband, it is better to repudiate her than to detain her" (On Mal. 2:16) — Calvin seeks both to liberate the "poor consciences" and to give marriage its profound morality. That is why he extols the greatness of marriage, which is of such social importance that Calvin and the reformers are led to condemn any marriage agreed to without the consent of the parents. Parental authority must be reestablished so that marriage is not just a matter of personal choice but regains its social function. In marriage, which is no longer considered to be a remedy against the dangers of sexual desire *(remedium concupiscentiae)* but considered to be an aid to human weakness, persons build themselves up and respond to their vocation. It is therefore important that marriage and family be protected by law. For Calvin and the Protestant tradition, in order to really protect the family, marriage has to be protected. That is undoubtedly a point on which the break from contemporary social morality is evident!

So we can see that Calvin made important contributions with regard to the three big questions that have always preoccupied human societies — power, sexuality, and money; in each case he sought to understand how to combine biblical teaching and knowledge of the real world. Thus in the political arena he took care to distinguish the foundation of the laws, that is, justice, and their contingent formulation, which depends on circumstances; he says so very clearly: "What I have said will become plain if in all laws we examine, as we should, these two things: the constitution of the law, and the equity on which its constitution is itself founded and rests. Equity, because it is natural, cannot but be the same for all, and therefore, this same purpose ought to apply to all laws, whatever their object. Constitutions have certain circumstances upon which they in part depend. It therefore does not matter that they are different, provided all equally press toward the same goal of equity" (*Inst.* IV,20,16). Political reality should take account of circumstances and adapt to them, all the while remaining faithful to the principle of justice, of equity, which is its foundation, which recalls God's Law.

155

The same logic is used with regard to money: taking the economic needs of the time seriously, Calvin is led to recognize the need to legitimize lending with interest insofar as it can be used for the good of the whole community by encouraging economic activity. There again, the principle of justice, in this case using personal goods to serve another, is the basis of the action.

Finally, when a man and a woman recognize that they are gifts from God for one another, they make an effort to register their relationship in a discipline of life that directs their desire with their responsibility to make their family an example that honors God and serves the community.

Thus each time we must distinguish what is drawn from the fundamental ethical principle and the manner of practicing it in view of the circumstances. God's Law is the source of ethics; the role of human intelligence is to translate this Law into moral laws that are adapted to the particular place and time. The Law is the critical authority for laws.

Conclusion: The Values and Difficulties of Calvin's Ethics

The question posed by reading Calvin's works is: Is it possible to build a Christian code of ethics based on the idea of providence? If God controls everything, including human will, how can you justify and develop a code of ethics, which can only make sense when coupled with the freedom of man? Without freedom there is no responsibility, and without responsibility, man is nothing but a toy in the hands of a God for whom the arbitrary has no need of justification. After taking the logic of his understanding of providence much further, Calvin writes that even sinners are necessary and wanted by providence, because in the end they serve the cause pursued by God; and that is not because God will correct their sinfulness through additional kindness, but because their sinfulness itself is part of God's design. While they are responsible for the sin they commit, God uses sinners to serve his glory. This is the awful logic of a system that in justifying God ends up making him detestable! God's mysterious and inscrutable omnipotence seems to have the upper hand on his love. Is man's only responsibility to accept what happens to him and to submit to it as if to God's will?

That is a danger that Calvin saw and overcame by highlighting the notion of promise. Divine providence assures us of the promise made to man that he can act and respond, using his intelligence and will informed by the Holy Spirit, to the gift of life that is given to him. Ethics is a responsibility because it is a response, a response based on God's providence that assures believers that their life is the object of a promise, a promise that they can take their life in their own hands without fear of the circumstances that they will have to face.

Therefore, to submit to the will of God is to try to discover evidence of it in the events of life and respond to it, with humility, as our knowledge in this field is uncertain, and with intelligence, by turning to God's Law, which interpreted in the light of the gospel will guide this endeavor.

Lastly, the word that best characterizes Calvin's ethics is *responsibility*. Throughout the *Institutes* he suggests a true spiritual and moral method that can help the believer respond to the call of God's word and thereby progressively reach Christian, and thus human, wholeness. Calvin's concern for education is evident and explains the considerable success of his writings. Though he is convinced that the grace of God gives us everything as soon as faith accepts God's promise, Calvin also knows that a lot of patience is required before this gift produces all of its spiritual and moral fruits.

Discernment and *responsibility* are both terms that imply consciousness of oneself and of God's gifts. To make progress in the Christian life we must abandon all pride and pretension; sin is always present to make us doubt the greatness and grace of God. Never forget that hating sin goes hand in hand with loving God's justice, in order "to hasten to God and yearn for him, . . . having been engrafted into the life and death of Christ" (*Inst.* III,3,20). Calvin does not want to give us any illusions about our spiritual capabilities but wants us to marvel at the gifts from God. The God whose greatness humbles any human pretension is also the God who through Jesus Christ showed himself to be a loving Father and a Creator with great care for his creation.

This emphasis on responsibility creates a tension in the spiritual and moral life of the person — tension between awareness that could easily become a form of self-hatred, constant self-underestimation, a lack of hope for oneself or for others, or complacence, abandonment of any critical thought. In both cases, ethics are forgotten; why worry about it if everything is going badly, if everything is going well? However, this tension can be fruitful if we understand that it qualifies ethical responsibility while keeping it from taking pride in its success. This is what leads to the practice known as Calvin's moderate asceticism, which puts the value of goods into perspective as moral values with regard to the fullness of promised eternal life. This perspective does not depreciate the goods, but rather it is a specific response to the concern of falling into the excesses of an asceticism that spurns God's gifts. Gifts should be used with gratitude and in moderation, so that a person does not become a slave to them.

It is this that the life of the church and the lives of believers should show, both in the discipline that they accept for themselves and in the courage of their ethical behavior with regard to political, economic, or cultural powers.

Today, it is important to respect the spirit, rather than the letter, of this program that Calvin implemented with such vigor. In today's largely secular society, the church no longer has restrictive power, and that is undoubtedly a gift of providence! More than ever, it still has the responsibility to tirelessly tell first believers, then society, that the gospel is not apart from the Law, or in modern terms, that there are no rights without a recognition of duties, or even that freedom cannot exist without solidarity.

Translated from French by Victoria Mendham, Bath, UK

Calvinism and Capitalism

Ulrich H. J. Körtner

God and Money

From time immemorial, God and money have often been placed in a complex and difficult relationship. While sociologist Niklas Luhmann (1927-1998) advises modern Christianity to follow the model of the modern monetary economy for a religious organization more suited to our times, and whereas other sociologists of religion view the religious diversity and competition of today's pluralistic society as a form of market in accordance with economic principles, Jesus confronts us with the alternative of either God or money and warns us that we cannot serve both masters at the same time (Matt. 6:24; Luke 16:13). In another context Jesus did speak in favor of making friends using the very mammon (Luke 16:9) that is, at the same time, deemed to be dishonest. And how, Jesus adds, can one expect to be entrusted with true riches when one has not proven faithful with dishonest wealth (Luke 16:11)?

Not only each individual Christian, but the church as a whole needs to address the matter of the complex relationship between God and money. In times of economic austerity, one must pay the greatest heed to thrift. This, time and again, leads to the question of whether the church, in its efforts to

---

In this essay, the quotations from the *Institutes* refer to *Institutes of the Christian Religion (1559)*, trans. F. L. Battles (Philadelphia/London, 1960).

reform, should fall in line with the spirit and exigencies of the modern economy, or whether other alternative ways of dealing with money can evolve from the spirit of Christ. Beginning with the question of where the church invests its money and how it raises funds to finance its personnel and real estate, this also involves matters such as church labor law and the broad topic of diaconal services, which in countries such as Germany represent one of the largest employment sectors and thus a major economic factor.

There is, without a doubt, a historical difference between the economy and monetary principles during the days of Jesus and the modern economy of today. The modern capitalist market economy is based on economic laws and principles that were unknown to that period of late antiquity. The system only began to emerge during the Reformation era. It remains a topic of discussion to historians of the Reformation and economic historians whether there was an inner connection between the religious and philosophical shifts of the Reformation and the development of modern-era capitalism.

The sociologist Max Weber (1864-1920) believed that this could indeed be shown. He saw a special connection between Calvinism and the spirit of modern capitalism. When one also takes into account the role that Calvinism played in the development of modern democracy, Weber's propositions contribute to the conclusion that Calvin and Calvinism, much more than Lutheranism or Zwingli, served as trailblazers for the modern era.

Setting aside the question of whether Weber's theory is at all historically correct, the theological question arises as to the attitude the Reformed churches of today should take with regard to the capitalism of our time. Is the capitalist market economy, from the perspective of the Reformed tradition, something to be affirmed as a matter of principle; are perhaps at most only certain excrescences to be criticized? Or is today's economic system, which emerged after the conflict between the capitalist and socialist global systems, to be rejected as a whole? If this is in fact the case, one must then ask to what extent the theological criticism of capitalism today is a continuation of the Reformed heritage, and to what degree it represents a theological watershed.

These questions are unavoidable when, for example, discussing topics such as the "confession of faith in the face of economic injustice and ecological destruction," as did the August 2004 General Council of the World Alliance of Reformed Churches in Accra. The Council requested of its member churches that they implement this confession, and that they, together with the ecumenical community, work for a just economy and the integrity of creation. The main point of the document is that the "current world (dis)order is rooted in an extremely complex and immoral economic system defended by empire. In using the term 'empire' we mean the coming together of economic, cultural, political and military power that constitutes a system of domination led by powerful nations to protect and defend their own interests" (Art. 11). This was tied to an explicit reference to the "government of the United States of America and its allies, together with international finance and trade institutions (International Monetary Fund, World Bank, World Trade Organization)." In all economic and ecological injustice, moreover, one can hear the "groaning of creation" (Rom. 8:22). The Accra Confession maintains the conviction that the current economic system represents a betrayal of God (Luke 16:13) and categorically denounces the system's underlying spirit and logic.

If Max Weber's theory is indeed correct, and the spirit of modern capitalism — at least in its beginnings — was greatly inspired by Calvinism, one is then faced with the question of the origins of the estrangement between today's Calvinism and capitalism. One must also ask what alternatives to the current economic system would mesh better with the basic convictions of the Reformed faith.

The Accra Confession speaks of an "economy of grace for the household of all of creation," which entails a preferential option for the poor and marginalized (Art. 20). This "economy of grace" leads to the rejection of the "current world economic order imposed by global neoliberal capitalism and any other economic system, including absolute planned economies, which defy God's covenant by excluding the poor, the vulnerable and the whole of creation from the fullness of life" (Art. 19). The World Alliance of Reformed Churches thus voiced a resounding "no"; but is there perhaps a concrete and therefore economically practicable "yes" as well? Can the "economy of grace" be transformed into concrete economic programs or a functioning economic system? Or is this just a case of religious rhetoric?

Before we come to terms with this question, we will first turn to a summary and discussion of Max Weber's theory on Calvinism and capitalism.

Calvinism and the Spirit of Capitalism according to Max Weber

A simple depiction of Calvinism as the intellectual breeding ground upon which modern-day capitalism could develop and prosper represents a gross oversimplification of Weber's ideas. Weber in fact treated the relationship between the two with greater subtlety.[1] When discussing his ideas, one should also take into account Weber's main concern: in his famed study, *The Protestant Ethic and the Spirit of Capitalism,* which he wrote between 1904 and 1906, Weber pursued neither a purely historical investigation of factors relevant to the history of ideas in the beginnings of modern-era economic history, nor did he seek to depict a Protestant or, more specifically, a Reformed social ethic as such. Weber was indeed more interested in the "emergence of modern . . . humanity."[2]

Weber did in fact derive the modern middle-class way of life, of which capitalist economic activity represents only a part, from the Protestant and, more specifically, Calvinist understanding of professional life. His historical derivation included, one must add, *criticism* with regard to contemporary capitalism. Weber begins his investigation by establishing that an unmitigated pursuit of gain and of the greatest possible amount of money has, per se, nothing to do with capitalism.[3] This is indeed of interest within the theological discussion on the position of the Reformed Church with regard to current forms of capitalism.

Put simply, Weber delineated the capitalism of the nineteenth century and his own time as the product of a decline from its commendable original form. This ideal — but not to say idealized — form of capitalism alone, according to Weber, was rooted in the Calvinist view of humanity. In contrast, contemporary capitalism stands in danger of losing the rationality it requires to work due to increasing bureaucratization. This rationality is indeed, according to Weber, Reformed in origin. Weber refers to Calvinism as being a critical force in opposition to a further deformation and perversion of capitalism. The question of the origins of capitalism in terms of history and the evolution of ideas gives way to a theoretical outlook on the future of capitalism, and thus also the future of modern democracy; Weber sees capitalist economics and democratic liberalism as being interconnected in their very essence.

Weber's use of the term *capitalism* must first be explored in order to be able to evaluate his individual theories and conclusions. The term *capitalism* has its roots in *capital,* which in turn derives from *capitale* (heads,

---

1. With regard to the following, cf. Körtner, *Reformiert,* pp. 80-97.
2. Wilhelm Hennis, cited in Ulrich, "Kapitalismus," p. 607.
3. Weber, *Protestant Ethic,* p. 17.

livestock). This stems from a time when livestock were used as a means of exchange.[4] The word is used today to mean any assets, whether in terms of cash or securities, land ownership, real estate, or means of production (real capital). The capitalist pursuit of profit aims at the expansion of one's fortune not for its own sake but as a means of investing in production or other manners of increasing value.

The term *capitalism,* to be certain, entails difficulties in terms of discourse theory. Ever since Karl Marx, it has been used chiefly by those who reject, as a matter of principle, the economic form in question. Capitalism is thus not a macroeconomic category independent of values, but is a term that always contains economic and political value judgments. The term is hence mostly avoided within the capitalist economic system itself. One speaks instead of a free or a social market economy.

According to Weber's definition, a capitalist economic action is "one which rests on the expectation of profit by the utilization of opportunities for exchange, that is on (formally) peaceful chances of profit."[5] Weber clearly differentiated between capitalist economic action and warlike forms of profit. The peculiarity of the modern-age capitalist economic form as derived in Europe is, however, "the rational capitalist [workplace] organization of (formal) *free labour.*"[6] Two further important developments of modern-era capitalism are the separation of household and workplace as well as rational bookkeeping. "However, all these peculiarities of Western capitalism have derived their significance in the last analysis only from their association with the capitalistic organization of labour."[7] In terms of cultural history, Weber placed the origins of the Western middle class in connection with the emergence of capitalism.[8]

Weber then continued to pursue the conditions, in terms of cultural history, that were necessary for the development of the modern middle class, conditions that are not identical but still closely tied to the origins of the capitalist organization of labor. In other words, Weber analyzes the history of ideas to inquire into what he calls "the spirit of capitalism."[9] Weber equates this spirit with a certain "*ethically* coloured maxim for the conduct

---

4. Cf. Hölscher and Hilger, "Kapital," pp. 402f.
5. Weber, *Protestant Ethic,* p. 17.
6. Weber, *Protestant Ethic,* p. 21.
7. Weber, *Protestant Ethic,* p. 22.
8. Weber, *Protestant Ethic,* p. 24.
9. Weber, *Protestant Ethic,* pp. 47-78.

of life."[10] More specifically, this idea of one's duty in a calling "is what is most characteristic of the social ethic of capitalist culture, and is in a sense the fundamental basis of it. It is an obligation which the individual is supposed to feel and does feel towards the content of his professional activity, no matter in what it consists in particular no matter whether it appears on the surface as a utilization of his personal powers, or only of his material possessions (as capital)."[11] Although capitalism is characterized by the highest measure of calculated rationality, Weber's view of professional activity involves an irrational aspect, at least from the viewpoint of a eudemonic or utilitarian ethic geared toward the principle of self-interest. Weber is indeed most interested in the origin of this putatively irrational element within capitalism.

What is, however, the derivation of the particular view of profession in the capitalist economic system? Weber's well-known and oft-discussed theory states that Calvinism played a large role in forming the ethic on which capitalism is based. One important supporting indication for this supposition is the striking fact that the modern history of industrial and capitalist economies began not in Roman Catholic areas nor in countries with a Lutheran background, but in the Netherlands, England, and North America, places with a Calvinist religious influence. In his broad-based investigation, Weber did not allude so much to the original form of Calvinism or Calvin himself but more so to later Calvinism and Puritanism. Weber also in no way simply equates Calvinism and what he refers to as the spirit of capitalism. He is instead more of the opinion that the capitalist ethic and the Calvinist professional ethic share common religious roots.

In Weber's view, the two are connected in their ethic of worldly asceticism *(innerweltliche Askese)*. With this term Weber explains how one important result of the Reformation was a completely new view of work and professional life in contrast with the medieval views and with Catholicism of the Late Middle Ages. This coincided with a fundamental criticism of monasticism and of the twofold set of ethics *(Zweistufenethik)* endorsed by the Catholic Church. Evolving in part from the ancient differentiation between the *vita activa* and *vita contemplativa,* this stipulated that while work was doubtless a necessity, a life of contemplation and meditation was to be held in higher esteem. God was to be sought and found not so much

10. Weber, *Protestant Ethic,* pp. 51f.
11. Weber, *Protestant Ethic,* p. 54.

in everyday life as in the cloistered life of the monastery. The classic biblical passage used in medieval theology to establish the difference between the *vita activa* and *vita contemplativa* was the story of Mary and Martha (Luke 10:38-42). According to the medieval interpretation, Martha, who tended to Jesus' needs, stood for the *vita activa,* while her sister Mary, rebuked for her choice by Martha, received words of praise from Jesus for choosing "the better part" (Luke 10:42), and stood for the monastic *vita contemplativa.* The medieval Church taught that one could give oneself fully to God only in the monastery, whereas common people living in marriage and families, who needed to work each day to earn a living, could only be considered to be incomplete Christians.

Monasticism, as it strove for perfection, was and continues to be ascetic by nature. Chastity, poverty, and obedience are the fundamental rules of every form of monastic life. Asceticism entails giving up the world for the sake of God, and becoming free from all that prevents a person from such undivided dedication. But as the Catholic Church of the Middle Ages indeed taught, this was not something for everyone. A life spent undividedly dedicated to God and in search of God required a particular vocation that was possible only for certain select Christians.

Martin Luther (1483-1546), in contrast, came to a fully different view of marriage, family, and work. Referring to 1 Corinthians 7:17-24, Luther stated that every Christian received a calling from God, each in his or her particular manner, such that there were no differences of rank between Christians and that a special monastic form of life did not follow biblical teachings. He wrote that every Christian was called to discipleship in equal measure, which was, however, not to be confused with an attempt to escape from the world. Christians, on the contrary, were called to service within and for the sake of the world. Luther thus rejected the traditional differentiation between *vita activa* and *vita contemplativa.* Christians, according to Luther, should serve God particularly in the *vita activa,* in marriage and work. One's daily work was to be seen as a divine calling or vocation.

Although Luther and the other reformers criticized the monastic form of life, they did not renounce the biblical concept of strict discipleship, but rather transposed the monastic ideals of chastity, poverty, and obedience onto everyday life in the world. In a sense, every Christian could therefore be seen to be called to lead a monastic life — not, however, behind monastery walls but in the context of the world. Perfection or indeed sanctification was seen as a continual task for all Christians, manifested for them in their families, marriages, and working lives.

As Max Weber pointed out, Calvin expanded on Luther's views on the matter. In the third chapter of the third book of his *Institutes of the Christian Religion* (*Institutio christianae religionis*, 3rd ed., 1559), Calvin established that while Christians were born again through faith, the consequence of this faith was their lifelong repentance. Calvin, however, differentiated between legal and evangelical forms of repentance (*Inst.* III,3,4). The essence of evangelical repentance is described in terms of mortification and quickening: "It is a true turning of our life to God, a turning that arises from a pure and earnest fear of him; and it consists in the mortification of our flesh and of the old man, and the vivification of the Spirit" (*Inst.* III,3,5). The Christian life in the framework of the everyday world was viewed by Calvin in terms of self-denial (*Inst.* III,7). According to Titus 2:12, this consists of "soberness, righteousness, and godliness," whereby Calvin interpreted soberness as "chastity and temperance as well as a pure and frugal use of temporal goods, and patience in poverty" (*Inst.* III,7,3).

Calvin also addressed the issue of one's calling within the framework of the doctrine of holiness. For Calvin, work was not the place for self-actualization in modern terms or merely a means to earning money and securing a living but was "a sort of sentry post" assigned by the Lord, so that we "may not heedlessly wander about throughout life" (*Inst.* III,10,6). Specific duties came with each vocation, leading each individual to self-discipline. According to Calvin, self-discipline was required from Christians also with regard to ownership and all earthly goods. Calvin was indeed able, as is often overlooked, to declare that food and clothing were not only there to satisfy basic needs, "but also for delight and good cheer" (*Inst.* III,10,2). At the same time, however, Christians were to despise the present life and aspire to celestial immortality. The evangelical freedom of believers in their use of earthly things is thus subject to law: "to indulge oneself as little as possible; but on the contrary, with unflagging effort of mind to insist upon cutting off all show of superfluous wealth, not to mention licentiousness" (*Inst.* III,10,4).

It is precisely this attitude that we see in Calvin and in later Calvinism — but also incorporated into Luther's view of occupation — that Max Weber termed "worldly asceticism." This was connected to the doctrine of election — not in fact in Calvin's writings but those of his student and successor, Theodore Beza (1519-1605). As is well known, Calvin and his followers espoused the doctrine of double predestination, in which God elects the faithful to eternal life, while nonbelievers are eternally damned. For Calvin (as indeed also for Luther!) the latter was the logical if, in his view, terrible consequence of the doctrine of election, a doctrine that does not, however, aim primarily at the damnation of nonbelievers, but at providing persecuted believers with solace and certainty. Weber would explain that, in later Calvinism, this doctrine of election, despite its original intent to provide solace, did not serve to boost the certainty of salvation but, in full contrast, led to a greater disquietude and anxiety of conscience. The doctrine of the so-called *Syllogismus practicus,* which posited that the personal welfare of an individual provided insight into his or her election, was then introduced within Calvinism to remedy this anxiety.

It was Weber's view that the concept of the *Syllogismus practicus* in conjunction with his demand for worldly asceticism brought forth the spirit of capitalism. The Calvinists sacrificed themselves for their vocations and pursued economic success in the hope of thus providing evidence of their own election. The precept of worldly asceticism, however, denied them the right to simply enjoy the fruit of their success. This would have constituted sin and, therefore, a break with God. People consequently reinvested much of their earnings in their businesses or production, making it possible for their successful work to increase their capital assets. This in turn made it necessary to search for useful new investments. Capitalism was born.

According to Weber, while capitalism developed as a world-changing economic system atop the roots of Calvinism, it did not in fact remain tied to Calvinism but soon departed from its religious tenets. Weber described this development by citing the Puritan Baxter:

> In Baxter's view the care for external goods should only lie on the shoulders of the "saint like a light cloak, which can be thrown aside at any moment." But fate [!] decreed that the cloak should become an iron cage. Since asceticism undertook to remodel the world and to work out its ideals in the world, material goods have gained an increasing and finally an inexorable power over the lives of men as at no previous period in history. To-day the spirit of religious asceticism — whether finally, who knows? — has escaped from this cage.[12]

12. Weber, *Protestant Ethic,* p. 181.

Weber, however, was not yet certain as to which spirit would predominate in modern capitalism. It was possible, in his dark vision, that capitalism would end in "mechanized petrification. . . . For of the last stage of this cultural development, it might well be truly said: 'Specialists without spirit, sensualists without heart; this nullity imagines that it has attained a level of civilization never before achieved.'"[13]

Criticism of Weber's Understanding of Capitalism

Weber's theory would prove to be a great success. But does it in fact hold up to criticism? From the perspective of social history, one must agree with Weber that among the major Christian confessions, the Reformed tradition or, to be more precise, Calvinism has played the largest active role with regard to modern capitalism. Even into the twentieth century, Catholic social doctrine had developed no real relationship with capitalism. Lutheranism as well did more in terms of simply tolerating capitalism than it did toward playing an active role in its development. Calvinism alone worked actively toward forming modern capitalism as a real economic system and way of life. This, however, by no means implies that capitalism as such was a direct outgrowth of Calvinism.

It is particularly striking that many important terms in modern-era banking derive from the Italian language. Western banking developed from coin and money-changing activities in large trading centers. Trade was particularly active in Lombardy and northern Italy, which explains the dominance of Italian as the language of banking. Even before the Reformation, banking spread into the Orient. In the fourteenth and fifteenth centuries, deposit and transfer transactions were introduced to supplement traditional money-changing activities. In any event, the origins of modern banking, which was so important for the rise of capitalism, are not to be found in Calvinism.

We can illustrate this using the Reformed attitude toward bank interest at the beginning of the modern era. The medieval church rejected the charging of interest as un-Christian, and even Luther condemned the practice. Calvin, however, maintained another attitude, although he in no way justified bank interest without qualification nor the rise of the mod-

13. Weber, *Protestant Ethic*, p. 182.

ern monetary economic system. Calvin was, however, of the opinion that interest was not always unethical — something that Luther indeed never said — while he, on the other hand, did not condone professional money lending and banking as a profession. Instead, he maintained that one should lend to the poor without charging interest, and that, when collecting permissible interest, one should not neglect the principle of loving one's neighbor. In other words, one should not work to one's own advantage but for the well-being of one's fellows.

In an essay on the question of interest and usury in the Reformed Church, the church historian Karl Holl (1866-1926) presented a case for Calvinism having been "the decided *opponent* of capitalist pursuits" through the middle of the seventeenth century. It was only later that Calvinism became, in a virtually tragic manner, a "chief supporter of capitalist pursuits . . . at least in England and America," due to a professional ethic that was partly compatible with capitalism.[14] Into the seventeenth century, bankers and moneylenders in France, Holland, and England were confronted often enough with church discipline in accordance with Calvin's strict regulations.

As has often been established, Weber took the historical evidence for his theory from the English Puritanism of the mid-seventeenth century, something that reduces the accuracy of his interpretation from the start.[15] Weber's postulated connection between Calvinism and capitalism does not hold for seventeenth-century French Protestantism either. His derivation of the capitalist pursuit of profit from the Reformed doctrine of predestination and the concept of *Syllogismus practicus* presupposes the strict doctrine of predestination upheld in Dordrecht and Westminster, which, however, did not in fact represent a good portion of French Protestantism.[16] This was equally the case for Moyse Amyraut (1596-1664), who taught in Saumur and whose six-volume *Morale Chrestienne* was exemplary for the Huguenot moral doctrine of the seventeenth century.[17]

In Amyraut's view, the differences of ownership and income that resulted from the individual's contribution to the community were to conform with natural justice. Amyraut approved of profits from trade and crafts, while he paid little heed to the newly emerging professions of his

14. Holl, "Frage," p. 402.

15. Cf. Strohm, *Ethik*, pp. 3f.

16. That Weber's theories are not even directly supported by the Westminster Confession is shown in Schellong, *"These,"* pp. 34-37.

17. On the following, cf. Kretzer, "Calvinismus-Kapitalismus-These," pp. 65-71.

time. He saw long-distance trade and monetary transactions as sources of wealth but not commercial production on the basis of a division of labor. "This social philosophy is practically timeless. It did not yet take the early capitalist mode of production into account, and thus did not yet reflect on the capitalist entrepreneur."[18]

Amyraut justifies tireless and intensive work. He permits money-lending for interest under certain circumstances, though he calls for moderation and modesty (without which, Christians would remain slaves to mammon). Profits earned should not be reinvested as in modern capitalism, but should instead be used for charity. Amyraut in no way preaches worldly asceticism but instead calls for a joyous Christianity, far from regulated piety or an exacting manner of living. He also rejects the implications of the *Syllogismus practicus,* in which poverty and need are seen as signs of a lack in grace.

Amyraut's moral doctrine is not far from Calvin, who introduced his view that Christians "should know how to bear poverty peaceably and patiently as well as to bear abundance moderately" (*Inst.* III,10,4). Abundance should, moreover, be received gratefully as a gift of God, but should not be pursued actively. Calvinism, according to the analysis of Ernst Troeltsch (1865-1923), was not in fact responsible for setting the capitalist pursuit of profit into motion; it was indeed Calvinism and its ethical qualms that attempted to keep this emerging modern trend in check. The main factors driving the development of modern capitalism were thus by no means to be found within Calvinism.[19]

While the Reformed-Protestant professional ethic seemingly provided an opening for the capitalist economic system to grow, it also had the potential for criticizing capitalism from the beginning. Modern Calvinism is, for example, marked by a radical individualism that Troeltsch and other researchers have rightly characterized as being un-Calvinist.[20] Manchester capitalism and Calvinism social doctrine are indeed worlds apart. The latter theologically views the world from the perspective of the church, which is set above the individual. Similarly, it is not the egocentric happiness of each individual but the well-being of the community that is placed at the center of the Calvinist social ethic. It is not the pursuit of

18. Kretzer, "Calvinismus-Kapitalismus-These," p. 70.
19. Troeltsch, *Soziallehren,* p. 795.
20. Cf. Biéler, *Pensée;* Lüthy, "Calvinisme"; Lüthi, "Calvinismus," pp. 185f.

profit but the commandment for brotherly love that drives the Calvinist view of work and profession and the use of money and property.[21] The economic ethic in later Calvinism, it must be added, has distanced itself increasingly from Calvin, becoming, as Troeltsch sees it, "bourgeois — one can say petit bourgeois-capitalist."[22] Originally, Calvinism was actually closer to a development toward a form of Christian socialism.

In order to describe the relation between Calvinism and capitalism, one cannot limit one's scope to worldly asceticism and Puritanism, but must also take into account Calvinist and Reformed influences and aspects of modern criticism of capitalism. In this context, we must especially emphasize the great significance of Reformed theology in the religious socialism of the twentieth century.[23] While large sections of the Protestant world attempted to solve the increasingly apparent darker side of capitalism in the nineteenth century and the pauperization of the industrial proletariat, and did so through the means of a patriarchal diaconal system, religious socialists worked toward structural change in politics and the economy. They adapted the criticism of capitalism put forward by the socialist movement, all while working to overcome the atheism and the anticlerical posture of the socialists.

One center of the religious socialist movement was located in Switzerland. Hermann Kutter's (1863-1931) book, *Sie müssen! Ein offenes Wort an die christliche Gesellschaft* [They must! A frank word to Christian society], appeared in 1903, around the same time that Weber was composing his study on the Protestant-Calvinist ethic and the spirit of capitalism. Kutter's book contained strong criticism of the Christian social movement, which he saw in reality as being un-Christian for limiting itself to attempts to alleviate the symptoms of Calvinism without fighting the root causes involved. While Kutter was at the center of the quietistic wing of the religious socialists, Leonard Ragaz (1868-1945) rose as a leader of the activist wing. The different religious socialist groups were linked in their efforts to unite the Christian hope of God's kingdom with the socialist utopia of a state founded in liberty, and to interpret the proclamation of God's kingdom — not as an opiate for the people or as an attempt to console the de-

---

21. Cf. Geiger, "Calvin," pp. 243-53.
22. Troeltsch, *Soziallehren,* p. 955.
23. Cf. Ruddies, "Religiöse Sozialisten"; Deresch, *Glaube;* Katterle and Rich, eds., *Religiöser Sozialismus.*

graded with the promise of a future world — but as a motivation for political and economic change within the society at hand. Karl Barth (1886-1968) belonged to this movement in his early years, although he was also influenced by the Swabian Pietist Christoph Blumhardt (1842-1919) in addition to the aforementioned Reformed theologians. While we must also note that Barth, in later years, stressed the differences between God and human, the kingdom of God and the economy, Barth and other representatives of dialectic theology continued to maintain the influence of religious socialism in their school of thought.

Reformed Economic Ethics Today

Not only does the historical and systematic question of the relationship between Calvinism and capitalism play a part in the political controversies concerning the moral legitimacy of capitalism as an economic form, this question is also present within the debate on the legitimacy of the modern era and the position of Christianity with regard to modernity. Church controversies and documents on capitalism and the criticism of capitalism, such as the Accra Confession (discussed at the beginning of this essay), must ultimately be interpreted within this context.

One must generally emphasize that it makes just as little sense to equate the spirit of Calvinism with the spirit of capitalism as with that of a planned socialist economy. Part of the heritage of Calvin and Calvinism involves a concerted effort — rooted in a gospel-based view of God, humankind, and the world — toward taking on the tasks involved in forming the economic and social spheres, and facing the challenges of modern economic life. It is of no less importance that Calvinism, throughout its history, has criticized the negative developments within capitalism and has supported the social, practical, and political efforts of the church. To this day, Calvinism is characterized by participation in the development of the economy while — anchored in a prophetic basic view of things — honing a critical awareness of the dangers involved.

This heritage is exemplary in its ethics of a humanity based on faith, hope, and love within the horizon of God's kingdom, as the Zurich-based theologian Arthur Rich (1910-1992) phrased it.[24] Rich derived important

---

24. Rich, *Business and Economic Ethics,* pp. 99-124 (= *Wirtschaftsethik,* vol. 1, pp. 105-28).

inspiration for his theological and ethical thinking from religious socialism. His economic ethic addresses the concept of an "economism" that
views the economic world as a system of processes, acting in accordance
with its own laws. He stipulates that the economy exists for the people's
sake, and not vice versa. The fundamental issue in economic ethics is thus
the question of what best serves humankind. From a Christian point of
view, Rich portrays service to life as the fundamental purpose of every economic activity.[25] In his view, however, a system cannot meet the people's
needs without also meeting those of the economy and of the environment.
All three together form a type of magical triangle of an ethically responsible economy.

From this point, Rich arrives at a critical yet positive and constructive understanding of the relationship between Christianity and capitalism. He views the so-called free market economy — when held up to the
basic human criteria of faith, hope, and love — as being ethically unac-
ceptable. A social market economy, one incorporating elements of comprehensive planning and state support, would, however, be ethically responsible, in his view. Rich clearly rejects forms of market economy that
view humanity purely in terms of individual freedom, but not in terms of
solidarity and social responsibility. Confronted with the alternative between a controlled, social market economy and a socialist planned economy, Rich opts for the former. The decision for one of the two basic systems is, however, as Rich accurately establishes, "not only a question of
human justice, but equally one of economic rationality."[26] Rich's decision
for a social market economy by no means entails a theological sanctioning
of the capitalist status quo and certainly not a view of economic forces
with their own laws, forming part of a sort of questionable "doctrine of
two kingdoms." According to Rich, this entails examining alternatives on
the basis of the market principle while maintaining a critical distance from
any specific economic system, as well as understanding the further development or, if necessary, reorientation of the economic system as a task required of Christians. A Christian social approach to ethics should not simply accept the extant economic system, but should also accept the task of
actively working to reform the world in line with the principle of loving

25. Rich, *Business and Economic Ethics*, pp. 277-82 (= *Wirtschaftsethik*, vol. 2, pp. 23-
27).

26. Rich, *Business and Economic Ethics*, p. 522 (= *Wirtschaftsethik*, vol. 2, p. 257).

one's neighbor. As Rich explains, this should constitute a "pragmatic optimization of the mutual relationship of the economic purposes now under consideration, with the aim of minimizing the opposing tensions. With that, however, one moves into the domain of the relative, which in this context also means that the question of meaning in the economy can never find more than a relative solution."[27]

The theologically well-founded criticism of errant developments in modern capitalism and present-day globalization loses, however, its plausibility if it is not, as Rich has it, coupled with a solid understanding of economics. The advocacy of the World Alliance of Reformed Churches in its aforementioned Accra Confession of 2004 on behalf of the weak and suffering is in full accordance with the Calvinist ethic and heritage. As we have seen, the fate of the poorest in society was already an ethical criterion with regard to the economy and professional life for Calvin and in early Calvinism. The Accra Confession is, in a sense, apocalyptically loaded in a way that does not correspond with the Reformed tradition. The document makes much of "signs of the times," criticizing and declaring its opposition to "globalization" and "Neoliberalism" in the strongest terms without making the effort necessary for a nuanced economic analysis. There is a fine line between biblically sound prophecy and ideological conspiracy theories. All this confessional rhetoric, again calling for a *status confessionis,* is still not able to hide the fact that the favored "economy of grace" remains a vague concept and not a real alternative to the economic system so strongly condemned. The criticism of capitalism in the context grows into a form of fundamentalism, rooted in historical theology and apocalyptically fueled. This makes it impossible to perceive and appreciate the penultimate, as Dietrich Bonhoeffer (1906-1945) put it, in which we need to live and bear responsibility. This type of theology, lastly, contributes to the self-marginalization of the church, which represents the precise opposite of the critical openness to the world that has distinguished Calvinism throughout its history.

Translated from German by David Dichelle, Leipzig

---

27. Rich, *Business and Economic Ethics,* p. 295 (= *Wirtschaftsethik,* vol. 2, p. 40).

Calvin and Religious Tolerance

Christoph Strohm

In 1936, Stefan Zweig (1881-1942) published a historical novel later translated as *The Right to Heresy: Castellio against Calvin* (original title: *Castellio gegen Calvin oder Ein Gewissen gegen die Gewalt*). In his book, Zweig placed Calvin's work in a clear analogy with the dictatorial conditions of the National Socialist era, in terms of epitomizing intolerance and inhumanity. Calvin was thus depicted not only as the instigator of a "clerical tyranny" but also as being responsible for the elimination of the freedom of conscience that had been upheld by the Reformation.[1] The renowned U.S. church historian Roland H. Bainton (1894-1984) viewed Calvin as representing "the peak of Protestant intolerance."[2] One can easily add an entire list of similar views.[3] Even more recently, Arnold Angenendt (b. 1934) has pointed to the negative effects of the Reformation in its treatment of heresies and adherents to heterodox beliefs in his comprehensive study of tolerance and violence in the history of Christianity.[4] From this perspective, the medieval Church Inquisition had not, as is today commonly thought, in fact been overcome. Instead, it was replaced by a repression

---

1. Cf. Zweig, *Castellio gegen Calvin,* pp. 9f.

2. "The peak of protestant intolerance: John Calvin" (Bainton, *Travail,* p. 52). Cf. critique by Cameron, "Scottish Calvinism and the Principle of Intolerance," pp. 113-15. A view similar to Bainton's is offered in Lecler, *Geschichte,* vol. 1, p. 485, and many others.

3. For further examples see Witte, "Moderate Religionsfreiheit," pp. 402f.

4. Cf. Angenendt, *Toleranz und Gewalt,* pp. 320-27.

perpetrated by secular powers, which had become all the more oppressive due to a failure of church norms to represent a source of moderation.

The criticism of Calvin's attitude toward tolerant positions has been repeatedly opposed by other views, which focus on Calvin's significance within the history of modern liberty. John Adams (1735-1826), the second president of the United States, made it clear that religious freedom owed much to Calvin's Geneva despite the Servetus affair.[5] And Abraham Kuyper (1837-1920), with reference to the U.S. historian George Bancroft (1800-1891), believed that a fanatic adherent of Calvinism was in fact a fanatic supporter of liberty.[6] Others were more reserved in their view that Calvin was unjustly tarnished with the "odium of intolerance."[7]

The execution of Michael Servetus (1511-1553) in Geneva has played a decisive role in the controversy surrounding the significance of Calvin for the spread of the modern view of tolerance and the establishment of freedoms of religion and conscience. We will thus address this matter in depth in the present essay. This can, however, only be understood properly if one takes into account both the context of Calvin's efforts to safeguard the Reformation in the face of a wide range of threats, as well as the legal and cultural situation of the time. We will operate within this framework in our efforts to evaluate the place that Calvin afforded tolerance in his works.

The Servetus Affair of 1553

Calvin had to fight to maintain his authority in Geneva, most immediately and extensively in matters concerning moral discipline. Long-established Geneva burghers did not want to be placed under the yoke of the French pastor immediately after attaining their independence from the bishopric.[8] Calvin's fight for authority and establishment of the Reformation in

---

5. "Let not Geneva be forgotten or despised. Religious liberty owes it much respect, Servetus notwithstanding" (Adams, *The Works*, vol. 6, p. 313).

6. "Every competent historian will without exception confirm the words of Bancroft: 'The fanatic for Calvinism was a fanatic for liberty, for in the moral warfare for freedom, his creed was a part of his army, and his most faithful ally in the battle'" (Kuyper, *Calvinism*, p. 99; with quote from Bancroft, *History of the United States*, vol. 1, p. 464). Cf. other relevant sources in Witte, "Moderate Religionsfreiheit," p. 402.

7. Neuser, *Calvin*, p. 80.

8. Cf. Philip Benedict's essay in this publication.

Geneva was linked, however, to questions of doctrine in the narrow sense of the word. The year 1551 saw Hieronymus Bolsec (d. 1584), a physician and former monk, put on trial. On October 16, he had rejected the doctrine of divine predestination at the weekly Bible interpretation meeting of preachers. Not only did he lend his support to previously expressed criticism but was so strongly adamant about it that he was immediately arrested by the town's chief constable. Assessments procured from Bern, Zurich, and Basel denounced Bolsec's views, and he was subsequently banished from Geneva. Two years later, disagreements with Philibert Berthelier, a member of a leading Geneva family, concerning the powers of the consistory and the pastor with regard to moral discipline led Calvin to voice his concern in September 1553 that he would have to leave Geneva.[9]

It was within this context, only a few weeks later, that Michael Servetus was arrested, beginning a legal process that would end with his execution at the stake on October 27, 1553.[10] This dramatic turn of events followed on a long-standing acquaintanceship between Calvin and the Spanish anti-Trinitarian. Servetus attempted to strike up a correspondence with Calvin, as he did with other Reformation leaders, but was not well received due to his rejection of Trinitarian doctrine. Numerous letters sent by the scholar, who had been active as a physician in Vienna since 1540, went unanswered by Calvin. The very title of *Christianismi Restitutio*,[11] which he wrote there, expressed the theological aim of his theological correspondence with the author of the *Institutes of the Christian Religion*. Servetus sent a copy of his work to Calvin before it was published, in fact, but this only served to incite Calvin's decided rejection. In place of the Trinitarian doctrine of the early church, which he rejected as unbiblical, Servetus supported a view, strongly influenced by Neoplatonism and bordering on pantheism, of a God immanent in the world.[12] Calvin had only severe words for the scholar, who self-confidently challenged him to a theological dispute: "Servetus lately wrote to me, and coupled with his letter a long volume of his delirious fancies, with the Thrasonic boast, that I should see something astonishing and unheard of. He takes it upon him to

9. Cf. Calvin's letter to Pierre Viret of September 4, 1553 (CO 14,606).

10. Cf. in particular Kingdon, Bergier, and Dufour, eds., *Registres*, vol. 2, pp. 1553-63.

11. Cf. Servet, *Christianismi Restitutio* (1553). Servetus had hitherto refuted Trinitarian doctrine in depth and, to an extent, rejected it polemically in two publications: *De Trinitatis erroribus libri septem* (1531); and *Dialogorum de Trinitate libri duo* (1532).

12. For more specifics, see Cottret, *Calvin*, pp. 260f.; Bainton, *Michel Servet*.

come hither, if it be agreeable to me. But I am unwilling to pledge my word for his safety, for if he shall come, I shall never permit him to depart alive, provided my authority be of any avail."[13]

Once Servetus's *Christianismi Restitutio* was published, the French refugee Guillaume de Trie, son-in-law of the famed humanist Guillaume Budé (1467-1540), provided information leading to the unveiling of the author's identity. After the Inquisition's investigation did not lead to his discovery, the Inquisition was able to continue its inquiry based on letters written by Servetus to Calvin, which Trie had asked to be sent to him.[14] Having escaped from jail on April 7, 1553, Servetus remained in hiding for a few months before traveling to Geneva. On August 13, he was recognized in a church service there and immediately arrested at Calvin's behest. It was Calvin's secretary, Nicolas de la Fontaine, who served as the accuser in the two-and-a-half-month trial for heresy and disruption of the church order. Since opponents of Calvin were among the judges, Servetus had reason for hope, but neither his counteraccusation against Calvin nor his desperate pleas for better prison conditions were able to help his cause. External statements were then requested to shed light on the case. Once, however, the evaluations of councilors and "servants of the word of God" had been received from Zurich, Schaffhausen, Bern, and Basel over the first half of October, all of which called for the execution of the dangerous heretic, Servetus was condemned to death at the stake on October 27, 1553. The sentence was carried out the same day.

The legal situation was clear and straightforward. Imperial law reserved the death penalty for the denial of Trinitarian doctrine. For one thing, the first book of the *Codex Iustinianus* called for the punishment of opponents of the orthodox doctrine (cf. Codex Iustinianus I,1,1) as well as other heretics (cf. Codex Iustinianus I,5). Moreover, Article 106 of the *Peinliche Gerichtsordnung,* the ordinance of criminal procedure of Charles V (1500-1558), reserved for blasphemers a strict punishment to their "body, life or members." The often-expressed opinion that it was Calvin himself who was responsible for Servetus being executed overlooks this. Calvin's behavior must also be placed in the context of a decades-long

---

13. Calvin's letter to Farel of February 13, 1547, in Calvin, *Letters,* vol. 2, p. 19; *Johannes Calvins Lebenswerk,* vol. 1, p. 332 (Schwarz dates the letter as February 13, 1546).

14. Calvin supposedly gave the letters to Trie only with reluctance (cf. Feld, "Michael Servet," p. 1475).

and complex personal relationship that can no longer be reconstructed in all of its dimensions. The peculiar fact that Servetus, faced with a great danger, left for Geneva of all places, can only, it would seem, be explained by a strongly apocalyptic mood. It must, however, be established in all clarity that Calvin was not capable of any measure of religious tolerance in his dealings with either Bolsec or Servetus. This leads us to ask what points of departure for tolerance can in fact be found in Calvin's works. Taking into account that the view of the idea of tolerance in the modern era has changed fundamentally, we must consider this question in the historical context of sixteenth-century reality.

The Concept of Tolerance in the Sixteenth Century

Any foray into the view of the concept of tolerance among Reformation leaders, and Calvin in particular, is met with the difficulty that the term *tolerance* was not, at the time, understood in its modern sense. It has rightly been pointed out that the tolerance of another viewpoint as an autonomous decision worthy of respect, as in the modern sense for the word, was not in fact connoted by the Latin term *tolerantia* or its derivatives in languages such as German.[15] One referred instead to terms like *freedom of conscience, freedom of religion,* or *autonomy.* One only spoke of tolerance when not enough could be done to counter a poor state of affairs or a deviant attitude. *Tolerance* as a term in this way was established in medieval theology and was so used in the Roman Catholic discourse of the sixteenth and seventeenth centuries.[16] Thomas Aquinas entertained the tolerance of pagans and heretics in order to prevent greater evil.[17]

The sixteenth century knew no right to the freedom of religion or conscience in the modern sense of the concept. At the same time, incipient support was on the rise for these rights and the related concept of tolerance, particularly in the spheres of humanism and the Reformation.[18] This was in part based on the ideas that were developed in scholastic theology[19] and the

15. Cf. Dreitzel, "Toleranz," pp. 118f.

16. Cf. Dreitzel, "Toleranz," pp. 119f.

17. Cf. Lecler, *Geschichte,* vol. 1, pp. 144-48 and 155f.

18. For an overview, see Schreiner and Besier, "Toleranz," pp. 445-605.

19. On Thomas Aquinas's criticism of the coercive conversion of pagans, see Aquinas, *Summa theologiae* 2.2. q.10, a.8.

mystical spirituality of the Middle Ages. Intensified religious individualism also played an early role in this development, a movement that spread among humanists and that stressed a view of human dignity that was anchored in authors of antiquity. Erasmus's efforts to unify Christendom, in the face of the division of the church that loomed as the result of the Reformation, also provided another point of departure. The question of tolerance arose for the great humanist in the context of the problem of which deviant doctrines could be "tolerated" in the interest of church unity. Erasmus tended toward an undogmatic religiosity, seeking to define dogma as little as possible in order to open up space for other religious views. Erasmus understood the parable of the wheat and tares as a call to refrain, through the end of time, from final verdicts concerning dissidents.[20]

Another point of departure for the development of the modern concept of tolerance could be seen in the Reformation's redefinition of the relationship between the spiritual and worldly regiments. In his paper, published in 1520, *To Christian Nobility of the German Nation: The Enhancement of the Christian State* (original title: *An den christlichen Adel deutscher Nation von des christlichen Standes Besserung)*, Martin Luther (1483-1546) stressed the particular value of secular authorities in the face of the clerical claim to greater authority.[21] This began the Reformation's tradition of clearly differentiating between the tasks and means of the worldly and spiritual regiments. The spiritual regiment, in this view, served to proclaim the gospel and thus to expand the kingdom of God. This was to occur without recourse to force, but only through the word alone *(sine vi sed verbo)*. The goal of the worldly regiment was to provide for peace and order in the face of the power of sin, as a means of making the orderly proclamation of the gospel possible. The actions of the secular authorities would thus relate to physical life and external behavior but not to questions of belief and conscience. This establishment of the relationship between the spiritual and worldly regiments led to the rejection of both tendencies toward the supremacy of the church over the state, in which the state acts as a secular arm of the church, and of the supremacy of the state over the church.

In his 1523 treatise *Temporal Authority: To What Extent It Should Be Obeyed* (original title: *Von weltlicher Obrigkeit wie weit man ihr Gehorsam*

---

20. Cf. Turchetti, "Une question mal posée."
21. Cf. Luther, *To Christian nobility* (1520) (= WA,6,[381],404–69, esp. 407,9–411,7).

schuldig sei), Luther, with great clarity, stated the significance this doctrine had for the treatment of false teachers: "Heresy is a spiritual matter which you cannot hack to pieces with iron, consume with fire, or drown in water. God's word alone avails here."[22] The proclamation of the gospel and the ensuing illumination of the heart by the divine spirit were thus the only appropriate means of overcoming false doctrine.

> Moreover, faith and heresy are never so strong as when men oppose them by sheer force, without God's word. For men count it certain that such force is for a wrong cause and is directed against the right, since it proceeds without God's word and knows not how to further its cause except by naked force, as brute beasts do. Even in temporal affairs force can be used only after the wrong has been legally condemned. How much less possible it is to act with force, without justice and God's word, in these lofty spiritual matters! See, therefore, what fine, clever nobles they are! They would drive out heresy, but set about it in such a way that they only strengthen the opposition, rousing suspicion against themselves and justifying the heretics. My friend, if you wish to drive out heresy, you must find some way to tear it first of all from the heart and completely turn men's wills away from it. With force you will not stop it, but only strengthen it. What do you gain by strengthening heresy in the heart, while weakening only its outward expression and forcing the tongue to lie? God's word, however, enlightens the heart, and so all heresies and errors vanish from the heart of their own accord.[23]

This potential foundation for religious freedom, freedom of conscience, and tolerance, was, however, soon seen to be relativized in Luther's thought. With a view to the peasant revolts, in which, according to Luther, Thomas Müntzer's (ca. 1488-1525) radical teachings played a decisive role, Luther stressed the responsibility of secular authorities to move against the public proclamation of errant doctrine. In later years, the secular summepiscopate *(landesherrliches Kirchenregiment),* with its diversity of theoretical foundations, led to a contamination of the original distinction between the spiritual and worldly regiments. In his later years, Luther was also not able to see his fundamental earlier ideas become reality with regard to the Jews, who in his view were unwilling to convert.

---

22. Luther, *Temporal Authority* (1523) (= WA 11,268,27-29).
23. Luther, *Temporal Authority* (1523) (= WA 11,268,33–269,15).

To conclude, we must mention one further point in the development of the concept of tolerance in the sixteenth century. The existence of two or more confessions within the Holy Roman Empire made it increasingly necessary to introduce regulations that provided for their peaceful coexistence. The Peace of Augsburg of 1555 established in the empire a system that, while based on a system of confessionally homogeneous territories, did in fact allow for confessional parity in some free imperial cities. In the First and Second Peaces of Kappel in 1529 and 1531, a quarter of a century earlier, agreements had to be made in Switzerland to guarantee the survival of the Confederation despite differences of confessional orientation. At the end of the sixteenth century, the Edict of Nantes of 1598 provided for a limited tolerance of Reformed Christians in France, after a similar solution had been found previously in the Kingdom of Poland.

Calvin's Early Steps toward Religious Tolerance

When, at the age of twenty-seven, Calvin wrote his *Institutes of the Christian Religion,* the publication that led to his immediate renown, he had already been forced into exile as the result of his faith. The fact of his persecution influenced his preface to the king that began the 1536 and all later editions. Calvin, in the preface, attempted to defend his brothers in faith from the accusations they faced. It is thus of little surprise that Calvin asked the king for tolerance with regard to Reformed Christians.[24] In his work, which was influenced in many ways by Luther's reforming efforts, Calvin expressly adopted his clear distinction between spiritual and worldly realms with all its consequences for the appropriate treatment of those with different or errant beliefs. It was characteristic of the worldly regiment that it solely governed the implementation of civil justice and the insurance of moral behavior, while the spiritual regiment extended to the life of the soul.[25]

It was Calvin's primary aim, in this regard, to emphasize the religious freedom of believers from legal regulations that could hamper the con-

24. Cf. OS I,21-36. Quotations from the *Institutes* (1536, 1559) refer to the following translations: *Institutes of the Christian Religion, 1536 Edition,* trans. F. L. Battles (Grand Rapids, 1995) and *Institutes of the Christian Religion (1559),* trans. F. L. Battles (Philadelphia/London, 1960).

25. Cf. *Inst.* VI (1536): OS I,232 and 258.

science of Christians.[26] He spoke out against those who sought to derive a freedom from worldly laws, courts, and authorities from the spiritual freedom that is granted to us. "But whoever knows how to distinguish between body and soul, between the present fleeting life and that future eternal life, will without difficulty know that Christ's spiritual Kingdom and the civil jurisdiction are things completely different."[27]

One also had to choose the methods of dealing with those who, through their teachings and actions, threatened to harm the community of believers, in line with the irrevocable distinction between the spiritual and worldly regiments. Such delinquents were not to be addressed with state force but with a temporally limited exclusion in the interest of their improvement or salvation. By whatever means, "whether by exhortation and teaching or by mercy and gentleness, or by our own prayers to God," one had to strive toward improvement and conversion to make it possible to return to the communion of the church. Calvin added that this type of behavior also had to be maintained with regard to adherents to other religions and the opponents of the true religion. "And not only those are to be so treated, but also Turks, Saracenes, and other enemies of religion."[28] Calvin expressly rejected conversion under force and violence: "Far be it from us to approve those methods by which many until now have tried to force them to our faith, when they forbid them the use of fire and water and the common elements, when they deny to them all offices of humanity, when they pursue them with sword and arms. Although, while we are as yet uncertain of God's judgment, we are not allowed to distinguish individually those who belong to the church or not."[29]

It is emblematic that these sentences, which connote a certain tolerance even toward adherents to other religions including Muslims, and which reject the use of force with regard to faith, were removed from later editions of the *Institutes*.[30] This is an indication of how Calvin's new responsibilities as a church leader — similarly to Luther — led to a problematic modification of the Reformation's distinction between the tasks and

26. Cf. *Inst.* VI (1536): OS I,224-32 and 238f.

27. *Inst.* VI (1536): OS I,258f.

28. *Inst.* II (1536): OS I,91.

29. *Inst.* II (1536): OS I,91.

30. On the lasting significance of the distinction between the spiritual and worldly regiments, see *Inst.* III,19,15 (1559): OS IV,449f.; *Inst.* IV,20,1 (1559): OS V,471f.; *Inst.* IV,11,3 (1559): OS V,199.

means of the spiritual and worldly regiments. This was all the more feasible since Calvin, with a background in legal schooling, emphasized from the very beginning the responsibility of the worldly regiment in fighting blasphemy and idolatry. As he wrote in the 1536 edition of the *Institutes* about its duties: "It . . . also prevents idolatry, sacrilege against God's name, blasphemies against his truth, and other public offenses against religion from arising and spreading among the people."[31] It was the task of the worldly authorities "to prevent the true religion, which is contained in God's law from being openly and with public sacrilege violated and defiled with impunity."[32]

Calvin's More Rigid Positions of Later Years

The way in which Calvin's views changed concerning dissenters, errant teachers, and adherents to other beliefs is demonstrated in the statement he wrote defending the course of force and violence taken against the anti-Trinitarian Servetus. Immediately following Servetus's execution, strong criticism was raised against Calvin and the Geneva authorities for returning to the methods of the hated Inquisition, among other things. Calvin then regarded it as necessary to write his comprehensive *Defensio orthodoxae fidei de sacra trinitate contra prodigiosos errores Michaelis Servetusi Hispani*,[33] which has been characterized by Joseph Lecler as a "categorical apology of intolerance" and "one of the most abominable treatises ever written to justify the persecution of heretics."[34] Yet again, Calvin strongly rejected the teachings of Servetus criticizing Trinitarian doctrine. He also closely examined the question whether Christian authorities should be allowed to punish heretics.[35] In this publication, as in others, Calvin underscored his view that the kingdom of Christ exists not by means of armed force but through the proclamation of the gospel. Nobody was to be forced to accept the faith. At the same time, however, the worldly authorities had

31. *Inst.* VI (1536): OS I,260.
32. *Inst.* VI (1536): OS I,260; cf. also *Inst.* IV,20,3 (1559): OS V,473f.; Sermon on Daniel 4:1-3 (CO 40,647-51).
33. Completed in late December 1553 and printed in February 1554; cf. CO 8,453-644; cf. also Plath, *Calvin und Basel*, pp. 120-28; H. Guggisberg, *Sebastian Castellio*, pp. 85-89.
34. Cf. Lecler, *Geschichte*, vol. 1, pp. 459 and 456.
35. "An christianis iudicibus haereticos punire liceat" (CO 8,461-81).

the responsibility to counter those who called for renouncement of true faith, and who undermined the peace of the church and the unity of the pious *(pietatis consensus)*.[36]

The death penalty was also to be implemented as the most extreme means of force against the spreaders of false teachings when — as in the case of Servetus — their stubbornness prevailed and the godlessness of their errors was no longer tolerable.[37] Some supporters of false teachings could, on the other hand, be treated with leniency and punished moderately if necessary. "But when the religion is shaken in its fundaments, when God is insulted in a reprehensible manner, when souls are brought to perdition through godless and ruinous teaching, and when one openly threatens to renounce the one God and his doctrine, it becomes necessary to turn to that final remedy so that the deadly poison does not continue to spread."[38]

Calvin's line of argument is focused on two types of opponents, *turbulenti homines* and *boni et simplices*. The latter group of good-willed and modest characters would deny the worldly authorities the right to punish heretics partly due to ignorance and partly due to their own negative experience with the Inquisition. The former group, people who are responsible for spreading confusion, were those who held fast to their own individual religious intuitions and who viewed every general rule of church doctrine as tyranny.[39] Calvin's response to these people was: "How will the religion persist, how will one be able to recognize the true Church, what will indeed Christ himself be, if the doctrine of piety *(pietatis doctrina)* becomes uncertain and doubtful?"[40] This brings Calvin's particular aim into a clear light. He saw the Reformation as being endangered at a basic level; this meant that the clarity and unity of the true church needed to be protected by all means. The struggle for survival of the true Church thus meant that there was no room for plurality and individual religiosity.

It therefore was a logical step for Calvin to strive ceaselessly toward the definition of true doctrine in the face of a variety of false teachings. These

36. Cf. CO 8,467f.

37. Cf. CO 8,480f.

38. CO 8,477. Calvin looked closely at the biblical passages that spoke against fighting heretics, in particular the parable of the wheat and tares (Matt. 13:24-30) and Gamaliel's counsel (Acts 5:34-39) (cf. CO 8,472f.).

39. Cf. CO 8,461-67; cf. also H. Guggisberg, *Sebastian Castellio*, pp. 85f.

40. CO 8,464.

writings on controversial theology comprise an important part of Calvin's legacy, in addition to his Bible interpretation, his systematic depiction of Christian teaching in the *Institutes,* and the texts he wrote directly addressing the formation of church life. As would be expected, he placed his greatest focus on his dispute with Roman Catholic theologians,[41] in addition to coming to terms with Baptists, Humanism and the Libertinists, the so-called Nicodemites, anti-Trinitarians, and some Gnesio-Lutherans.[42] These debates influenced the revisions of the *Institutes* and showcased his redoubled efforts to maintain the correct biblical and Christian doctrine that Calvin and other Reformation leaders believed they had rediscovered.[43]

Calvin's entire body of writings on controversial theology is characterized by the fact that they do not focus, as such, on tolerance for divergent teachings, but more on rejecting them as unbiblical errors that worked against the true worship of God. The severity with which Calvin fought divergent teachings cannot be explained in psychological terms alone. It is more a reaction of his view that the Reformed Church in France and in Geneva, in light of the persecutions and perceived fundamental threats, could survive only with a strict orientation toward the Word of God. Strong personal experiences that had led to this view were very common among the exiled French refugees of faith living in Geneva. And there seemed to be less leeway for liberality and plurality as the threat increased, especially under the reign (1547-59) of Henry II, the son and successor of Francis I, when it began to coincide with the ruinous defeat of the Protestants of the empire in the 1547 Schmalkaldic War. This sort of perception was only boosted by the fact that Calvin remained in an insecure and precarious situation in his Geneva exile through 1555.

41. Such as with Cardinal Sadolet (1539), Albertus Pighius, and the Sorbonne theologians (1544), as well as the Council of Trent and the Augsburg Interim.

42. For a good overview comprising various registers as well as comments on the background situations for various writings, see Peter and Gilmont, *Bibliotheca Calviniana;* cf. esp. vol. 3, pp. 650-54.

43. On the place of writings on controversial theology in Calvin's body of literary work and the significance of polemics in Calvin's style of theological argument, see Higman, *The Style of John Calvin;* Higman, "Calvin polémiste"; Higman: "I Came Not to Send Peace, but a Sword," esp. pp. 432f. for a list of Calvin's writings in opposition to Catholic authors, "radicals," "compromisers," and anti-Trinitarians.

Calvin versus Castellio — Intolerance versus Tolerance?

In addition to Servetus, we should mention his earlier friend Sebastian Castellio (1515-1563) as among the "agitators" who were the target of Calvin's *Defensio orthodoxae fidei de sacra trinitate*.[44] From Savoy, Castellio taught in the Geneva Latin school through 1544, only to enter into conflict with the Geneva pastors due to his denial of the canonicity of the Song of Songs and his interpretation of discussions on Christ's descent into hell. After leaving Geneva with Calvin's letters of recommendation, he worked in Basel as a corrector and after 1553 as a professor of Greek. Castellio reacted to Servetus's execution and Calvin's justification for it with a pseudonymously written 1554 publication, which remains a milestone in the history of tolerance to this day. Entitled *De haereticis an sint persequendi et omnino quomodo sit cum eis agendum, Luteri et Brentii, aliorumque multorum tum veterum tum recentiorum sententiae*, the 175-page-long, octavo-format edition comprised a collection of texts and quotes, all of which served to reject capital punishment for heretics.[45]

As the title already emphasized, the publication focused on relevant statements of Luther from his earlier years[46] and related passages from the works of Johannes Brenz (1499-1570),[47] a Reformation leader in Württemberg. In addition to a large number of early Christian authors, Castellio also quoted contemporaries of the first half of the sixteenth century, Erasmus of Rotterdam (ca. 1466-1536) and Sebastian Franck (1499-1542) in particular. Castellio even included two Calvin quotes, in which Calvin seemed to have spoken out against the execution of heretics.[48] In addition to the aforementioned passage in the first edition of the *Institutes*, in which Calvin supported clemency even toward Turks and opponents of the true religion,[49] Castellio included a quote from the preface to the Commentary on Acts.[50] In the latter, Calvin stated that the power of the Holy Spirit in the kingdom of Christ not only tamed wild animals, but in fact turned wolves, lions, and bears into lambs. Bellius's

---

44. Cf. H. Guggisberg, *Sebastian Castellio*, p. 86.
45. Martinus Bellius [= Sebastian Castellio], *De haereticis* (1554).
46. Quoted in part in "The Concept of Tolerance in the Sixteenth Century," above.
47. On Brenz, see Seebaß, "An sint persequendi haeretici?"
48. Bellius [= Castellio], *De haereticis*, pp. 107f.
49. Cf. *Inst.* II (1536), OS I,91.
50. Cf. CO 14,293f.

preface to the collection also addressed the rejection of capital punishment as a means of fighting heretics. In line with the humanistic understanding of tolerance of those like Erasmus, Castellio supported the tolerance of deviant religious views, a focus on basic biblical tenets, and the teaching of adherents of other beliefs as a practical means of following Christ.

This seems to confirm the opposition, mentioned at the beginning of this essay, between Castellio and Calvin that was popularized by Stefan Zweig, a sort of "conscience against force." It is, however, too simple to attribute tolerance and intolerance to these two names like that. This view is countered by the fact that Castellio also shared basic attitudes characteristic of the sixteenth century that are incompatible with the modern understanding of tolerance. He, for example, sought to make a distinction between heretics and blasphemers, in that only heretics, that is, those who took divergent positions in matters of doctrine and church order, were worthy of tolerance. Blasphemers, on the other hand, who denied God and scripture, were, in Castellio's view, to be handed over to the magistrate for punishment. Worldly powers were therefore most certainly authorized to send subjects into exile, when they held fast to the denial of the most basic religious truths such as the idea of creation, the immortality of the soul, or the resurrection of Christ.[51] In his treatise *Contra libellum Calvini,* which was not published until the early seventeenth century, Castellio looked into this more closely in his thorough treatment of Calvin's *Defensio orthodoxae fidae.* Castellio, in this text, held fast to the view that the laws of the Old Testament did not apply to heretics, who simply erred, but in fact to the godless, blasphemers, and idolaters. These, by contrast, could justifiably be charged with having insulted the divine majesty, and could therefore also be liable to punishment by the worldly authorities.[52]

The statements made by Calvin, in which he allowed no room for tolerance, were at least mitigated in part by the fact that he, at least in certain cases, maintained a different attitude with regard to Judaism.[53] One

---

51. Cf. Bellius [= Castellio], *De haereticis,* pp. 3-28; cf. also Lecler, *Geschichte,* vol. 1, pp. 468f.

52. Cf. Castellio, *Contra libellum Calvini,* Nr. 122-125, f. H 2^v-I 1^v; cf. also Lecler, *Geschichte,* vol. 1, pp. 482f.

53. Cf. Detmers, *Reformation und Judentum,* pp. 264-68 and 297-311; on Calvin's limited understanding of Islam and the "Turks," see White, "Castellio against Calvin."

can also find evidence of Calvin having called for moderation in the treatment of heretics.[54] This does not, however, change the overall picture, in which we see that Calvin's way of thinking and acting left little room for religious tolerance. This did not, moreover, apply only to the later Calvin, who was caught up in a struggle to maintain the achievements of the Reformation, but also for his earlier years. Faced with the question of which of the thought structures inherent to his theology were compatible with or supported the development of the modern view of tolerance, and which instead posed obstacles, we may observe the following.

It is generally helpful to mention the clear distinction made between the worldly and spiritual regiments, which was not only reflected in differences in the tasks to be carried out but also in the means used to do so. Calvin's work also consistently shows an appreciation of spiritual freedom in contrast with the tethering of conscience through church orders[55] or the support of a limitation of the worldly authorities' claims to power.[56] This did not, however, extend to possible consequences for the development of the right to freedom of conscience or to the concept of tolerance. The idea among humanists of focusing on fundamental doctrine while tolerating a variety of individual teachings or even trends toward an individualized religiosity played virtually no role for Calvin.

We can identify four main patterns of thought in Calvin's works that made religious tolerance difficult or impossible. First, we must refer to the consistent observance of the Roman law of the Christian emperors, which Calvin knew well from his legal training.[57] The relevant sections of the *Codex Iustinianus* and the *Novellae,* which comprised the decrees of the emperors since Constantine, viewed as a matter of course the responsibility that the Christian rulers held for the correct worship of God within their states, to the inclusion of the means and sanctions necessary to carry out this responsibility.

---

54. Cf. Calvin, Commentary on Titus 3:10 (CO 52,434f.); cf. also Commentary on 1 Cor. 11:6 (CO 49,479).

55. See above, n. 26.

56. Cf. Calvin, Commentary on 1 Pet. 2:16 (CO 55,206); Commentary on Gen. 39:1 (CO 23,502); Sermon on 1 Sam. 8 (CO 29,544); Sermon on Deut. 16:18f. (CO 27,410f.); Sermon on Deut. 17:14-18 (CO 27,459); Sermon on Deut 5:17 (CO 26,321); further passages in Witte, "Moderate Religionsfreiheit," p. 419; Höpfl, *Christian Polity,* pp. 156-60; Millet, "Le thème," pp. 34f.

57. For an overview, see Strohm, "Recht und Kirchenrecht."

This is closely tied to a high esteem for the Law of the Old Testament, which Calvin was less willing to relativize, as compared with others such as Luther who looked to the gospel or the New Testament parenesis. One must mention, in particular, the strict Pentateuch laws against idolatry, blasphemy, heresy, and magic, which provided Calvin with a model for using capital punishment to fight heretics.[58] It must, however, be stressed that Calvin, as a principle, viewed not only Old Testament ceremonial law but also the judicial law as being no longer applicable to Christians. And yet, they remained relevant as a model. Calvin's successor in Geneva, Theodore Beza (1519-1605), went significantly far beyond this in his 1554 treatise in opposition to Castellio's writings.[59] It was Beza's aim to highlight the difference between the judicial law and the fully dismissed ceremonial law. He criticized Castellio for, as he phrased it using an old legal term, "dissimulating" this difference.[60] He set forth that the ceremonial law had been valid for all but limited in temporal scope, while the judicial law was only valid for the Jewish people but, in principle, unlimited in time.[61] While the ceremonial law was superseded by the gospel, the continued relevance of the Old Testament judicial law had to be determined according to criteria of appropriateness.[62] There were indeed clearer consequences ensuing from Beza's legally schooled treatment of Old Testament religious law than had been the case with Calvin. Both shared the view, influenced both by Roman law and by the Old Testament, that God could punish an entire community for tolerating false teachings, idolatry, and blasphemy among its ranks.

One particular view closely connected with humanism also continued to slow down the development of a basis for tolerance in Calvin's thought. Calvin believed, together with all the Reformed and Reformed Catholic theologians with an appreciation for Plato, that true being was not external and material but mental and spiritual. This entailed that offenses of a mental and spiritual nature should be seen as particularly serious. If indeed the worldly powers could react strongly to injury and the theft of material goods, how much more strongly would they have to sanction spiritual offenses such as heresy, idolatry, and blasphemy?

58. Cf. esp. Lev. 24; Deut. 13.

59. Cf. Beza, *De haereticis a civili Magistratu puniendis libellus, aduersus Martini Bellii farraginem, et novorum Academicorum sectam* (1554).

60. Cf. Beza, *De haereticis,* p. 220.

61. Cf. Beza, *De haereticis,* pp. 221f.

62. Cf. Beza, *De haereticis,* p. 222.

Among the factors that prevented Calvin from developing attitudes of tolerance was, finally, his perception of an imminent threat to the Reformation. This impression was assured by the experience of persecuted brothers in faith in France, Calvin's home country, and was magnified by the precarious position of his Geneva exile as well. This affected Calvin in his later years by dampening what would have been his main point of departure for a system of tolerance and individual freedom of conscience: a clear distinction between the spiritual and worldly regiments. This would, however, change soon thereafter; Calvinist-Reformed Protestantism was faced with entirely different historical challenges in later years. In the centuries that would follow, social milieus with a Calvinist background would indeed play an important role in bringing about our modern history of liberty, particularly in the United States.

Translated from German by David Dichelle, Leipzig

The Contribution of Calvin and Calvinism to the Birth of Modern Democracy

Mario Turchetti

The most widely held view is that Calvin's inspiration for organizing the church of Geneva — his life's work — and, at least to a degree, organizing Genevan society, came from an aristocratic conception of the tainted power of democracy. However, not all researchers, even the highest authorities on his doctrine, agree. Some of them instead think that the reformer gave a decisive launch to what was to become modern democracy, because he had carved out the elements of fundamental freedoms. The leading proponent of this view may be Émile Doumergue (1844-1937), who dedicated a monumental work to Calvin's life, showing the work of the "founder of modern freedoms."[1] According to this viewpoint, Calvinist ideas spread to the four corners of the Protestant European world, particularly in French- and English-speaking countries, including the American colonies, where modern democracy took root. After more methodologically rigorous research, Jakobus M. Vorster arrives at a similar conclusion: Calvin "provided a

---

1. "Fondateur des libertés modernes" was the title of his speech given on November 18, 1898, at the Faculty of Protestant Theology at Montauban (edited in 1898). Cf. Doumergue, *Jean Calvin*. Other works "favorable" to this theory, but with each author's own nuances, are Troeltsch, *Bedeutung des Protestantismus;* Troeltsch, *Soziallehren;* Froidevaux, *Ernst Troeltsch;* Baron, *Calvins Staatsanschauung;* Baron, "Calvinist Republicanism"; Koenigsberger, "Organization of Revolutionary Parties"; Walzer, *Revolution of the Saints;* Skinner, *Foundations of Modern Political Thought.*

This essay contains parts of a fuller text that could not be included here for editorial reasons.

sound basis on which Reformed theology can contribute to the establishment of an ethos of human rights in the present society."[2] Many historians oppose this view, judging it to be inconceivable that Calvin could have contributed in any way to modern democracy, as he himself was a defender of the aristocracy and against any democratic trend. Charles Mercier wrote that "it would be a serious mistake to claim to discover a precursor to modern democracy in Calvin."[3] "Calvin opposes everything coming under what we have called democratism," insists Marc-Édouard Chenevière. "The central dogma of democratism is, in fact, popular sovereignty. Yet the profoundly theocratic doctrine taught by Calvin is absolutely opposed to the doctrine of popular sovereignty."[4] Faced with very different opinions, so rich in nuance, but which we do not believe to be opposing, moderate positions are drawn. I will mention that of Robert M. Kingdon, one of the leading experts in the political doctrine of Calvin and the Genevan institutions of his time. Having studied the debate between Calvin and Jean Morély (ca. 1524-1594), one of his disciples who was the most attached to the democratic method of organizing the church, Kingdon notes the aversion of Calvin and Theodore Beza (1519-1605), his right-hand man, to this method, and, taking everything into account, concludes that "the quarrel illustrates neatly one of the many perennial problems in the relations between state and church."[5] At the end of another study dealing specifically with this matter, he says, with more precision and after the same consideration, that "Calvinism marked a decisive step in the evolution of Christianity towards democracy by creating a representative ecclesiastical government."[6]

2. Vorster, "Calvin and Human Rights," p. 218. Cf. Koetsier, *Natural Law and Calvinist Political Theory;* Little, "Religion and Human Rights"; Egmond, "Calvinist Thought and Human Rights."

3. Mercier, "L'esprit de Calvin et la démocratie," p. 30. For historians less favorable or not favorable, cf. the in-depth research of Lagarde, *Recherches sur l'esprit politique de la Réforme;* Chenevière, *La pensée politique de Calvin;* Sabine, *History of Political Theory.*

4. Chenevière, *La pensée politique de Calvin,* p. 178.

5. Kingdon, "Calvin and Democracy," p. 401. I thank Mr. Kingdon for sending me his personal copy of an opuscule printed for students, which I recommend reading: Kingdon and Linder, eds., *Calvin and Calvinism.* In this "moderate" field, cf. Bohatec, *Calvins Lehre von Staat und Kirche;* Foster, "Political Theories"; McNeill, *History and Character of Calvinism;* McNeill, "Democratic Element in Calvin's Thought"; McNeill, "John Calvin on Civil Government"; McNeill, "Calvinism and European Politics"; Monter, *Studies in Genevan Government;* Monter, *Calvin's Geneva;* Linder, "Rezension zu Douglas F. Kelly," p. 911.

6. Kingdon, "Calvin et la démocratie," p. 54; a "very favourable" collection of texts by

Synchronic and Diachronic Analysis

On the subject of Calvinism, it is pertinent to note that many authors, faced with the objective difficulty of placing Calvin's sixteenth-century theological and political ideas into other eras, have decided to take into account Calvin's disciples, his spiritual successors and epigones, to study the possible relationship with modern democracy through them, through the development of their ideas in the face of the various and sometimes dramatic circumstances of history. Those are the most fascinating results, because they show how the ideas evolved differently when submitted to different situations that could not have been predicted at the outset, in Calvin's doctrine and his historical circumstances. Certainly, in this method, the question of history requires some thought, particularly with regard to methodology. Even so, there is no proof that Calvin would have changed his doctrine if he had been faced with Cromwell's English Independents in the 1640s, or with the Puritan settlers in Pennsylvania in 1776, or even with the Parisian revolutionaries in 1789, not to mention if he had been confronted with the nineteenth-century doctrine of liberal Protestantism. The vanity of such speculations is evident: we would be leaving history and entering the realm of historical fiction. To avoid falling into the trap of these "badly formed" questions, the historian will attempt to measure the reach of the ideas at the moment in history that they flowed into the mind of their inventor. I therefore let Calvin express himself in his own words and not through the prism of our preferences or commentaries. That is synchronic analysis. Second, I will follow the evolution or change in meaning that contemporary authors, including some most faithful Calvinists, have attributed to Calvin's doctrines under differing circumstances. That is diachronic analysis.

Following these methodological precisions (other authors consulted for this study appear to have hardly addressed this point), I have chosen for the purposes of this essay to expound on a significant and central aspect of Calvin's contribution to modern democracy — the conscience and its freedom — despite knowing that in Calvin's time it was not accorded the status of a right subject to public law, as it is today. I believe that in freedom of conscience, Calvin gave the future of humanity a vital element;

Marc Liénhard, Lucien Carrive, Liliane Crété, André Encrevé, Jean Baubérot, and Alain Boyer are to be found in Viallaneix, ed., *Réforme et Révolutions.*

he gave the religious and political identity of a person a "free" conscience, so that person could therefore behave as an accomplished citizen in civil society and in the legal state.

Calvin's Notion of Democracy

Focusing my attention on "modern democracy," rather than looking at the building of the current state systems claiming to be democracies, I look at the founding notions of democracy during the period when it was being formed, becoming first a theory and then a program. The two classic references are still John Locke (1632-1704) and Jean-Jacques Rousseau (1712-1778), whose intellectual training, though different in each case, must have felt the effects of Calvinism to a certain degree, even if they could not define themselves as Calvinists. These founding elements bring us to the basic tenets of democracy, such as nation, community, equality, election, representativeness, citizenship, individual rights and duties, and many others like them. These were and are the basis of the notion and form of a republic, with the differences stemming from being a democracy, on the one hand, and, on the other, the doctrinal, legal, and political system for modern freedoms.[7]

Before looking at Calvin's text, we should consult one of the major sources, one that all intellectuals of the time knew by heart. It is essential to quote — in a note — a passage from Aristotle (384-322 BCE), because he sheds light on Calvin's use of the words *politia,* in Latin, *policie,* in French.[8]

---

7. Cf. Doumergue, "Calvin, le fondateur des libertés modernes," pp. 21-49.

8. In quoting this text, we remain conscious of the political terminology of both Aristotle's Greek and Guillaume de Mœrbeke (ca. 1215-1286), who in around 1260 was the first to review and render into Latin the key words of Aristotle's politics, in the terms that his friend Thomas would then comment on. Aristotle's Greek and Guillaume's Latin are shown in brackets. Here is the page, which will be useful for us hereafter, taken from *Politics,* III, 7.2-5 (page numbers from the Bekker edition: 1279 a 26-b 10):

> But inasmuch as "constitution" *(politeía; politia)* means the same as "government" *(políteuma; politeuma),* and the government is the supreme power in the state, and this must be either a single ruler or a few *(olígoi; pauci)* or the mass *(polloí; multi)* of the citizens, in cases when the one or the few or the many govern with an eye to the common interest *(tò koinòn sumphéron; ad commune conferens),* these constitutions must necessarily be right ones *(orthas politéas; rectas politias),* while those adminis-

For now we will simply note the three elements that the Greek philosopher highlights. (1) Democracy is considered to be a deviant form of government. (2) The term *politia* specifies unequivocally Aristotle's view on the best form of mixed government and, therefore, had been included in Latin, as a neologism, by Guillaume de Mœrbeke in the thirteenth century. Nicole Oresme (d. 1382; translator of *Nicomachean Ethics*) translated it as *policie* in the fourteenth century, as did Christine de Pizan (1363–ca. 1430; *Le livre du Corps de Policie*) in the fifteenth century. This word has unfortunately not been used in French since Rousseau, who had tried to reuse it spelled *politie* (Contrat social, III, 8; for obvious reasons, the word *police* — from the Latin *politia* and the Greek *politeia,* according to Littré — is not suitable; but we may be tempted to use *politie,* in moderation). The term had also drawn the attention of Thomas Aquinas (ca. 1224-1274), who translated it into Latin as *respublica.*[9] (3) We will find this passage of Aristotle's in Calvin's writings again and again; he summarized it faithfully.

---

tered with an eye to the private interest of either the one or the few or the multitude are deviations *(parekbaseis; transgressiones)*. For either we must not say that those who are part of the state are citizens, or those who are part of the state must share in the advantage of membership. Our customary designation for a monarchy that aims at the common advantage is "kingship"; for a government of more than one yet only a few "aristocracy" (either because the best men rule or because they rule with a view to what is best for the state and for its members); while when the multitude *(plethos; multitudo)* govern the state with a view to the common advantage, it is called by the name common to all the forms of constitution, "constitutional government" *(politeia; omnium politiarum politia)*. (And this comes about reasonably, since although it is possible for one man or a few to excel in virtue, when the number is larger it becomes difficult for them to possess perfect excellence in respect of every form of virtue, but they can best excel in military valor, for this is found with numbers; and therefore with this form of constitution the class that fights for the state in war is the most powerful, and it is those who possess arms who are admitted to the government.) Deviations from the constitutions mentioned are tyranny corresponding to kingship, oligarchy to aristocracy, and democracy to constitutional government; for tyranny is monarchy ruling in the interest of the monarch, oligarchy government in the interest of the rich, democracy government in the interest of the poor, and none of these forms governs with regard to the profit of the community.

We use this translation as is, even though we do not agree with the usage of the terms *constitution* and *constitutional* because of their anachronism.

9. Thomas Aquinas, *In octo libros politicorum Aristotelis expositio*, p. 139: "Sed quando multitudo principatur intendens ad utilitatem commune, vocatur respublica, quod est nomen commune omnibus politiis."

One thing is significant: in his immense body of work, Calvin only used the word *democracy* once, when dealing with the debate over the form of government best adapted for societies of people (and which is not democracy). Calvin observes that "this question admits of no simple solution but requires deliberation, since the nature of the discussion depends largely upon the circumstances. And if you compare the forms of government among themselves apart from the circumstances, it is not easy to distinguish which of them excels in usefulness, for they contend on such equal terms." And he adds this thought, which is not contained in the Latin text: "There are three kinds of civil government; namely, Monarchy, which is the domination of one only, whether he be called King or Duke, or otherwise; Aristocracy, which is a government composed of the chiefs and people of note; and Democracy *(democratie),* which is a popular government, in which each of the people has power."[10]

Wanting to include this classic quotation, Calvin probably felt obliged to use the word *democracy (democratie),* for the first and final time in the foundation of his doctrine.[11] This uniqueness arouses our curiosity about the significance given to it by the author, who goes on to add that "it is true that a King or other with dominion can easily descend to being a tyrant. But it is just as easy when people of note have the superiority, for them to conspire to raise up an iniquitous dominion; and again it is even easier, when the people have the authority, for sedition" — this is, word for word, the quotation from Aristotle. Taking account of the corruptibility of each, Calvin seemed to show a timid preference for the mixed form of aristocracy and *politie;* he doesn't use the term *democracy.*

> It is true that if we compare the three forms of government as I laid out above, the preeminence of those who govern with the people at liberty, would be best [in the Latin edition of 1559, Calvin wrote: *Equidem si in se considerentur tres illae, quas ponunt philosophi regiminis formae, minime negaverim vel aristocratiam, vel temperatum ex ipsa et politia statum, aliis omnibus longe excellere];* not indeed in itself, but because

10. *Inst.* IV,20,8 (French edition of 1560: CO 4,1133; Latin edition of 1559: CO 2,1098). All quotations from the *Institutes* of 1559 refer to *Institutes of the Christian Religion (1559),* trans. F. L. Battles (Philadelphia/London, 1960).

11. And, we will add, in French. Calvin of course knows the Latin word, which he uses to describe ancient Rome, once in his commentary on Seneca's *De clementia* (CO 5,32) and a second time in his exegesis of the prophecy of Daniel (Lecture on Dan. 2:44; CO 40,604).

it very rarely happens that kings so rule themselves as never to dissent from what is just and right, or are possessed of so much acuteness and prudence as always to see correctly.[12]

It is therefore not in and of itself that the combination of aristocracy and *politie* would be the best, only insofar as it would guarantee good government where the monarchy could not do so. What therefore should we think of the aristocracy itself? "Owing, therefore, to the vices or defects of men, it is safer and more tolerable when several bear rule, that they may thus mutually assist, instruct, and admonish each other, and should any one be disposed to go too far, the others are censors and masters to curb his excess."[13]

Aristocracy would be the most tolerable form of government (*magis tolerabile plures tenere gubernacula*) on condition that its members could help each other by controlling and censuring each other, to avert the danger of seeing the aristocracy descend into oligarchy (*in paucorum factione*).

Democracy or Aristocracy in Electing Pastors?

The most direct application of this concept is reflected in Geneva's electoral systems in all their different forms. Charles Mercier, whose position I am aware of, excludes any democratic tendency of Calvin's and refutes anybody holding such an opinion.[14] Mercier recognizes that, while Calvin

---

12. French Edition of 1560 = CO 4,1134; Latin edition of 1559 = CO 2,1098. It is surprising that one of the foremost scholars of Calvin's political doctrine could have ignored this subtlety, giving the translation of this Latin passage as follows: "For if the three forms of government which the philosophers discuss be considered in themselves, I will not deny that aristocracy, or a system compounded of aristocracy and democracy *(vel aristocratiam vel temperatum ex ipsa et politia statum)* far excels all others"; McNeill, "John Calvin on Civil Government," p. 37. If Calvin had wanted to write *democratiam*, he would not have written *politia*. Be that as it may, the difference between the Latin (1559) and the French (1560) from the same Calvin is worthy of attention. The error or the confusion between *democratia* and *politia* is fairly widespread, as demonstrated in the article by Meier et al., "Demokratie," p. 837 and especially pp. 840-42.

13. CO 4,1134. This alludes to the "grabot," a custom in all Genevan committees, companies, and institutions: an annual meeting dedicated to mutual criticism known as "grabot."

14. "Supporters of the latter interpretation appear to us to have not always sufficiently distinguished the principles of ecclesiastical and civil government, professed by Cal-

did not give believers the right of suffrage, he consolidated an electoral practice that validated the role of the people's representatives — though, we might add, the people of the parishes had the ability to tacitly approve or reject the chosen candidates. Nonetheless, the author remarks that "this essentially aristocratic concept of society appears notably in the appointment of elders or presbyters."[15] In my view, this judgment seems quite balanced, in spite of a certain, possibly inescapable, anachronism, as for a twentieth-century historian it is not easy to evaluate with certainty the so-called democratic concepts of the sixteenth century. Having said that, this judgment becomes even more plausible when compared to a similar criticism made by certain of Calvin's disciples, reproaching him for using methods that were not very democratic in ecclesiastical organization and for having aristocratic tendencies, particularly in depriving believers of their right of direct suffrage for the election of ministers. The most sensational case was that of Jean Morély — whom I mentioned earlier — whose *Traité de la discipline ecclésiastique* (Lyon, 1562) was met with such disapproval that it was burned in the public square in 1563 on the orders of the council. Unlike Calvin, who had always insisted on the clear distinction between civil and ecclesiastical governments, Morély establishes an analogy between them to demonstrate that, according to the word of God as set out in scripture, the type of government desired was a democratic one. This "democratic government" is not to be considered in the abstract, in the forms that it took in the distant republics of Athens and Rome, but becomes feasible when adapted to the requirements of the various congregations according to the models given in the holy scripture, which is able to provide it with a body of laws and an organizational system.[16] The theory was also refuted by Antoine de la Roche-Chandieu (1534-1591; *La confirmation de la discipline ecclésiastique observée des églises réformées du royaume de France, avec la response aux objections proposées à l'encontre* [Geneva/La Rochelle, 1566]), who tried to dismantle the central theory of the analogy between the two powers.

---

vin, on one hand, from his constant preoccupation with defending the essential freedoms of the governed people, on the other hand. The distinction is however crucial in this matter. One can believe in what we call individual freedoms in politics, without proclaiming the people's right to govern themselves; which is strictly speaking the essence of the democratic regime"; Mercier, "L'esprit de Calvin et la démocratie," p. 30.

15. Mercier, "L'esprit de Calvin et la démocratie," p. 33.

16. See Kingdon, "Calvin and Democracy," p. 397.

Nobody synthesized this argument better than Theodore Beza, in a letter written in 1571, which is precious because it also summarizes the process for the election and removal of ministers. In this letter, Calvin's successor explains to Heinrich Bullinger (1504-1575), Zwingli's successor, the intrigues of those who wished to sow discord in the churches of Zurich and Geneva. In particular, Beza denounces Morély's slander and that of his fellows, who accused him of having "in some way introduced oligarchy or tyranny into the Church, those who had refused to establish the most confused and pernicious democracy therein (quasi oligarchiam aut tyrannidem in Ecclesiam invehant, qui perturbatissimam et seditiosissimam democratiam stabilire in Ecclesia recusarint)." On the contrary, Beza explains to his counterpart in Zurich, the churches of France "have always had and continue to have in common with us the aristocratic principle of the Consistory (aristocratiam Consistorii nobiscum communem)"[17] — a shocking sentence that rightly attracted the attention of historians.[18]

The significance of this letter goes beyond the chronological boundaries of the matters discussed within it, because it incisively sets out the terms that form the basis of the debate between Presbyterians and Congregationalists, between aristocratic principles and democratic principles that are sometimes difficult to distinguish. While it was already being formed at that time, this debate among Puritans would take on considerable proportions in English-speaking countries during the seventeenth century, and continue in the New World. There is considerable literature showing the continuance of this debate, the consequences of which are linked on the one hand to the troubles in England that led to the Glorious Revolution, and on the other hand, to the American Revolution.[19] But the

17. Theodore Beza's letter to Heinrich Bullinger, Geneva, November 13, 1571, in *Correspondance de Théodore de Bèze*, vol. 12, no. 871, pp. 215-27, here p. 220.

18. Cf. Kingdon, *Geneva and the Consolidation of the French Protestant Movement*, pp. 209-15.

19. On the relationship between continental Calvinism and English political thought, cf. Cremeans, *Reception of Calvinistic Thought in England*; Salmon, *French Religious Wars in English Political Thought*; Collinson, *Elizabethan Puritan Movement*; Mosse, *Holy Pretence*; Hill, *Society and Puritanism in Pre-Revolutionary England*; Flynn, *Influence of Puritanism in the Political and Religious Thought of the English*; Mosse, *Struggle for Sovereignty*; Howse, *Saints in Politics*; Morris, *Political Thought in England*. On the origins of democracy with regard to Puritanism in the Old and New World, cf. Simpson, *Puritanism in Old and New England*; Mead, "William Brewster and the Independents"; Miller and Johnson, eds., *Puritans*; Miller, *New England Mind*; Perry, *Puritanism and Democracy*; Johnson, ed., *Foundations of Democracy*.

farther we get from Calvin's time, the more we must call on Calvinism, looking at the works of the disciples, a reasonable step and one that offers elements of continuity from one century to another right up to the present day.

Let us stay with Calvin's texts and try to understand how the notion of freedom is developed in the author's reasoning, as he departs from Christian freedom to reach freedom of conscience.

The Conscience and Its Freedom

Calvin dedicates a chapter of his *Institutes* to "Christian liberty." He uses the phrase *libertas christiana,* which Paul had used (1 Cor. 10:29; 2 Cor. 3:17) to mean the Christian's freedom from servitude and the ceremonies of the Law, the Law of Moses. Over the centuries, the fathers of the church, such as Jerome (347-420), Augustine (354-430), and Ambrose (339-397), and the theologians of the Middle Ages, such as Bernard of Clairvaux (ca. 1090-1153), Peter Abelard (1079-1142), and Thomas Aquinas, worked to clarify the notion of *conscientia* more than that of *libertas christiana,* so the former thereby acquired particular theological importance as the preferred place for faith.[20] But it was the sixteenth-century reformers who gave center stage to freedom of conscience. Martin Luther (1483-1546), Huldrych Zwingli (1484-1531), Philipp Melanchthon (1497-1560), and Calvin outlined a doctrine of Christian freedom that gradually became a doctrine of freedom of conscience. To find the shift from one to the other, let us follow Calvin, who began by explaining his doctrine:

> Christian freedom, in my opinion, consists of three parts. The first: that the consciences of believers, in seeking assurance of their justification before God, should rise above and advance beyond the law, forgetting all law righteousness. . . . The second part, dependent upon the first, is that consciences observe the law, not as if constrained by the necessity of the law, but that freed from the law's yoke they willingly obey God's will. . . . The third part of Christian freedom lies in this: regarding outward things that are of themselves indifferent, we are not bound before God by any religious obligation preventing us from

20. Turchetti, "À la racine de toutes les libertés: la liberté de conscience."

sometimes using them or other times not using them, indifferently. And the knowledge of this freedom is very necessary for us.[21]

Close to the "heart" and the "soul," the conscience is deep down inside the human being and in direct contact with God. Like "a keeper assigned to man, that watches and observes. . . . Hence that ancient proverb: conscience is a thousand witnesses,"[22] the conscience rules the believer's internal judgment mechanism, whose first concern is his or her justification and salvation. That is why it can be raised above the Law (the Old Testament Law of Moses), "forgetting all law righteousness" of "outward things" and themselves "indifferent," because it must account only to God. It is free in the sense that it must obey only the word of God. While, on the one hand, it is subject to divine will and ruled by it, on the other hand, it remains free with regard to any external or human law when those are not in accordance with divine law. This happens when human law does not follow the natural equity and natural law, which are akin to divine law. So that we do not lose ourselves in the midst of all these laws, let me try to clarify things and explain which laws the conscience can freely disobey and, on the other hand, which laws it must obey.

The Law of Moses, Moral Law, Equity

When Calvin affirms that the conscience is free from the Law of Moses, he refers to its three constituent parts: the "moral, ceremonial, and judicial laws." With regard to the two other laws, "the ceremonial law of the Jews was a tutelage," while "the judicial law, given to them for civil government . . . had something distinct from that precept of love. Therefore, as ceremonial laws could be abrogated while piety remained safe and unharmed, so too, when these judicial laws were taken away, the perpetual duties and precepts of love could still remain."[23] In this regard the conscience is freed from all obligation.[24] With regard to customs, little store should be set by

21. *Inst.* III,19,2-7; CO 4,344, 346, 349. See Lecler, "Liberté de conscience"; Dufour, "La notion de liberté de conscience," pp. 15-20; Millet, "Le thème."

22. *Inst.* IV,10,3; CO 4,761.

23. *Inst.* IV,20,14-16; CO 4,1143-44.

24. We note that Calvin added a comment at this point, into which a modern reader might read a principle destined to have a great democratic future: "But if this is true, surely

their value with regard to "ceremonial and judicial laws," which can "be changed or abrogated," but instead by what they entail with regard to "the true holiness of morals," that is to say, moral laws. Moral law "is the true and eternal rule of righteousness, prescribed for men of all nations and times," because it contains "two heads, one of which simply commands us to worship God with pure faith and piety; the other, to embrace men with sincere affection." Moral law thus laid out is enriched by another element, equity, for which Calvin underlines the prerogatives when one must decide the validity of laws in general. We must observe two elements in all laws: "the constitution of the law, and the equity on which its constitution is itself founded and rests. Equity, because it is natural, cannot but be the same for all, and therefore, this same purpose ought to apply to all laws, whatever the object." By drawing out one by one the characteristics of God's law, which surpass those of simply natural law, and by highlighting their permanence and validity for all people in all times, the author makes a link between these various characteristics and the conscience: "It is a fact that the law of God which we call the moral law is nothing else than a testimony of natural law and of that conscience which God has engraved upon the minds of men. Consequently, the entire scheme of this equity of which we are now speaking has been prescribed in it. Hence, this equity alone must be the goal and rule and limit of all laws."[25]

The conscience reveals to us the elements of God's law, particularly equity, which it must find in human laws in order to know whether they are to be obeyed or not. That is the responsibility of the individual, the citizen and the believer, who are intrinsically linked, whose conscience is both free to obey God's law immediately and to obey man's law after judging it to be equitable. Obeying civil laws "motivated by conscience" is an instruction given to us by Paul (Rom. 13:1-6), referring implicitly to good and just laws.

---

every nation is left free to make such laws as it foresees to be profitable for itself. Yet these must be in conformity to that perpetual rule of love, so that they indeed vary in form but have the same purpose" (CO 4,1144).

25. *Inst.* IV,20,16; CO 4,1145.

"Heavenly Regime and Earthly Ordinance"

It is in these terms that we can understand the dual religious and civil register in which Calvin explains the dual attitude of the conscience when faced with the duty to obey, because "human and civil jurisdictions are quite different from those which touch the conscience." His explanation of the two areas of action becomes even more coherent when paired with the distinction made by the theologian between ecclesiastical government and civil government — in other words, between the "heavenly regime and earthly ordinance." With regard to the heavenly regime, which is more specifically the realm of the conscience, if "conscience refers to God," we are in the presence of a "clear conscience": "A good conscience, then, is nothing but inward integrity of heart."[26] Meanwhile, in the "earthly" governed by human laws, the conscience can act as a shield to protect ourselves from these laws "if they were passed to lay scruples upon us"; sometimes, in this world that is under "the densest darkness of ignorance," it is like a "tiny little spark of light," lighting the way to show us that "man's conscience [is] . . . higher than all human judgments." In fact, "God still willed that some testimony of Christian freedom appear to rescue consciences from the tyranny of men." The conscience, as Calvin describes it, becomes the defender of the individual from the encroachments of an oppressive power, even if the author does not describe it in those terms. "For if we must obey rulers not only because of punishment but for conscience' sake, it seems to follow from this that the rulers' laws also have dominion over the conscience. Now if this is true, the same also will have to be said of church laws." Calvin maintains a prudent but firm attitude when specifying that two things must be taken into consideration.

> I answer, that the first thing to be done here is to distinguish between the genus and the species. For though individual laws do not reach the conscience, yet we are bound by the general command of God, which enjoins us to submit to magistrates. And this is the point on which Paul's discussion turns — viz. that magistrates are to be honoured, be-

---

26. *Inst.* III,19,16; CO 4,360. The phrase is repeated again in the text in Book IV,10,4; CO 4,761, as follows: "Therefore, just as works concern men, so the conscience relates to God in such a way that a good conscience is nothing but an inward uprightness of heart. In this sense, Paul writes that 'the fulfilment of the law is love, out of a pure . . . conscience and faith unfeigned [1 Tim 1:5].'" These two paragraphs are in fact identical.

cause they are ordained of God (Rom. 13:1). Meanwhile, he does not at all teach that the laws enacted by them reach to the internal government of the soul, since he everywhere proclaims that the worship of God, and the spiritual rule of living righteously, are superior to all the decrees of men. Another thing also worthy of observation, and depending on what has been already said, is, that human laws, whether enacted by magistrates or by the Church, are necessary to be observed (I speak of such as are just and good), but do not therefore in themselves bind the conscience, because the whole necessity of observing them respects the general end, and consists not in the things commanded.[27]

Obedience to Civil Laws

As we can see, obedience to civil laws is due to the magistrates insofar as they are good magistrates. The second consideration is that "all human laws (I speak of good and just laws) do not bind the conscience," but these must be observed in consideration of "the general end, that there should be good order and ordinance among us." Calvin could not have said any more about freedom of conscience, even though he only used that phrase twice in all of his writings, on the same page, to reiterate that "a pious and ready inclination to obey" ecclesiastical edicts in order to "cherish mutual charity" takes nothing away from the "freedom of conscience": "The conscience will not cease to be free and frank."[28] There was no need to repeat the expression itself more often, because his argument had already built a solid theory of the conscience and its freedom.

Therefore, when it comes to the conscience, Calvin is faultlessly precise and coherent. The conclusions we can draw from one chapter — in this case, Book IV, Chapter 10, on the power of the church and the tyranny of the pope — join those that we can draw from another chapter, one more specific about disobedience and resistance, in Book IV, Chapter 20, *in fine,* as I have already mentioned. The discussion on the subject of the conscience and its liberty in the field of politics is inevitably linked to the question of knowing "how much deference private individuals ought

27. *Inst.* IV,10,5; CO 4,763.
28. *Inst.* IV,10,31; CO 4,794.

to yield to their magistrates *(supérieurs)*, and how far their obedience ought to go."[29] We already know the reasoning and the answer, so they do not need to be repeated here. I would, however, like to suggest several reflections on the essence of Calvin's doctrine on the freedom of conscience and its scope, which sometimes goes beyond what its author had imagined.

The Contradictions (or "Vitality") of a Doctrine When Put to the Test of Time

While recognizing that he owed much to his predecessors, Luther and particularly Melanchthon, in drawing up his theory on the freedom of conscience, Calvin had given center stage to a creature that — we could say — would develop a life of its own and could not die with its author. This is also true for other things, including Calvin's contribution to modern democracy. By separating the two spheres, the religious and the political, the conscience became a separate protagonist in the history of nations, asserting itself both in moral theology, as a place deep down inside for the action of individual will, and in political law, as an individualizing identity of the legal person. If — following Calvin's prescriptions — in religious life the conscience should free itself from the Law of Moses and the tyrannical regulations of the papacy, it would acquire an autonomous status in political life giving it the right to obey only the equitable laws of just and God-fearing magistrates, to "commit the judgement to the matter of the magistrate *(remonstrer au superieur/ad magistratum cognitionem deferre)*,"[30] to

---

29. *Inst.* IV,20,17: CO 4,1146.

30. *Inst.* IV,20,23; CO 4,1152-53: "Under this obedience, I comprehend the restraint which private men ought to impose on themselves in public, not interfering with public business, or rashly encroaching on the province of the magistrate, or attempting anything at all of a public nature. If it is proper that anything in a public ordinance should be corrected, let them not act tumultuously, or put their hands to a work where they ought to feel that their hands are tied, but let them leave it to the cognisance of the magistrate, whose hand alone here is free. My meaning is, let them not dare to do it without being ordered. For when the command of the magistrate is given, they too are invested with public authority. For as, according to the common saying, the eyes and ears of the prince are his counsellors, so one may not improperly say that those who, by his command, have the charge of managing affairs, are his hands." Ibid., CO 2,1111: "If anything in a public ordinance requires amendment, let them not raise a tumult, or put their hands to the task — all of them ought to keep their

resist the iniquitous edicts of kings by applying the "exception or rather the rule" intrinsic to the Petrine precept ("We must obey God rather than men" [Acts 5:29]). In highlighting the elements of contestation, which are the structures leading toward future democracies, we should not lose sight of the fact that, in Calvin's construction, they were joining a theory of civil obedience due to the magistrate and respect for the established order. There is no contradiction if we consider these elements to have arisen from an exceptional situation, as Calvin understood it. There may, however, be a contradiction between the theory and the practice, that is to say, between Calvin's claims in writing his doctrine on the freedom of conscience and their application in his own life. To examine this aspect — which could interest some readers — we must look at the question as a historian, being sure to make allowances and, to begin with, not placing Calvin in a role as precursor or prophet, which would lead us into error just as it has many researchers who were stubbornly convinced that they could prove that Calvin was the father of modern democracy.

The Conscience and Its Rights

We have discussed the autonomy of the conscience — an element with great significance for future democracies — but Calvin never used this term, just as he never used the phrase "rights of the conscience." Why? Because he did not need to. He had provided all the essential ingredients for the conscience to have its obvious rights. The proof of this is that his contemporaries, and even his adversaries, had taken note of this element of the Calvinist movement, by including the right in a royal edict of 1563, the Edict of Amboise (Arts. 1, 4 and 6), which ended the first civil war. This inclusion, as I have noted elsewhere,[31] marks a shift in French legislative language: the disappearance of the term *heretic* to describe "those of the new religion," a forerunner of the expression "those of the so-called reformed religion." Calvin's Protestant contemporaries spoke about the rights of the

---

hands bound in this respect — but let them commit the matter to the judgement of the magistrate *(ad magistratus cognitionem deferant),* whose hand alone here is free." In the interests of brevity, we have not examined this important passage, for which see Millet, "Le thème," p. 33.

31. Turchetti, "À la racine de toutes les libertés," pp. 627-28. Cf. Turchetti, "Une question mal posée."

conscience, which they put at the center of their claims *(vindiciae)* throughout the civil wars of the sixteenth and seventeenth centuries. Provisionally recognized by the Edict of Nantes in 1598, these theological rights would once again take their place at the forefront of the political scene with the progressive erosion of the liberal clauses of the edict, and be more solemnly proclaimed toward the end of the seventeenth century in the titles of famous works such as *Droits des deux Souverains en matière de Religion, la Conscience et le Prince* (1687, by Pierre Jurieu [1637-1713]) or *Réflexions sur les droits de la conscience* (1697, by Élie Saurin [1639-1703]). Even the rights of the "mistaken" conscience or the conscience of the heretic convinced of his orthodoxy were confirmed: that is what Pierre Bayle (1647-1706) calls "true freedom of conscience," since "error disguised as truth binds us to the same things as truth." But we must pause here to retrace our steps and open the chapter on contradictions, which I have already said a few words about.

Freedom of Conscience: For All Consciences?

When Calvin was creating his doctrine of Christian freedom, he knew that the Reformed believers of France were living under a regime of persecution. By putting forward his theories, he was sure to contribute to the advancement of the gospel and of reform in the kingdom, because, by trying to make freedom of conscience acceptable, he wanted the authorities to accept freedom of worship. Yet, when he dealt with the conscience, he spoke about the conscience of humans in general and the conscience of believers in particular. Which believers? — believers of all confessions? The question may seem rhetorical, but for the author and his followers it was undoubtedly about the conscience of Reformed believers, that is to say, those professing the true religion ("since of two religions, only one can be the true religion"), perhaps that of recognized Protestants, such as Lutherans or Zwinglians, and questions remained over that of papists. As for the conscience of the anti-Trinitarians, the Anabaptists, and the heretics of all kinds, there was no doubt. What historians have called the "exclusivity" of Calvin's religion was not without foundation, because, with regard to freedom of conscience and certainly with regard to freedom of worship, the reformer of Geneva only thought of the Reformed. This exclusivity — which for those of us today with little sense of history, would appear to be a failing — at the time was a great support, particularly for the persecuted, as they were thus reassured of the validity of their endurance, being witnesses to the true faith. If we say that Calvin asked himself this question, which is unlikely, he should have specified in his writings that when he spoke of freedom of conscience, he meant freedom of conscience for the Reformed. Why did he not do this? Because it was obvious. But the message was interpreted differently by other readers of his works, including some of his disciples — to name but one to represent them all, Sebastian Castellio (1515-1563). He, having worked with Calvin as a minister in Geneva, decided to move to Basel. The Michael Servetus episode and its repercussions, particularly the debate that followed, reveals the ambiguity in Calvin's doctrine on freedom of conscience that I wish to highlight.

Castellio advocated freedom of conscience throughout his life; he had taken the doctrine straight from the source, from Calvin himself. The controversy that flared up between master and disciple, and that was one of the most violent of the century, centered on freedom of conscience, which Castellio (the author of *Traité des hérétiques* in 1554) extended to all men, to all believers, and maybe even to heretics. This is why, when he implemented this principle by publishing his *Conseil à la France désolée* during the first civil war (October 1562: "admit two Churches into France"), he attracted even greater anger from Calvin, for whom Castellio's action amounted to "opening the door to all kinds of heresy." Modern readers might wonder what caused this argument, since Castellio simply wanted what the reformers wanted, the freedom to worship in France. That is one thing that all the histories of the Wars of Religion have trouble explaining, which is why they sidestep the question.[32] In 1562, the situation was not the same as it was in 1598: the aim of Calvin and his associates was not to be "tolerated," but rather to change the religion of the kingdom in order to achieve confessional unity, a "reformed" concord. Later on, toward the end of the civil wars, their goals would be — if I may be so bold — scaled down.

It is nevertheless the case that Castellio was right: he had found the fault in Calvin's doctrine on freedom of conscience, even if his interpretation was different from that of the master, the author of the *Institutes*. What Calvin implied in his pages — freedom of conscience for the Reformed — was not there to help the reader. I could of course discuss the

---

32. Cf. Turchetti, "Calvin face aux tenants de la concorde."

work and its interpretations. What I would say here is intended as innocent provocation, to underline a point of doctrine whose effects have been
"catastrophic" for the history of Calvinism. In addition, we could find
proof of the historical relevance of what we are saying here in the judgment of Calvin's closest collaborator, Theodore Beza, who perfectly understood the dangers that his master's doctrine on freedom of conscience
could be exposing itself to: "Would we say that freedom of conscience
should be permitted? Not in the least, if it means the freedom for everyone
to worship God however they please: that is a diabolical dogma (est enim
diabolicum dogma)."[33]

Beza too had been right and his interpretation, we must admit, coincided with Castellio's, although with a diametrically different assessment.
Let us put it another way. According to Beza, who followed Calvin's doctrine to the letter, the conscience in question was that of the Reformed,
while for Castellio it was the conscience of everybody. They were thus both
Calvinists, but in very different ways! To conclude this aspect of the contradictions between the theory and the practice (contradictions that in
some way prove the vitality of his ideas), that is, between the innocence of
a doctrine forged to edify humanity and the dramatic circumstances of life
imposing on its implementation, we turn to irony. The irony of the "heter-
ogeneity of purpose" meant that the principle of freedom of conscience,
which was destined for a dazzling future in modern democracy and judged
worthy of inclusion in the various declarations of human rights from 1776
to the present day, was implemented in the form conceived and spread by
Castellio and not as originally created by Calvin. However — risking a
gloss — we could say that what was to become known as Castellionism is
at its origin simply pure Calvinism.

And the Erroneous Conscience?

In conclusion, let us return to a subject which, because of its significance,
is linked to modern democracy: the erroneous conscience. Toward the end
of the seventeenth century, this debate inflamed theologians and French-

---

33. Theodore Beza's letter to Andreas Dudith, Geneva, June 18, 1570, in *Correspondance de Theodore de Bèze*, vol. 12, no. 780, pp. 168-85, here p. 179. On this issue see the article
by Dufour, "La notion de liberté de conscience," p. 15.

speaking Protestant intellectuals in France and the Netherlands, while for the English-speakers, who were also very involved in the reflections on freedom of conscience, it was rare (with John Locke and his set), and for Catholics it was tangled up in the doctrines of probabilism, laxism, tutiorism, and probabiliorism. In France the Calvinists were divided into three streams, explains Élie Saurin: the Indifferent, led by Bayle; the Intolerant, represented by Jurieu; and the Moderately Tolerant, also known as Charitably Zealous, a group Saurin was proud to belong to. The debate on this matter was to have an immediate effect on a political level, because its outcome would dictate, on the one hand, the resolution of the problem of religious tolerance, and on the other hand, the legality of the persecutions and the legitimacy of the revocation of the Edict of Nantes. Having re-examined in turn the bold speculations of Thomas Aquinas on the conscience blinded by insurmountable error, Bayle astonished his readers when he claimed, with implacable logic, that an error disguised as truth had all the same rights as truth. This was like putting orthodoxy and heresy on an equal footing: equal rights between an enlightened conscience and an erroneous one, parity between orthodoxy and heresy, equivalence between truth and insurmountable error.[34] According to this theory, freedom of conscience was clearing a new path to take it on the road to a new freedom, religious freedom, the freedom to profess all religions — another pillar of modern democracy.

Toward Parity for Truth and Error

Aware of how much this perhaps inevitable turn toward religious freedom would have displeased Calvin, we arrive at the threshold of another chapter on the contradictions or "vitality" of Calvin's ideas when put to the test of time. Which obliges us once again to take a step back. Let us pause to consider an author who could — cautiously, of course — play the role of Calvin: Pierre Jurieu, who believed himself to be a *Calvinus redivivus*.[35] At the dawn of the Age of Enlightenment, the doctrine of

---

34. See Turchetti, "La liberté de conscience et l'autorité du Magistrat."

35. I could not share, without criticism, Jurieu's opinion of himself (an opinion categorically refuted by Ms Elisabeth Labrousse, which I clearly remember discussing with her at a Colloquium on Jurieu). I come to this author because his ideas enter my discussion at a

freedom of conscience was fatally implicated in an intellectual climate where skepticism and "indifferentism" (in the form of Latitudinarianism) seemed to rule. Bayle embodied this trend, according to his adversaries, among whom Jurieu seemed to occupy the place of honor. The latter fought "the great source of delusion for our libertines" bitterly, saying that the erroneous conscience had the same rights as the orthodox conscience. In the same way, on a political level, he refuted the consequence categorically, that is to say, "that an idolatrous Prince has the same right to defend idolatry as an orthodox Prince for truth."[36] Jurieu understood perfectly that, after the Revocation, the tolerants, like Bayle, wanted to establish the rights of the erroneous conscience at the expense of those of the prince to ease the lot of the persecuted Protestants. But this enlargement of freedom of conscience represented an injustice, because even Jews, Turks, and pagans could benefit from it — not to mention what it would mean depriving sovereigns of their right to intervene in religious affairs; that would be to "relieve the kings of France and Spain of the authority to chase Papism from their States, as the kings of England and Sweden have done. . . . Be assured that this must happen here."[37] This is one of Jurieu's reflections that would seem to join Calvin's view of a certain notion of religious tolerance, which would nevertheless give way to the perception of their respective adversaries, who were also Calvinists in their own way: first Castellio, then Bayle.

"The Sovereignty of the People" —
The First Formulations, the First Debates

In these same debates at the end of the seventeenth century, another idea, perhaps the idea dearest to the supporters of modern democracy, comes to light: "popular sovereignty." In various controversial writings, such as his *Lettres Pastorales,* Jurieu reexamined and developed the theory drawn up by Calvinists, direct disciples of Calvin, such as François Hotman (1524-

---

certain point. In addition, one should recognize that there are elements in his method of imposing his ideas and in his attitudes that remind us of Calvin, for better or worse, but always with a certain affinity.

36. Jurieu, *Des droits des deux Souverains,* pp. 285-87, 289, 294.

37. Jurieu, *Des droits des deux Souverains,* pp. 283-84; cf. Turchetti, "La liberté de conscience," p. 343.

1590), Theodore Beza, Innocent Gentillet, George Buchanan (1506-1582), Junius Brutus, and others in the 1570s, in the heat of the wars of religion after the St. Bartholomew's Day Massacre. Now, in the heat — we can use the image again — of the Revocation, the ideas of the disciples of yesteryear became more explicit. Jurieu conferred on them such fire and aggression that he would even attract the disapproval of his Protestant contemporaries themselves. In the middle of the reign of Louis XIV (1638-1715), he wrote *Les soupirs de la France esclave* "with a view . . . to reignite in the hearts of the French the spirit of freedom that Tyranny has extinguished," because it was common knowledge that "the Court of France has built its Despotic Power" by diminishing the "Freedom of the People" to the point of abolishing "the Nation's General Assemblies, where the Sovereign Power lay."[38] This is why he wanted to show "the extremes to which Tyranny had gone, the means it used to establish and preserve itself."[39] As a result of his extraordinary historical, legal, and political knowledge, Jurieu proposed "reforming the State," regenerating the monarchy that was at that time reduced, in his view, to a pitiful level, which was "an effect of the Despotic and Arbitrary Power that is pure Tyranny."[40] The basis of his theory was that "the Sovereign Power" should be put back "into the hands of the People and of Assemblies composed of their Deputies," the people should be given back their rights and their liberty, which irresponsible kings, particularly "Louis the fourteenth, the most imperious and authoritative of all the kings," had taken away from them.

In the works of Calvinist authors of that period, we find expressions like "freedom of Peoples," and calls for "sovereign power" of which the people are guardians. Could we say that these contributed to modern democracy? Yes, of course, though it is important to note that they were writ-

---

38. Jurieu, *Les soupirs de la France,* pp. 296-97.

39. Jurieu, *Les soupirs de la France,* p. 543.

40. Jurieu, *Les soupirs de la France,* p. 107. In this and many other writings, using phrases such as this one about "the infidelity with which the Court supports the Tyranny of its Despotic Power," with numerous variations, Jurieu showed that he could no longer distinguish between despotism and tyranny, in fact just like other authors of this time. On this important historical confusion, important because it prevented thorough political analysis, not to mention the resulting improper usage of the "tyrannicide" theory, see my study of comparative terminological history, Turchetti, "Droit de Résistance à quoi?" pp. 831-77. Jean Hubac does not appear to have recognized this confusion — which Jurieu was not the only one to display — in his otherwise very interesting article: Hubac, "Tyrannie et tyrannicide selon Jurieu," pp. 583-609.

ing around a century before the Revolution, for which the idea has not yet appeared. It is not surprising that this theory of popular sovereignty (*ante litteram,* the origin of which is commonly said to be the Age of Enlightenment) must have hurt the ears of the Catholics and all those who were close to royal politics. In fact, first Jacques Bénigne Bossuet (1627-1704) did not hesitate to virulently oppose the theory of popular sovereignty in his *Avertissements aux Protestants sur les lettres du Ministre Jurieu contre l'Histoire des variations* (Paris, 1689). But within the scope of our research, it is the reaction of another Calvinist that interests us more: Pierre Bayle, who refuted the positions of his fellow Protestant on the basis of the same sources, with a view, like him, to protecting the interests of the Protestants in France. As for knowing which of them was the more Calvinist of the two, an analysis of their works — which we can do here — could tell us, at least to a degree. What were the arguments that led to such contrast between the two Calvinists? Bayle laid the blame on the "Republican lampoons" and the "Satirists," "infected with Political Heresies," who supported the "Sovereignty of the people."

> The main reason that leads you to teach that Sovereignty comes from the people, and that they only ever give it up for the faculty of atonement, or rather that they always confer it like a stronghold moving its Crown on the charge of reversion, is that you believe you can easily justify civil wars and the destitution of Kings with this theory. Yet beware, Sir, as if only the whole multitude of the people had the right to inspect and examine the conduct of the Prince, and that of his People; if it was necessary for each individual person to submit to the will of the Court, even when they found it injust: it would only be possible to remedy the disorder of the Government through the rebellion of an infinite number of individuals, which would render your theory completely absurd.[41]

The Protestants in exile, who were waiting for the time to return to France, did not realize that by spreading "Monarchomach dogmas" in their lampoons, renewed by the new "Presbyterien dogma of the accountability of Monarchs," they were undermining the principles of their own religion and declaring themselves to be in substance enemies of the state. The numerous references to the "parricide of Charles the First" led the au-

---

41. Bayle, *Avis important aux Refugiez sur leur prochain retour en France,* pp. 133-34.

thor to question the basis of the Presbyterian theories like that of George Buchanan, applied by the Independents according to the suggestions of John Milton, which are both in an anonymous text, printed in Magdeburg in 1550, *Du droit des Magistrats sur leurs sujets,* and in another text printed in 1579 under the pseudonym Stephanus Junius Brutus, *Vindiciae contra tyrannos.* Bayle refuted the theories of these two authors with arguments from the most subtle political philosophy, after which he could more easily demolish the theories that were attached to it, those of Jurieu, Jean Claude, and other makers of "insurgent pamphlets" that were circulating in France and elsewhere at the time. In particular, he attacked the new dogma of the sovereignty of the people.

> Where then is this supposed Sovereignty of the people that you have been so extolling for several months; this most monstrous, favoured illusion, which at the same time is the most pernicious dogma with which we could infatuate the world? Those for whom you have revived it from the graves of Buchanan, Junius Brutis, and Milton, the infamous Cromwell apologist, would be greatly embarrassed, if the inhabitants of Great Britain wanted to use the gift that you are offering them: as if this Sovereignty means that the people can force Monarchs to give an account of their administration, and nominate Commissioners for this, it can also mean the examination by other Commissioners of the conduct of a Convention or a Parliament. Who can deny it? And what could be more ridiculous than claiming that the Sovereignty of a people gives it the right to oppose a king but not an Assembly of around four or five hundred people?[42]

To expose the vicious circle in which the theories of "inferior Magistrates" and the right to resistance were fatally engaged, Bayle also relied on the argument of another Calvinist, the author of *De jure belli ac pacis,* Hugo Grotius (1583-1645), wanting to warn his fellow Protestants against their ideas, which were a threat to their very survival.

---

42. Bayle, *Avis important aux Refugiez sur leur prochain retour en France,* pp. 86-87.

Freedom of Conscience First in the
Secular Democracy of the Twentieth Century

Let us stop here, resisting the pull of these fascinating pages, to ask ourselves another question at the end of our study. At the end of the seventeenth century, just before entering the age of revolutions and Enlightenment, we are faced with two streams of thought both claiming to represent Calvinism, and which were battling for recognition, particularly in the kingdom of France: one, through resistance, in the footsteps of Beza-Buchanan-Jurieu; the other, through tolerance, in the footsteps of Castellio-Grotius-Bayle. Which side would Calvin have come down on? This is a question that cannot be answered, we admit. Let us try to change the terms. On the basis of what we know of him through his writings, we would say that both of these lines of conduct would find supporting points in his doctrine, especially if we remember not only the famous last page of the *Institutes,* which alludes to the right to resistance, but also the dozens of preceding pages, discussing the duty of obedience. Let us note that both of these streams are essential for modern democracy to blossom and would be prolonged, on the one hand, in the affirmation of the right to revolution — in the United Provinces, in England, in the United States, and in France — and on the other hand, in the affirmation of human rights. Of course, Calvin is not alone in these various processes, which we are unavoidably outlining far too simply. But it is without doubt that among the numerous legal, theological, and political elements that contributed to both of these developments, there is a place for Calvin and Calvinism. We believe we can definitely discern his mark in the idea that is at the heart of both of these streams of thought: freedom of conscience. This idea made its way, in particular — not alone, of course[43] — in the incisive form that Calvin gave it, through the centuries between debates and revolutions, to establish itself, at the beginning of the twentieth century, at the heart of the most areligious (not anti-religious) and atheological (not antitheological) law that there could be, to serve as the perpetual foundation of the "dogma" of laicism. We find it in its essential brevity, as power-

---

43. In other denominations and particularly among Catholics, there is considerable debate on freedom of conscience in very different forms; for an initial introduction to it in Catholic theology, cf. Baucher, "Liberté morale." Readers should also look at what is perhaps the best account of the issue from the perspective of ecclesiastical law and moral philosophy, Ruffini's treatise *La libertà religiosa.*

ful as it is profound, in the first line of the first article of the French Constitution: "The Republic ensures freedom of conscience. It guarantees the freedom to worship with only the restrictions decreed hereafter in the interest of public order."[44]

We now reach another important conclusion for our subject, Calvin and modern democracy, touching on the primordial element that is at the heart of every human being, that place deep down inside. Freedom of conscience is now destined to be affirmed in its legal status as a subjective and inalienable right that is worthy of appearing in constitutions and in conventions and declarations on human rights, the rights of women, and the rights of the child. It is so central that it would be worthy of its own convention or declaration on the rights of the conscience.[45] It is in light of this experience that we should consider perfecting the structures of modern democracy.

Translated from French by Victoria Mendham, Bath, UK

---

44. Act of December 9, 1905, on the separation of church and state, Chapter 1, Principles, Article 1. Cf. Passy, *Soyons laïques!*

45. Cf. Turchetti, "La liberté de conscience," p. 798.

Bibliography

Primary Sources

John Calvin

Calvin, John. *Calvin-Studienausgabe.* Ed. Eberhard Busch, Alasdair Heron, Christian Link, Peter Opitz, Ernst Saxer, and Hans Scholl. 8 vols. Neukirchen-Vluyn: Neukirchener Verlag, 1994-2008.

———. *Calvin's Commentary on Seneca's De Clementia.* Trans. and ed. Ford Lewis Battles and Andre Malan Hugo. Renaissance Text Series, vol. 3. Leiden: Brill, 1969.

———. *Calvin's New Testament Commentaries.* Ed. David W. Torrance and Thomas F. Torrance. 12 vols. Edinburgh/London/Grand Rapids: Eerdmans, 1961-74 (1994-96).

———. *Christliche Glaubenslehre, nach der ältesten Ausgabe vom Jahre 1536.* Trans. Bernhard Spiess. Wiesbaden: Limbarth, 1887. Reprinted Zurich, 1985.

———. *Commentaires de Jehan Calvin sur le Nouveau Testament. Le tout reveu diligemment et comme traduit de nouveau, tant le texte que la glose.* 4 vols. Paris: Meyrueis, 1854-55.

———. *Concerning the Eternal Predestination of God by John Calvin.* Trans. and ed. J. K. S. Reid. Louisville: Westminster John Knox, 1997.

———. "Congregation on Eternal Election." In Philip C. Holtrop, *The Bolsec Controversy on Predestination from 1551 to 1555,* vol. 1, pp. 695-720. Lewiston/Queenston/Lampeter: Edwin Mellen, 1993.

———. *De aeterna Dei praedestinatione. Consensus Pastorum Geneviensis ecclesiae = Von der ewigen Vorherbestimmung Gottes.* Trans. and ed. Wilhelm H. Neuser. Schriften des Archivs der Evangelischen Kirche im Rheinland, vol. 18. Düsseldorf: Archiv der Evangelischen Kirche im Rheinland, 1998.

————. *De aeterna Dei praedestinatione = De la prédestination éternelle*. Ed. Wilhelm H. Neuser. Ioannis Calvini opera omnia, Serie 3: Ioannis Calvini Scripta ecclesiastica, vol. 1. Geneva: Droz, 1998.

————. *The Epistles of Paul the Apostle to the Romans and to the Thessalonians*. Trans. Ross Mackenzie. Ed. David W. Torrance and Thomas F. Torrance. Calvin's New Testament Commentaries, vol. 8. Edinburgh: T & T Clark; Grand Rapids: Eerdmans, 1961; repr. 1996.

————. *The First Epistle of Paul, the Apostle, to the Corinthians*. Trans. John W. Fraser. Ed. David W. Torrance and Thomas F. Torrance. Calvin's New Testament Commentaries, vol. 9. Edinburgh: T & T Clark; Grand Rapids: Eerdmans, 1960; repr. 1996.

————. *Institutes of the Christian Religion (1559)*. Trans. Ford Lewis Battles. Ed. John T. McNeill. 2 vols. Library of Christian Classics, vols. 20-21. Philadelphia: Westminster, 1960.

————. *Institutes of the Christian Religion: Embracing Almost the Whole Sum of Piety, & Whatever Is Necessary to Know of the Doctrine of Salvation . . . , 1536 Edition*. Trans. Ford Lewis Battles. Grand Rapids: Eerdmans, 1986; repr. 1995.

————. *L'Institution chrétienne*. [Aix-en-Provence]/[Fontenay-sous-Bois], Kerygma-Farel, 1978. Reprinted as *Institution de la religion chrétienne*. 4 vols. Geneva: Labor et Fides, 1955-58.

————. *Institution de la religion chrestienne (édition 1559)*. Ed. Jean-Daniel Benoît. 5 vols. Paris: Vrin, 1957-63.

————. *Institution de la religion chrestienne. Texte de la première édition française 1541*. Ed. Jacques Pannier. 4 vols. Paris: Les belles lettres, 1936-39 (^{2}1961).

————. *Ioannis Calvini opera exegetica*. Ed. Brian G. Armstrong, Cornelis Augustijn, Irena Backus, Christoph P. M. Burger, Olivier Fatio, Helmut Feld, Francis Montgomery Higman, Wilhelm H. Neuser, Bernard Roussel, Willelm van't Spijker, and David F. Wright. 7 vols. Ioannis Calvini opera omnia, Serie 2. Geneva: Droz, 1994-2001.

————. *Ioannis Calvini opera omnia. Denuo recognita et adnotatione critica instructa notisque illustrata. Auspiciis praesidii Conventus internationalis studiis calvinianis fovendis*. Ed. Brian G. Armstrong, Cornelis Augustijn, Irena Backus, Christoph P. M. Burger, Olivier Fatio, Helmut Feld, Francis Montgomery Higman, Wilhelm H. Neuser, Bernard Roussel, Willelm van't Spijker, and David F. Wright. Series 1-7. 13 vols. Geneva: Droz, 1992-2007.

————. *Ioannis Calvini Opera quae supersunt omnia*. Ed. Wilhelm Baum, Eduard Kunitz, and Eduard Reuss. 59 vols. Corpus Reformatorum, vols. 29-88. Brunschwick: C. A. Schwetschke et Fils, 1863-1900.

————. *Joannis Calvini Opera Selecta*. Ed. Peter Barth and Wilhelm Niesel. 5 vols. Munich: Kaiser, 1926-36.

————. *Johannes Calvins Lebenswerk in seinen Briefen. Eine Auswahl von Briefen Calvins in deutscher Übersetzung*. Ed. Rudolf Schwarz. 3 vols. Neukirchen-Vluyn: Neukirchener Verlag, ^{2}1961-62.

————. *Letters of John Calvin.* Comp. Jules Bonnet. Trans. David Constable. 2 vols. Edinburgh: T. Constable, 1855.

————. *Lettres de Jean Calvin.* Ed. Jules Bonnet. 2 vols. Paris: Meyrueis, 1854.

————. *Oeuvres choisies.* Ed. Olivier Millet. Paris: Gallimard, 1995.

————. *The Second Epistle of Paul the Apostle to the Corinthians and the Epistles to Timothy, Titus and Philemon.* Trans. T. A. Smail. Ed. David W. Torrance and Thomas F. Torrance. (Calvin's New Testament Commentaries, vol. 10). Edinburgh: T & T Clark; Grand Rapids: Eerdmans, 1964; repr. 1996.

————. *Supplementa Calviniana. Sermons inédits.* Iussu Corporis presbyterianorum universalis (World Alliance of Reformed Churches). Ed. Erwin Mülhaupt. 10 vols. Neukirchen-Vluyn: Neukirchener Verlag, 1936-2006.

————. *Tracts and Treatises,* vol. 1: *On the Reformation of the Church;* vol. 2: *On the Doctrine and Worship of the Church;* vol. 3: *In Defense of the Reformed Faith.* Trans. Henry Beveridge. Ed. Thomas F. Torrance. Grand Rapids: Eerdmans, 1958.

————. *Unterricht in der christlichen Religion. Institutio christianae religionis, nach der letzten Ausgabe.* Trans. and ed. Otto Weber. Neukirchen-Vluyn: Neukirchener Verlag, ³1984.

Gilmont, Jean-François, and Rodolphe Peter. *Bibliotheca Calviniana. Les œuvres de Calvin publiées au XVIe siècle.* 3 vols. Travaux d'humanisme et renaissance, vols. 255, 281, and 339. Geneva: Droz, 1991-2000.

Other Primary Sources

Adams, John. *The Works.* Ed. Charles Francis Adams. 10 vols. Boston: Little, Brown, 1851-65.

Aquinas, Thomas. *S. Thomae Aquinatis Doctoris Angelica Summa theologiae.* Ed. Pietro Caramello. 3 vols. Turin/Rome: Marietti, 1948-63.

————. *S. Thomae Aquinatis In octo libros politicorum Aristotelis expositio.* Ed. Raymondi Spiazzi. Turin/Rome: Marietti, 1966.

————. *Somme théologique.* Vol. 2.2. Paris: Cerf, ³2002.

Arbenz, Emil, and Hermann Wartmann, eds. *Die Vadianische Briefsammlung der Stadtbibliothek St. Gallen.* 7 vols. Mitteilungen zur vaterländischen Geschichte, publié par Historischen Verein des Kantons St. Gallen, vols. 24-25, 27-30a. St. Gallen: Fehr, 1890-1913.

Aristotle. *Aristotelis Opera.* Ed. der Academia Regia Borussica. 5 vols. Berlin, 1831-70.

————. *Les politiques.* Trans. Pierre Pellegrin. Paris: Flammarion, 1990.

————. *Werke in deutscher Übersetzung.* Trans. Ernst Grumach. Ed. Hellmut Flashar. Vols. 1-20. Berlin/Darmstadt: Akademie Verlag/Wissenschaftliche Buchgesellschaft, 1964-2007.

Aubert, Hippolyte, Alain Dufour, Claire Chimelli, and Béatrice Nicollier, eds. *Correspondance de Théodore de Bèze.* Vol. 11: 1570. Geneva: Droz, 1983.

Aubert, Hippolyte, Alain Dufour, Béatrice Nicollier, and Mario Turchetti, eds. *Correspondance de Théodore de Bèze.* Vol. 12: 1571. Geneva: Droz, 1986.

Augustine. *Oeuvres de Saint Augustin.* Ed. Institut d'Etudes Augustiniennes. Vols. 1-75. Bibliothèque augustinienne, vols. 1-75. Paris: Desclée du Brouwer, 1947-2005.

————. *Opera omnia.* In *Patrologiae Cursus Completus,* Serie Latinae. Vols. 32-47. Ed. Jaques-Paul Migne. Paris, 1835-39.

Bayle, Pierre. *Avis important aux Refugiez sur leur prochain retour en France, donné pour Estrennes à l'un d'eux en 1690. Par Monsieur C. L. A. A. P. D. P.* Paris: chez la Veuve de Pierre Marten, 1692.

Bellius, Martinus [= Sebastian Castellio]. *De haereticis an sint persequendi et omnino quomodo sit cum eis agendum, Luteri et Brentii, aliorumque multorum tum veterum tum recentiorum sententiae.* Magdeburg: Georg Rausch, 1554. Reprinted with introduction by Sape van der Woude; Geneva: Droz, 1954.

Beza, Theodore. *Correspondance de Théodore de Bèze.* Trans. Hippolyte Aubert, Fernand Aubert, Henri Meylan, Arnaud Tripet, Alexandre de Henseler, Claire Chimelli, Mario Turchetti, Reinhard Bodenmann, Alain Dufour, Béatrice Nicollier, and Hervé Genton. 29 vols. Geneva: Droz, 1960-2007.

————. *De haereticis a civili Magistratu puniendis libellus, adversus Martini Bellii farraginem, et novorum Academicorum sectam.* Geneva: Oliva Roberti Stephani, 1554.

Borel-Girard, Gustave, ed. *Guillaume Farel 1489-1565. Biographie nouvelle écrite d'après les documents originaux, par un groupe d'historiens, professeurs et pasteurs de Suisse, de France et d'Italie.* Neuchâtel/Paris: Delachaux & Niestlé, 1930.

Bullinger, Heinrich. *Briefwechsel.* Ed. Ulrich Gäbler, Endre Zsindely, Matthias Senn, Kurt Jakob Rüetschi, Hans Ulrich Bächtold, Rainer Henrich, Alexandra Kess, and Christian Moser. 13 vols. Heinrich Bullinger Werke, sec. 2. Zurich: Theologischer Verlag, 1973-2008.

Castellio, Sebastian. *Contra libellum Calvini in quo ostendere conatur Haereticos jure gladii coercendos esse.* 1612.

————. *De haereticis an sint persequendi et omnino quomodo sit cum eis agendum, Luteri et Brentii, aliorumque multorum tum veterum tum recentiorum sententiae.* Magdeburg: Georg Rausch, 1554.

Crespin, Jean. *Histoire des Martyrs persécutez et mis à mort pour la vérité de l'Evangile, depuis le temps des Apostres jusques à présent (1619).* Ed. Daniel Benoit and Matthieu Lelièvre. 3 vols. Toulouse: Société des livres religieux, 1885-89.

Du Moulin, Pierre. *Enodatio gravissimarum quæstionum: De providentia Dei. De statu innocentiae. De peccato originali. De libero arbitrio. De praedestinatione. De perseverantia.* Leiden: Elzevir, 1632.

Fatio, Olivier, ed. *Confessions et catéchismes de la foi réformée.* Publications de la Faculté de théologie de l'Université de Genève, vol. 11. Geneva: Labor et Fides, 1986.

Herminjard, Aimé Louis, ed. *Correspondance des Réformateurs dans les pays de langue française. Recueillie et publiée avec d'autres lettres relatives à la réforme et des notes historiques et biographiques.* 9 vols. Geneva/Paris: Georg-Lévy, 1866-97.

Jurieu, Pierre. *Des droits des deux Souverains en matière de religion, la conscience et le prince: Pour détruire le dogme de l'indifférence des Religions et de la tolérance universelle; contre un livre intitulé Commentaire Philosophique sur ces paroles de la Parabole Contrains-les d'entrer*. Rotterdam: Graef, 1687.

————. *Les soupirs de la France esclave qui aspire après la liberté*. 1689.

Jussie, Jeanne de. *Kleine Chronik. Bericht einer Nonne über die Anfänge der Reformation in Geneva*. Trans. and ed. Helmut Feld. Veröffentlichungen des Instituts für Europäische Geschichte. Abteilung abendländische Religionsgeschichte, Beiheft, vol. 40. Mainz: von Zabern, 1996.

————. *Petite chronique*. Trans. and ed. Helmut Feld. Veröffentlichungen des Instituts für Europäische Geschichte. Abteilung abendländische Religionsgeschichte, vol. 167. Mainz: von Zabern, 1996.

————. *The Short Chronicle: A Poor Clare's Account of the Reformation of Geneva*. Trans. and ed. Carrie F. Klaus. Chicago: University of Chicago Press, 2006.

Kingdon, Robert M., Jean-Françoise Bergier, and Alain Dufour, eds. *Registres de la compagnie des pasteurs de Geneva au temps de Calvin*. 13 vols. Geneva: Droz, 1962-2001.

Knox, John. *The Works*. Ed. David Laing. 6 vols. New York, 1966. Reprinted Edinburgh: Thin, 1854-95.

Lambert, Thomas A., and Isabella M. Watt, eds. *Registres du Consistoire de Geneva au temps de Calvin*. 4 vols. Geneva: Droz, 1996-2007.

Loi du 9 décembre 1905 concernant la séparation des Eglises et de l'Etat, Titre Ier, Principes, Article 1. Journal officiel de la République Française. Paris: Journaux Officiels, 1905.

Luther, Martin. *A la noblesse chrétienne de la nation allemande sur l'amendement de l'état chrétien*. Trans. Pierre Jundt. Martin Luther, Œuvres, vol. 2. Geneva: Labor et Fides, 1966.

————. *D. Martin Luthers Werke. Kritische Gesamtausgabe*. Vols. 1-67. Weimar: Böhlau, 1883-1997.

————. *De l'authorité temporelle et des limites de l'obéissance qu'on lui doit*. Trans. Franck D. C. Gueutal. Martin Luther, Œuvres, vol. 4. Geneva: Labor et Fides, 1958.

————. *Du serf arbitre*. Trans. Jean Carrère. Martin Luther, Œuvres, vol. 5. Geneva: Labor et Fides, 1958.

————. *Luther's Works*. Ed. Jaroslav Pelikan and Helmut T. Lehmann. 56 vols. Philadelphia: Fortress; St. Louis: Concordia, 1957-86.

————. *Oeuvres*. 17 vols. Geneva: Labor et Fides, 1957-93.

Migne, Jaques-Paul, ed. *Patrologiae Cursus Completus, Serie Latinae*. Vols. 1-221. Paris, 1844-90.

Rivoire, Emile, and Victor Van Berchem, eds. *Les sources du droit du canton de Genève*, vol. 2: *From 1461 to 1550*. Les sources du droit suisse, vol. 22. Aarau: Sauerländer, 1930.

Ronsard, Pierre de. *Oeuvres complètes.* Ed. Paul Laumonier. Vols. 1-20. Paris: Hachette, 1924-82.

Servet, Michel. *Christianismi Restitutio.* [Vienne en Dauphiné]: [Balthazar Arnollet], 1553.

———. *De Trinitatis erroribus libri septem.* [Haguenau]: [Johann Setzer], 1531.

———. *Dialogorum de Trinitate libri duo.* [Haguenau]: [Johann Setzer], 1532.

Viret, Pierre. *De la vertu et usage du ministère de la parolle de Dieu et des sacremens dépendans d'icelle.* [Geneva], 1548.

Wolleb, Johannes. *Christianae Theologiae Compendium.* Basel: Genath, 1626.

———. *Johannis Wollebii Christianae Theologiae Compendium.* Ed. Ernst Bizer. Neukirchen : Buchhandlung des Erziehungsvereins, 1935.

Secondary Sources

Ahlstrom, Sydney Eckman. *A Religious History of the American People.* New Haven/London: Yale University Press, 1972 ([9]1979).

Angenendt, Arnold. *Toleranz und Gewalt. Das Christentum zwischen Bibel und Schwert.* Münster: Aschendorff, [3]2007.

Assonville, Victor E. d'. *Der Begriff "doctrina" bei Johannes Calvin. Eine theologische Analyse.* Rostocker Theologische Studien, vol. 6. Münster: LIT, 2000.

Augustijn, Cornelis. "Farel und Calvin in Bern 1537-1538." In *Calvin im Kontext der Schweizer Reformation. Historische und theologische Beiträge zur Calvinforschung,* ed. Peter Opitz, pp. 9-23. Zurich: Theologischer Verlag, 2003.

Bächthold, Hans Ulrich. "Ein Volk auf der Flucht. Die Schweiz als Refugium der Waldenser." In *Jahrbuch für Europäische Geschichte,* ed. Heinz Durchhardt, vol. 7, pp. 23-42. Munich: Oldenbourg, 2006.

Bähler, Eduard. *Nikolaus Zurkinden von Bern 1506-1588. Ein Vertreter der Toleranz im Jahrhundert der Reformation.* Zurich: Beer & Cie, 1912.

———. "Petrus Caroli und Johannes Calvin. Ein Beitrag zur Geschichte und Kultur der Reformationszeit." In *Jahrbuch für schweizerische Geschichte,* vol. 29, pp. 39-168. Zurich: Beer & Cie, 1904.

Bainton, Roland H. *The Hunted Heretic: The Life and Death of Michael Servetus.* Boston: Beacon, 1953.

———. *Michel Servet 1511-1553.* Trans. Senta Bergfeld, Agnes Müller Brockhusen, and Gustav Adolf Benrath. Schriften des Vereins für Reformationsgeschichte, vol. 178. Gütersloh: Mohn, 1960.

———. *The Travail of Religious Liberty: Nine Biographical Studies.* London: Lutterworth, 1953.

Balserak, Jon. *Divinity Compromised: A Study of Divine Accommodation in the Thought of John Calvin.* Studies in Early Modern Religious Reforms, vol. 5. Dordrecht: Springer, 2006.

Bancroft, George. *History of the United States, from the Discovery of the American Continent.* 10 vols. Boston: Little, Brown, 1834-74.

Barilier, Etienne. *Sébastien Castellion, Contre le libelle de Calvin. Après la mort de Michel Servet.* Carouge: Zoé, 1998.

Baron, Hans. "Calvinist Republicanism and Its Historical Roots." *Church History* 8 (1939): 30-42.

————. *Calvins Staatsanschauung und das konfessionelle Zeitalter.* Historische Zeitschrift Beiheft, vol. 1. Munich: Oldenbourg, 1924.

Barth, Karl. *Church Dogmatics.* Ed. Geoffrey W. Bromiley and Thomas F. Torrance. 14 vols. Edinburgh: T & T Clark, 1975-77.

————. *Dogmatique.* Trans. Fernand Ryser. 27 vols. Geneva: Labor et Fides, 1953-80.

————. *Die Kirchliche Dogmatik.* 12 vols. Zurich: Theologischer Verlag, 1932-67.

————. *Die Theologie Calvins. Vorlesung Göttingen Sommersemester 1922.* Ed. Hans Scholl. Karl Barth Gesamtausgabe II: Akademische Werke, 1922. Zurich: Theologischer Verlag, 1993.

————. *The Theology of John Calvin.* Trans. Geoffrey W. Bromiley. Grand Rapids: Eerdmans, 1995.

Baucher, J. "Liberté (V. Liberté morale, de conscience et des cultes)." In *Dictionnaire de théologie catholique,* vol. 9, pp. 684-703. Paris: Letouzey et Ane, 1926.

Becht, Michael. *Pium consensum tueri. Studien zum Begriff consensus im Werk von Erasmus von Rotterdam, Philipp Melanchthon und Johannes Calvin.* Reformationsgeschichtliche Studien und Texte, vol. 144. Münster: Aschendorff, 2000.

Belt, Hendrik van den. *Autopistia: The Self-Convincing Authority of Scripture in Reformed Theology.* Leiden, 2006; repr. 2008.

Benedict, Philip. *Christ's Churches Purely Reformed: A Social History of Calvinism.* New Haven: Yale University Press, 2002.

Biéler, André. *Calvin's Economic and Social Thought.* Trans. James Greig. Ed. Edward Dommen. Publications de la Faculté des sciences économiques et sociales de l'Université de Genève, vol. 13. Geneva: Georg, 2005.

————. *L'Homme et la femme dans la morale calviniste.* Geneva: Labor et Fides, 1963.

————. *La pensée économique et sociale de Calvin.* Publications de la Faculté des sciences économiques et sociales de l'Université de Genève, vol. 13. Geneva: Georg, 1959; repr. 1961.

Bizer, Ernst. *Studien zur Geschichte des Abendmahlsstreits.* Beiträge zur Förderung christlicher Theologie, série 2, vol. 46. Munich: Kaiser, 1940.

Blacketer, Raymond A. *The School of God: Pedagogy and Rhetoric in Calvin's Interpretation of Deuteronomy.* Studies in Early Modern Religious Reforms, vol. 3. Dordrecht: Springer, 2006.

Bohatec, Josef. *Calvins Lehre von Staat und Kirche.* Breslau: Gierke, 1937.

Bohatec, Josef, ed. *Festschrift zum 400. Geburtstage Johann Calvins.* Leipzig: Haupt, 1909.

Bouwsma, William J. *John Calvin: A Sixteenth-Century Portrait.* New York/Oxford: Oxford University Press, 1988.

————. "The Peculiarity of the Reformation in Geneva." In *Religion and Culture in the Renaissance and Reformation,* ed. Steven Ozment, pp. 65-77. Sixteenth Century Essays and Studies, vol. 11. Kirksville, Mo.: Sixteenth Century Journal Publishers, 1989.

Bratt, James D. *Dutch Calvinism in Modern America: A History of a Conservative Subculture.* Grand Rapids: Eerdmans, 1984.

Bratt, James D., ed. *Antirevivalism in Antebellum America: A Collection of Religious Voices.* New Brunswick, N.J.: Rutgers University Press, 2006.

Bruening, Michael W. *Calvinism's First Battleground: Conflict and Reform in the Pays de Vaud, 1528-1559.* Studies in Early Modern Religious Reforms, vol. 4. Dordrecht: Springer, 2005.

Brunner, Otto, Werner Conze, and Reinhart Koselleck, eds. *Geschichtliche Grundbegriffe: historisches Lexikon zur politisch-sozialen Sprache in Deutschland.* Stuttgart: Klett-Cotta, 1972-97.

Burger, Christoph. "Calvins Beziehungen zu Weggefährten in der Schweiz." In *Calvin im Kontext der Schweizer Reformation. Historische und theologische Beiträge zur Calvinforschung,* ed. Peter Opitz, pp. 41-55. Zurich: Theologischer Verlag, 2003.

————. "Werben um Bullingers Beistand. Calvins Briefe von 1537/38." In *Die Zürcher Reformation. Ausstrahlungen und Rückwirkungen. Wissenschaftliche Tagung zum Hundertjährigen Bestehen des Zwinglivereins (29. Oktober bis 2. November 1997 in Zürich),* ed. Alfred Schindler and Hans Stickelberger, pp. 101-20. Zürcher Beiträge zur Reformationsgeschichte, vol. 18. Bern: Peter Lang, 2001.

Busch, Eberhard. *Gotteserkenntnis und Menschlichkeit. Einsichten in die Theologie Johannes Calvins.* Zurich: Theologischer Verlag, [2]2006.

Büsser, Fritz. *Calvins Urteil über sich selbst.* Quellen und Abhandlungen zur Geschichte des schweizerischen Protestantismus, vol. 7. Zurich: Zwingli-Verlag, 1950.

————. *Heinrich Bullinger (1504-1575). Leben, Werk und Wirkung.* 2 vols. Zurich: Theologischer Verlag, 2004/2005.

Cameron, James K. "Scottish Calvinism and the Principle of Intolerance." In *Reformatio Perennis: Essays on Calvin and the Reformation in Honor of Ford Lewis Battles,* ed. Brian A. Gerrish, pp. 113-28. The Pittsburgh Theological Monograph Series, vol. 32. Pittsburgh: Pickwick, 1981.

Chenevière, Marc-Édouard. *La pensée politique de Calvin.* Geneva/Paris: Labor-Je sers, 1937.

Chute, Anthony L. *A Piety above the Common Standard: Jesse Mercer and the Defense of Evangelistic Calvinism.* Macon, Ga.: Mercer University Press, 2004.

Clarke, Erskine. *Our Southern Zion: A History of Calvinism in the South Carolina Low Country, 1690-1990.* Tuscaloosa/London: University of Alabama Press, 1996.

Coalter, Milton J. *Gilbert Tennent, Son of Thunder.* Contributions to the Study of Religion, vol. 18. New York: Greenwood, 1986.

Collinson, Patrick. *The Elizabethan Puritan Movement.* London: Cape, 1967.

Conforti, Joseph A. *Saints and Strangers: New England in British North America.* Baltimore: Johns Hopkins University Press, 2006.

Cottret, Bernard. *Calvin. Biographie.* Paris: Jean-Claude Lattès, 1995.

―――. *Calvin. Eine Biographie.* Trans. Werner Stingl. Stuttgart: Quellverlag, 1998.

Cremeans, Charles Davis. *The Reception of Calvinistic Thought in England.* Illinois Studies in the Social Sciences, vol. 31/1. Urbana: University of Illinois Press, 1949.

Deresch, Wolfgang. *Der Glaube der religiösen Sozialisten.* Hamburg: Furche, 1972.

Detmers, Achim. *Reformation und Judentum. Israel-Lehren und Einstellungen zum Judentum von Luther bis zum frühen Calvin.* Judentum und Christentum, vol. 7. Stuttgart/Berlin/Cologne: Kohlhammer, 2001.

Doumergue, Émile. "Calvin, la fondation des libertés modernes." In *Séance publique de rentrée, 17 novembre 1898,* pp. 21-29. Montauban: Université de théologie protestante de Montauban, 1898.

―――. *Jean Calvin. Les hommes et les choses de son temps.* 7 vols. Lausanne/Paris: Armand-Delille, 1899-1927.

Dreitzel, Horst. "Toleranz und Gewissensfreiheit im konfessionellen Zeitalter. Zur Diskussion im Reich zwischen Augsburger Religionsfrieden und Aufklärung." In *Religion und Religiosität im Zeitalter des Barock,* ed. Dieter Breuer, vol. 1, pp. 115-28. Wolfenbütteler Arbeiten zur Barockforschung, vol. 25. Wiesbaden: Harrassowitz, 1995.

Dufour, Alain. "Le mythe de Geneva au temps de Calvin." *Revue suisse d'histoire* 9 (1959): 489-518.

―――. "La notion de liberté de conscience chez les Réformateurs." In *La liberté de conscience (XVIe-XVIIe siècle), Actes du colloque de Mulhouse et Bâle (1989),* ed. Hans Rudolf Guggisberg, Frank Lestringant, and Jean-Claude Margolin, pp. 15-20. Études de philologie et d'histoire, vol. 44. Geneva: Droz, 1991.

Egmond, A. van. "Calvinist Thought and Human Rights." In *Human Rights and Religious Values: An Uneasy Relationship?* ed. Ahmed An-Na'im Abdullahi, pp. 192-202. Amsterdam: Rodopi, 1995.

Eliot, Samuel A., ed. *Pioneers of Religious Liberty in America.* Boston: American Unitarian Association, 1903. Reprinted East Sussex, 2007.

Elwood, Christopher. *The Body Broken: The Calvinist Doctrine of the Eucharist and the Symbolization of Power in Sixteenth-Century France.* New York: Oxford University Press, 1999.

Engel, Mary Potter. *John Calvin's Perspectival Anthropology.* American Academy of Religion series, vol. 52. Atlanta: Scholars, 1988.

Farmer, James Oscar, Jr. *The Metaphysical Confederacy: James Henley Thornwell and the Synthesis of Southern Values.* Macon, Ga.: Mercer University Press, 1986.

Feld, Helmut. "Einleitung." In *Ioannis Calvini opera omnia. Denuo recognita et adnotatione critica instructa notisque illustrata. Auspiciis praesidii Conventus internationalis studiis calvinianis fovendis,* series 2, vol. 15: Commentarii in secundam Pauli epistolam ad Corinthios, ed. Helmut Feld, xi-xlv. Geneva: Droz, 1994.

―――. "Michael Servet." In *Biographisch-Bibliographisches Kirchenlexikon,* ed. Traugott Bautz, vol. 9, cols. 1470-79. Hamm (Westphalia): Bautz, 1995.

Flynn, John Stephen. *The Influence of Puritanism in the Political and Religious Thought of the English.* New York: Dutton, 1920.

Foster, Herbert Darling. "The Political Theories of Calvinists before the Puritan Exodus to America." *American Historical Review* 21 (1916): 481-503.

Fowler, James W. *To See the Kingdom: The Theological Vision of H. Richard Niebuhr.* Nashville: Abingdon, 1974.

Fox, Richard Wightman. *Reinhold Niebuhr: A Biography.* Ithaca: Cornell University Press, 1996.

Friedman, Jerome. *Michael Servetus: A Case Study in Total Heresy.* Travaux d'humanisme et renaissance, vol. 163. Geneva: Droz, 1978.

Froidevaux, Camille. *Ernst Troeltsch, la religion chrétienne et le monde moderne.* Paris: Presses Universitaires de France, 1999.

Fuchs, Eric. *L'Ethique protestante.* Paris/Geneva: Les Bergers et Les Mages/Labor et Fides, 1990.

―――. *La morale selon Calvin.* Paris: Les Editions du Cerf, 1986.

Fuchs, Eric, and Christian Grappe. *Le Droit de résister. Le protestantisme face au pouvoir.* Entrée libre, vol. 7. Geneva: Labor et Fides, 1990.

Gäbler, Ulrich. "Das Zustandekommen des Consensus Tigurinus im Jahre 1549." *Theologische Literaturzeitschrift* 104 (1979): 321-32.

Gäbler, Ulrich, and Erland Herkenrath, eds. *Heinrich Bullinger, 1504-1575. Gesammelte Aufsätze zum 400,* vol. 2: *Beziehungen und Wirkungen.* Zürcher Beiträge zur Reformationsgeschichte, vol. 8. Zurich: Theologischer Verlag, 1975.

Ganoczy, Alexandre. *Calvin théologien de l'Eglise et du ministère.* Paris: Cerf, 1964.

―――. *Ecclesia ministrans. Dienende Kirche und kirchlicher Dienst bei Calvin.* Ökumenische Forschungen 1. Ekklesiologische Abteilung, vol. 3. Freiburg i. Br.: Herder, 1968.

Geiger, Max. "Calvin, Calvinismus, Kapitalismus." In *Gottesreich und Menschenreich. Ernst Staehelin zum 80. Geburtstag,* ed. Max Geiger, pp. 229-86. Basel: Helbing und Lichtenhahn, 1969.

Gilmont, Jean-François. *Jean Calvin et le livre imprimé.* Études de philologie et d'histoire, vol. 50. Geneva: Droz, 1997.

―――. *John Calvin and the Printed Book.* Trans. Karin Maag. Sixteenth Century Essays and Studies, vol. 72. Kirksville, Mo.: Sixteenth Century Journal Publishers, 2005.

―――. "La mauvaise foi de Calvin." *Bulletin de la Classe des Lettres de l'Académie Royale de Belgique* 6, no. 17 (2006): 21-42.

―――. *Le livre réformé au XVIe siècle.* Paris: Bibliothèque nationale de France, 2005.

Gilson, Étienne. *Introduction à l'étude de Saint Augustin.* Paris: Vrin, ⁴1969 (orig. ed. 1939).

Gordon, Bruce. "Calvin and the Swiss Reformed Churches." In *Calvinism in Europe, 1540-1620,* ed. Andrew Pettegree, Alastair Duke, and Gillian Lewis, pp. 64-81. Cambridge: Cambridge University Press, 1994.

Grosse, Christian. *L'excommunication de Philibert Berthelier. Histoire d'un conflit d'identité aux premiers temps de la Réforme genevoise, 1547-1555.* Les cahiers, vol. 3. Geneva: Droz, 1995.

Guggisberg, Hans Rudolf. *Sebastian Castellio 1515-1563. Humanist und Verteidiger der religiösen Toleranz im konfessionellen Zeitalter.* Göttingen: Vandenhoeck & Ruprecht, 1997.

Guggisberg, Kurt. "Calvin und Bern." In *Festgabe Leonhard von Muralt zum siebzigsten Geburtstag, 17. Mai 1970, überreicht von Freunden und Schülern,* ed. Martin Haas and René Hauswirth, pp. 266-85. Zurich: Berichthaus, 1970.

Haas, Martin, and René Hauswirth, eds. *Festgabe Leonhard von Muralt zum siebzigsten Geburtstag 17. Mai 1970, überreicht von Freunden und Schülern.* Zurich: Berichthaus, 1970.

Hambrick-Stowe, Charles E. *Charles G. Finney and the Spirit of American Evangelicalism.* Grand Rapids: Eerdmans, 1996.

Hamstra, Sam, and Arie J. Griffioen, eds. *Reformed Confessionalism in Nineteenth-Century America: Essays on the Thought of John Williamson Nevin.* Lanham, Md.: Scarecrow, 1995.

Hart, Darryl G. *Defending the Faith: J. Gresham Machen and the Crisis of Conservative Protestantism in Modern America.* Baltimore: Johns Hopkins University Press, 1994.

Hart, Darryl G., and John Muether. *Fighting the Good Fight: A Brief History of the Orthodox Presbyterian Church.* Philadelphia: Orthodox Presbyterian Church, 1995.

Hesselink, I. John. *Calvin's Concept of the Law.* Princeton Theological Monograph Series, vol. 30. Allison Park, Pa.: Pickwick, 1992.

Higman, Francis Montgomery. "Calvin polémiste" [1994]. In *Lire et découvrir. La circulation des idées au temps de la Réforme,* pp. 403-18. Travaux d'humanisme et renaissance, vol. 326. Geneva: Droz, 1998.

———. "I Came Not to Send Peace, but a Sword" [1997]. In *Lire et découvrir. La circulation des idées au temps de la Réforme,* pp. 419-33. Travaux d'humanisme et renaissance, vol. 326. Geneva: Droz, 1998.

———. *The Style of John Calvin in His French Polemical Treatises.* London: Oxford University Press, 1967.

Hill, Christopher. *Society and Puritanism in Pre-Revolutionary England.* London: Secker & Warburg, 1964.

Hillar, Marian. *The Case of Michael Servet (1511-1553): The Turning Point in the Struggle for Freedom of Conscience.* Texts and Studies in Religion, vol. 74. Lewiston/Queenston/Lampeter: Edwin Mellen, 1997.

Hillar, Marian, and Claire S. Allen. *Michael Servetus: Intellectual Giant, Humanist, and Martyr.* Lexington: University Press of America, 2002.

Holl, Karl. "Die Frage des Zinsnehmens und des Wuchers in der reformierten Kirche" [1922]. In *Gesammelte Aufsätze zur Kirchengeschichte,* vol. 3, pp. 385-403. Tübingen: Mohr Siebeck, 1928.

Hölscher, Lucian, and Marie-Elisabeth Hilger. "Kapital, Kapitalist, Kapitalismus." In *Geschichtliche Grundbegriffe,* vol. 3, pp. 399-454. Stuttgart: Klett-Cotta, 1982.

Holtrop, Philip C. *The Bolsec Controversy on Predestination, from 1551 to 1555: The Statements of Jerome Bolsec, and the Responses of John Calvin, Theodore Beza, and Other Reformed Theologians.* 2 vols. Lewiston/Queenston/Lampeter: Edwin Mellen, 1993.

Hood, Fred J. *Reformed America: The Middle and Southern States, 1783-1837.* Tuscaloosa: University of Alabama Press, 1980.

Höpfl, Harro. *The Christian Polity of John Calvin.* Cambridge Studies in the History and Theory of Politics. Cambridge: Cambridge University Press, 1982; repr. 1985.

Howse, Ernest Marshall. *Saints in Politics: The Clapham Sect and the Growth of Freedom.* Toronto: University of Toronto Press, 1952.

Hubac, Jean. "Tyrannie et tyrannicide selon Jurieu." *Bulletin de la Société de l'Histoire du Protestantisme Français* 152 (2006): 583-609.

Hundeshagen, Karl Bernhard. "Das Partheiwesen in der Bernischen Landeskirche von 1532 bis 1558 (Fortsetzung)." In *Beiträge zur Geschichte der Schweizerisch-reformirten Kirche, zunächst derjenigen des Kantons Bern,* ed. Friedrich Trechsel, pp. 3-69. Bern: Jenni, 1842.

Hunt, George L., and John T. McNeill, eds. *Calvinism and the Political Order: Essays Prepared for the Woodrow Wilson Lectureship of the National Presbyterian Center, Washington, D.C.* Philadelphia: Westminster, 1965.

Janse, Wim. "Calvin's Eucharistic Theology: Three Dogma-Historical Observations." In *Calvinus sacrarum literarum interpres: Papers of the International Congress on Calvin Research,* ed. Herman J. Selderhuis, pp. 37-69. Göttingen: Vandenhoeck & Ruprecht, 2008.

Johnson, F. Ernest, ed. *Foundations of Democracy: A Series of Addresses.* New York: Harper & Brothers, 1947.

Johnson, Gary L. W. *B. B. Warfield: Essays on His Life and Thought.* Phillipsburg, N.J.: P&R Publishing, 2007.

Jüngel, Eberhard. "Quae supra nos, nihil ad nos. Eine Kurzformel der Lehre vom verborgenen Gott." *Evangelische Theologie* 32 (1972): 197-240.

Katterle, Siegfried, and Arthur Rich, eds. *Religiöser Sozialismus und Wirtschaftsordnung.* Gütersloh: Mohn, 1980.

Kelly, Douglas F. *The Emergence of Liberty in the Modern World: The Influence of Calvin on Five Governments from the Sixteenth through the Eighteenth Centuries.* Phillipsburg, N.J.: P&R Publishing, 1992.

Kidd, Thomas S. *The Great Awakening: The Roots of Evangelical Christianity in Colonial America.* New Haven: Yale University Press, 2007.

Kingdon, Robert M. *Adultery and Divorce in Calvin's Geneva.* Harvard Historical Studies, vol. 118. Cambridge, Mass./London: Harvard University Press, 1995.

———. "Calvin and Democracy: Some Political Implications on Debates on French Reformed Church Government, 1562-1572." *American Historical Review* 69, no. 2 (1964): 393-401.

———. "Calvin et la démocratie." In *Réforme et Révolutions. Aux origines de la démocratie moderne,* ed. Paul Viallaneix, pp. 41-54. [Millau]: Presses du Languedoc, 1990.

————. "The Calvinist Reformation in Geneva." In *The Cambridge History of Christianity,* vol. 6: *Reform and Expansion 1500-1660,* ed. R. Po-Chia Hsia, pp. 90-103. Cambridge: Cambridge University Press, 2007.

————. *Geneva and the Consolidation of the French Protestant Movement 1564-1572: Contribution to the History of Congregationalism, Presbyterianism, and Calvinist Resistance Theory.* Geneva: Droz, 1967.

Kingdon, Robert M., and Robert D. Linder, eds. *Calvin and Calvinism: Sources of Democracy.* Lexington, Mass.: Heath, 1970.

Klappert, Bertold. "Erwählung und Rechtfertigung. Martin Luther und die Juden." In *Miterben der Verheißung. Beiträge zum jüdisch-christlichen Dialog,* ed. Bertold Klappert, pp. 105-47. Neukirchener Beiträge zur systematischen Theologie, vol. 25. Neukirchen: Neukirchener Verlag, 2000.

Kling, David W. *A Field of Divine Wonders: The New Divinity and Village Revivals in Northwestern Connecticut, 1792-1822.* University Park: Pennsylvania State University Press, 1993.

Knight, Janice. *Orthodoxies in Massachusetts: Rereading America Puritanism.* Cambridge, Mass.: Harvard University Press, 1993.

Koenigsberger, H. G. "The Organization of Revolutionary Parties in France and the Netherlands during the Sixteenth Century." *Journal of Modern History* 27, no. 4 (1955): 335-51.

Koetsier, Lora Suzanne. *Natural Law and Calvinist Political Theory.* Victoria: Trafford, 2002.

Kolfhaus, Wilhelm. "Der Verkehr Calvins mit Bullinger." In *Calvinstudien. Festschrift zum 400. Geburtstage Johann Calvins,* ed. Josef Bohatec, pp. 27-125. Leipzig: Haupt, 1909.

Körtner, Ulrich H. J. *Reformiert und ökumenisch. Brennpunkte reformierter Theologie in Geschichte und Gegenwart.* Salzburger theologische Studien, vol. 7. Innsbruck: Tyrolia-Verlag, 1998.

Kretzer, Hartmut. "Die Calvinismus-Kapitalismus-These Max Webers vor dem Hintergrund französischer Quellen des 17. Jahrhunderts." In *Calvinismus versus Demokratie respektive "Geist des Kapitalismus"? Studien zur politischen Theorie und zur Sozialphilosophie des französischen Protestantismus im 17. Jahrhundert,* pp. 59-71. Oldenburg: Bibliothek und Informationssystem der Universität, 1988.

Kuhr, Olaf. *Die Macht des Bannes und der Busse. Kirchenzucht und Erneuerung der Kirche bei Johannes Oekolampad (1482-1531).* Basler und Berner Studien zur historischen und systematischen Theologie, vol. 68. Bern: Peter Lang, 1999.

Kuropka, Nicole. "Calvins Römerbriefwidmung und der consensus piorum." In *Calvin im Kontext der Schweizer Reformation. Historische und theologische Beiträge zur Calvinforschung,* ed. Peter Opitz, pp. 147-67. Zurich: Theologischer Verlag, 2003.

Kutter, Markus. *Celio Secondo Curione. Sein Leben und sein Werk (1503-1569).* Basler

Beiträge zur Geschichtswissenschaft, vol. 54. Basel: Helbing und Lichtenhahn, 1955.

Kuyper, Abraham. *Calvinism: Six Stone Lectures.* Amsterdam/Pretoria: Höveker & Wormser, [1899].

Lagarde, Georges de. *Recherches sur l'esprit politique de la Réforme.* Paris: A. Picard, 1926.

Lane, Anthony N. S. *John Calvin: Student of the Church Fathers.* Edinburgh: T & T Clark, 1999.

Lecler, Joseph. *Geschichte der Religionsfreiheit im Zeitalter der Reformation.* 2 vols. Stuttgart: Schwabenverlag, 1965.

———. *Histoire de la tolérance au siècle de la réforme.* 2 vols. Paris: Aubier Montaigne, 1955.

———. "Liberté de conscience, origines et sens divers de l'expression." *Recherches de sciences religieuses* 54, no. 3 (1966): 370-406.

Lehmann, Hartmut. "Asketischer Protestantismus und ökonomischer Rationalismus: Die Weber-These nach zwei Generationen." In *Max Webers Sicht des okzidentalen Christentums. Interpretation und Kritik,* ed. Wolfgang Schluchter, pp. 529-53. Frankfurt a. M.: Suhrkamp, 1988.

Lindemann, Andreas. "'Erwählt vor Grundlegung der Welt' (Eph 1,4). Zum Verständnis der Prädestination im Römer- und im Epheserbrief und bei Johannes Calvin." In *Gottes freie Gnade. Studien zu Lehre von der Erwählung,* ed. Michael Beintker, pp. 41-67. Wuppertal: Foedus, 2004.

Linder, Robert D. "Rezension zu: Douglas F. Kelly, The Emergence of Liberty in the Modern World. The Influence of Calvin on Five Governments from the Sixteenth through the Eighteenth Centuries, Phillipsburg (N.J.) 1992." *Journal of Church and State* 35 (1995): 911-12.

Link, Christian. "Calvins Erwählungslehre zwischen Christologie und Providenz." In *Calvin im Kontext der Schweizer Reformation. Historische und theologische Beiträge zur Calvinforschung,* ed. Peter Opitz, pp. 169-93. Zurich: Theologischer Verlag, 2003.

———. "Das Thema der Erwählung als Rahmen einer geschichtsbezogenen Theologie." In *Gottes freie Gnade. Studien zu Lehre von der Erwählung,* ed. Michael Beintker, pp. 119-40. Wuppertal: Foedus, 2004.

Little, David. "Religion and Human Rights: A Personal Testament." *Journal of Law and Religion* 18 (2002-3): 57-77.

Locher, Gottfried W. "Bullinger und Calvin. Probleme des Vergleiches ihrer Theologien." In *Heinrich Bullinger 1504-1575. Gesammelte Aufsätze zum 400. Todestag, Bd. 2: Beziehungen und Wirkungen,* ed. Ulrich Gäbler and Erland Herkenrath, pp. 1-33. Zürcher Beiträge zur Reformationsgeschichte, vol. 8. Zurich: Theologischer Verlag, 1975.

Lüthi, Kurt. "Calvinismus und Kapitalismus (Die Max-Weber-These: Darstellung — Kritik — Aktualität)." In *Über Gesellschaft hinaus. Kultursoziologische Beiträge im Gedenken an Robert Heinrich Reichardt,* ed. Michael Benedikt, Reinhold

Knoll, and Kurt Lüthi, pp. 179-90. Klausen-Leopoldsdorf: Verlag der Synergeia, 2000.

Lüthy, Herbert. "Calvinisme et capitalisme. Les thèses de Max Weber devant l'histoire." *Preuve* 161 (1964): 3-22.

Marsden, George M. *The Evangelical Mind and the New School Presbyterian Experience: A Case Study of Thought and Theology in Nineteenth-Century America.* New Haven: Yale University Press, 1970.

———. *Fundamentalism and American Culture.* New York: Oxford University Press, ²2006.

———. *Jonathan Edwards: A Life.* New Haven: Yale University Press, 2003.

Mathis, James R. *The Making of the Primitive Baptists: A Cultural and Intellectual History of the Antimission Movement, 1800-1840.* New York: Routledge, 2004.

McCoy, Marjorie Casebier. *Frederick Buechner: Novelist/Theologian of the Lost and Found.* San Francisco: Harper & Row, 1988.

McKim, Donald, ed. *The Cambridge Companion to John Calvin.* Cambridge: Cambridge University Press, 2004.

McNeill, John T. "Calvin as an Ecumenical Churchman." *Church History* 32 (1963): 379-91.

———. "Calvinism and European Politics in Historical Perspective." In *Calvinism and the Political Order: Essays Prepared for the Woodrow Wilson Lectureship of the National Presbyterian Center, Washington, D.C.,* ed. George L. Hunt and John T. McNeill, pp. 11-22. Philadelphia: Westminster, 1965.

———. "The Democratic Element in Calvin's Thought." *Church History* 18 (1949): 153-71.

———. *The History and Character of Calvinism.* New York: Oxford University Press, ²1967.

———. "John Calvin on Civil Government." In *Calvinism and the Political Order: Essays Prepared for the Woodrow Wilson Lectureship of the National Presbyterian Center, Washington, D.C.,* ed. George L. Hunt and John T. McNeill, pp. 23-45. Philadelphia: Westminster, 1965.

Mead, Edwin D. "William Brewster and the Independents." In *Pioneers of Religious Liberty in America,* ed. Samuel A. Eliot, pp. 3-46. Boston: American Unitarian Association, 1903. Reprinted East Sussex, 2007.

Meier, Christian, Hans Leo Reimann, Hans Maier, Reinhart Koselleck, and Werner Conze. "Demokratie." In *Geschichtliche Grundbegriffe,* vol. 1, pp. 821-99. Stuttgart: Klett-Cotta, 1972.

Mercier, Charles. "L'esprit de Calvin et la démocratie." In *Revue d'histoire ecclésiastique,* vol. 30, pp. 5-53. Louvain: Bureaux de la revue, 1934.

Miller, Perry. *The New England Mind,* vol. 1: *The Seventeenth Century.* New York, 1939. Reprinted Boston: Beacon, 1966.

Miller, Perry, and Thomas H. Johnson, eds. *The Puritans.* New York: American Book Company, 1938.

Millet, Olivier. "Le thème de la conscience libre chez Calvin." In *La liberté de conscience*

(XVIe-XVIIe siècle), Actes du Colloque de Mulhouse et Bâle (1989), ed. Hans Rudolf Guggisberg, Frank Lestringant, and Jean-Claude Margolin, pp. 21-37. Études de philologie et d'histoire, vol. 44. Geneva: Droz, 1991.

Millet, Olivier, ed. *Calvin et ses contemporains. Actes du colloque de Paris (1995).* Cahiers d'humanisme et renaissance, vol. 53. Geneva: Droz, 1998.

Moltmann, Jürgen. *Prädestination und Perseveranz. Geschichte und Bedeutung der reformierten Lehre "de perseverantia sanctorum."* Beiträge zur Geschichte und Lehre der Reformierten Kirche, vol. 12. Neukirchen: Neukirchener Verlag, 1961.

Monter, E. William. *Calvin's Geneva.* New York: Wiley, 1967.

————. "The Consistory of Geneva, 1559-1569." *Bibliothèque d'humanisme et renaissance* 38 (1976): 467-84.

————. "Crime and Punishment in Calvin's Geneva." *Archiv für Reformationsgeschichte* 64 (1973): 281-86.

————. "Historical Demography and Religious History in Sixteenth-Century Geneva." *Journal of Interdisciplinary History* 9 (1979): 399-427.

————. *Studies in Genevan Government (1536-1605).* Travaux d'humanisme et renaissance, vol. 62. Geneva: Droz, 1964.

————. "Women in Calvinist Geneva (1550-1800)." *Signs* 6 (1980): 189-209.

Morris, Christopher. *Political Thought in England: Tyndale to Hooker.* London: Oxford University Press, 1953.

Mosse, George L. *The Holy Pretence: A Study in Christianity and Reason of State from William Perkins to John Winthrop.* Oxford: Blackwell, 1957.

————. *The Struggle for Sovereignty in England: From the Reign of Queen Elizabeth to the Petition of Right.* East Lansing: Michigan State College Press, 1950.

Mottu-Weber, Liliane. *Economie et refuge à Genèva au siècle de la Réforme. La draperie et la soierie (1540-1630).* Paris: Champion; Geneva: Droz, 1987.

Mühling, Andreas. *Heinrich Bullingers europäische Kirchenpolitik.* Zürcher Beiträge zur Reformationsgeschichte, vol. 19. Bern: Peter Lang, 2001.

Muller, Richard A. *Christ and the Decree: Christology and Predestination in Reformed Theology from Calvin to Perkins.* Studies in Historical Theology, vol. 2. Durham: Labyrinth, 1986.

————. *The Unaccommodated Calvin: Studies in the Foundation of a Theological Tradition.* New York/Oxford: Oxford University Press, 2000.

Murray, Andrew. *Presbyterians and the Negro: A History.* A Publication of the Presbyterian Historical Society, vol. 7. Philadelphia: Presbyterian Historical Society, 1966.

Naef, Henri. *Les origines de la Réforme à Genève.* 2 vols. Travaux d'humanisme et renaissance, vol. 100, 1/2. Geneva: Droz, 1968.

Naphy, William G. *Calvin and the Consolidation of the Genevan Reformation.* Manchester: Manchester University Press, 1994.

Neuser, Wilhelm H. *Calvin.* Sammlung Göschen, vol. 3005. Berlin: Walter de Gruyter, 1971.

————. "Calvin als Prediger." In *Gottes freie Gnade. Studien zu Lehre von der Erwählung,* ed. Michael Beintker, pp. 69-91. Wuppertal: Foedus, 2004.

Neuser, Wilhelm H., ed. *Calvinus Ecclesiae Genevensis Custos.* Frankfurt a. M./Bern: Peter Lang, 1984.

Neuser, Wilhelm H., Herman J. Selderhuis, and Willelm van't Spijker, eds. *Calvin's Books: Festschrift Dedicated to Peter De Klerk on the Occasion of His Seventieth Birthday.* Heerenveen: J. J. Groen, 1997.

Nichols, James Hastings, ed. *The Mercersburg Theology.* New York: Oxford University Press, 1966.

Niesel, Wilhelm. *Die Theologie Calvins.* Einführung in die evangelische Theologie, vol. 6. Munich: Kaiser, ²1957.

Noll, Mark A. *Das Christentum in Nordamerika.* Kirchengeschichte in Einzeldarstellungen 4: Neueste Zeit, vol. 5. Leipzig: Evangelische Verlagsanstalt, 2000.

——. *A History of Christianity in the United States and Canada.* Grand Rapids: Eerdmans, 1992; repr. 1999.

——. *Princeton and the Republic, 1768-1822: The Search for a Christian Enlightenment in the Era of Samuel Stanhope Smith.* Princeton, N.J.: Princeton University Press, 1989.

Noll, Mark A., ed. *The Princeton Theology, 1812-1921: Scripture, Science, and Theological Method from Archibald Alexander to Benjamin Breckinridge Warfield.* Grand Rapids: Baker, 1983; repr. 2001.

Oberman, Heiko A. *De erfenis van Calvijn: grootheid en grenzen.* Kampen: Kok, 1988.

Opitz, Peter. "Calvins Gebrauch des Begriffs 'religio.'" In *Calvinus Evangelii Propugnator. Calvin, Champion of the Gospel. Papers Presented at the International Congress on Calvin Research, Seoul 1998,* ed. David F. Wright, Anthony N. S. Lane, and Jon Balserak, pp. 161-74. Grand Rapids: Calvin Studies Society, 2006.

——. *Calvins theologische Hermeneutik.* Neukirchen: Neukirchener Verlag, 1994.

Opitz, Peter, ed. *Calvin im Kontext der Schweizer Reformation. Historische und theologische Beiträge zur Calvinforschung.* Zurich: Theologischer Verlag, 2003.

Otten, Heinz. *Calvins theologische Anschauung von der Prädestination.* Forschungen zur Geschichte und Lehre des Protestantismus, vol. 1. Munich: Kaiser, 1938.

Parker, Thomas Henry Louis. *Calvin's Preaching.* Louisville: Westminster John Knox, 1992.

Passy, Paul. *Soyons laïques! Quelques notes de sérieux avertissement aux protestants français.* Paris, 1905.

Perrenoud, Alfred. *La population de Geneva XVIe-XIXe-siècles.* Geneva: Jullien; Paris: Champion, 1979.

Perry, Ralph Barton. *Puritanism and Democracy.* New York: Vanguard, 1944.

——. *Puritanisme et démocratie.* Trans. Françoise Meaulnes. Paris: Laffont, 1952.

Peter, Rodolphe. "Geneva dans la prédication de Calvin." In *Calvinus Ecclesiae Genevensis Custos. Die Referate des Congrès international des recherches Calviniennes, International Congress on Calvin Research, des Internationalen Kongresses für Calvinforschung vom 6. bis 9. September 1982 in Geneva,* ed. Wilhelm H. Neuser, pp. 23-48. Bern: Peter Lang, 1984.

Peter, Rodolphe, and Jean-Françoise Gilmont. *Bibliotheca Calviniana. Les œuvres de Calvin publiées au XVIe siècle.* Geneva: Droz, 2000.

Pettegree, Andrew, Alastair Duke, and Gillian Lews, eds. *Calvinism in Europe 1540-1620.* Cambridge: Cambridge University Press, 1994.

Plath, Uwe. *Calvin und Basel in den Jahren 1552-1556.* Basler und Berner Studien zur historischen und systematischen Theologie, vol. 22. Zurich: Theologische Verlag, 1974.

Plomp, Johannes. *De kerkelijke tucht bij Calvijn.* Kampen: Kok, 1969.

Reventlow, Henning Graf. *Epochen der Bibelauslegung.* 4 vols. Munich: C. H. Beck, 1990-2001.

Rich, Arthur. *Business and Economic Ethics: The Ethics of Economic Systems.* Leuven, 2004.

———. *Ethique économique.* Trans. Anne-Lise Rigo and Irène Minder-Jeanneret. Ed. Roland J. Campiche and Denis Müller. Le Champ éthique, vol. 24. Geneva: Labor et Fides, 1994.

———. *Wirtschaftsethik.* 2 vols. Gütersloh: Gütersloher Verlagshaus, 1984/1990.

Richard, Willy. *Untersuchungen zur Genesis der reformierten Kirchenterminologie der Westschweiz und Frankreichs mit besonderer Berücksichtigung der Namengebung.* Romanica Helvetica, vol. 57. Bern: Francke, 1959.

Ritschl, Dietrich. *Zur Logik der Theologie: Kurze Darstellung der Zusammenhänge theologischer Grundgedanken.* Munich: Kaiser, [2]1988.

Robinson, Marilynne. *The Death of Adam: Essays on Modern Thought.* Boston: Houghton Mifflin, 1998; repr. 2000.

Roget, Amédée. *Histoire du peuple de Geneva depuis la Réforme jusqu'à l'Escalade.* 7 vols. Geneva: Jullien, 1870-83.

Rorem, Paul. *Calvin and Bullinger on the Lord's Supper.* Bramcote/Nottingham: Grove, 1989.

Roset, Michel. *Les chroniques de Geneva.* Geneva: Georg, 1984.

Ruddies, Hartmut. "Religiöse Sozialisten (I. Europa)." In *Religion in Geschichte und Gegenwart: Handwörterbuch für Geschichte und Religionswissenschaft,* ed. Hans Dieter Betz, vol. 8, pp. 409-12. Tübingen: Mohr Siebeck, [4]2004.

Rüegg, Arnold. "Die Beziehungen Calvins zu Heinrich Bullinger und der von ihm geleiteten Zürcher Kirche." In *Universitas Turicensis Academiae Genevensi 1559-1909.* Zurich: Orell Füssli, 1909.

Ruffini, Francesco. *La libertà religiosa come diritto pubblico subiettivo.* Bologna: Il mulino, 1992.

Rüsch, Ernst Gerhard. "Die Beziehungen der St. Galler Reformatoren zu Calvin." In *Zwingliana* vol. 11, pp. 106-16. Zurich: Berichthaus, 1959.

Sabine, George Holland. *A History of Political Theory.* Ed. Thomas Landon Thorson. Hinsdale, Ill.: Dryden, [4]1981.

Salmon, John Hearsey M. *The French Religious Wars in English Political Thought.* Oxford: Clarendon, 1959.

Sassi, Jonathan D. *A Republic of Righteousness: The Public Christianity of the Post-*

Revolutionary New England Clergy. Oxford/New York: Oxford University Press, 2001.

Schellong, Dieter. *Wie steht es um die "These" vom Zusammenhang von Calvinismus und "Geist des Kapitalismus"?* Paderborner Universitätsreden, vol. 47. Paderborn: Universität-Gesamthochschule, 1995.

Schnucker, Robert V., ed. *Calviniana: Ideas and Influence of John Calvin.* Kirksville, Mo.: Sixteenth Century Journal Publishers, 1988.

Schreiner, Klaus, and Gerhard Besier. "Toleranz." In *Geschichtliche Grundbegriffe,* vol. 6, pp. 445-605. Stuttgart: Klett-Cotta, 1990.

Seebaß, Gottfried. "An sint persequendi haeretici? Die Stellung des Johannes Brenz zur Verfolgung und Bestrafung der Täufer" [1970]. In *Die Reformation und ihre Außenseiter. Gesammelte Aufsätze und Vorträge zum 60. Geburtstag des Autors,* ed. Irene Dingel and Christine Kress, pp. 283-335. Göttingen: Vandenhoeck & Ruprecht, 1997.

Selderhuis, Herman, ed. *Calvin-Handbuch.* Tübingen: Mohr Siebeck, 2008.

Simpson, Alan. *Puritanism in Old and New England.* Chicago: University of Chicago Press, 1955.

Skinner, Quentin. *The Foundations of Modern Political Thought.* 2 vols. Cambridge: Cambridge University Press, 1978.

———. *Les fondements de la pensée politique moderne.* Trans. Jérôme Grossmann and Jean-Yves Pouilloux. Paris: Albin Michel, 2001.

Smith, Gary Scott. *The Seeds of Secularization: Calvinism, Culture, and Pluralism in America, 1870-1915.* Grand Rapids: Christian University Press, 1985.

Stam, Frans Pieter van. "Le livre de Pierre Caroli de 1545 et son conflit avec Calvin." In *Calvin et ses contemporains. Actes du colloque de Paris 1995,* ed. Olivier Millet, pp. 21-41. Cahiers d'humanisme et renaissance, vol. 53. Geneva: Droz, 1998.

———. "Das Verhältnis zwischen Bullinger und Calvin während Calvins erstem Aufenthalt in Geneva." In *Calvin im Kontext der Schweizer Reformation. Historische und theologische Beiträge zur Calvinforschung,* ed. Peter Opitz, pp. 25-40. Zurich: Theologischer Verlag, 2003.

Stauffer, Richard. *Dieu, la création et la Providence dans la prédication de Calvin.* Basler und Berner Studien zur historischen und systematischen Theologie, vol. 33. Bern: Peter Lang, 1978.

Steinmetz, David C. "The Judaizing Calvin." In *Die Patristik in der Bibelexegese des 16. Jahrhunderts. Vorträge gehalten anläßlich eines Arbeitsgespräches vom 20. bis 23. März 1994 in der Herzog-August-Bibliothek,* ed. David C. Steinmetz, pp. 135-45. Wolfenbütteler Forschungen, vol. 85. Wiesbaden: Harrassowitz, 1999.

———. *Luther in Context.* Grand Rapids: Baker, 1995.

Steinmetz, David C., ed. *Die Patristik in der Bibelexegese des 16. Jahrhunderts. Vorträge gehalten anläßlich eines Arbeitsgespräches vom 20. bis 23. März 1994 in der Herzog-August-Bibliothek.* Wolfenbütteler Forschungen, vol. 85. Wiesbaden: Harrassowitz, 1999.

Stewart, John W., and James H. Moorhead, eds. *Charles Hodge Revisited: A Critical Appraisal of His Life and Work*. Grand Rapids: Eerdmans, 2002.

Strohm, Christoph. *Ethik im frühen Calvinismus. Humanistische Einflüsse, philosophische, juristische und theologische Argumentationen sowie mentalitätsgeschichtliche Aspekte am Beispiel des Calvin-Schülers Lamberts Danaeus*. Arbeiten zur Kirchengeschichte, vol. 65. Berlin/New York: de Gruyter, 1996.

————. "Recht und Kirchenrecht." In *Calvin-Handbuch,* ed. Herman Selderhuis. Tübingen: Mohr Siebeck, 2008.

————. "Wirkungen der juristischen Schulung auf Bezas theologisches Œuvre." In *Théodore de Bèze (1519-1605). Actes du Colloque de Geneva (septembre 2005)*, ed. Irena Backus, pp. 517-35. Travaux d'humanisme et renaissance, vol. 424. Geneva: Droz, 2007.

Sweeney, Douglas A. *Nathaniel Taylor, New Haven Theology, and the Legacy of Jonathan Edwards*. Oxford/New York: Oxford University Press, 2003.

Thompson, Ernest Trice. *Presbyterians in the South*. 3 vols. Richmond: John Knox, 1963-73.

Troeltsch, Ernst. *Die Bedeutung des Protestantismus für die Entstehung der Modernen Welt. Vortrag, gehalten auf der 9. Versammlung deutscher Historiker zu Stuttgart am 21. April 1906*. Sonderdruck aus der Historischen Zeitschrift, vol. 97. Munich, 1906.

————. *Die Soziallehren der christlichen Kirchen und Gruppen*. 2 vols. Tübingen: Mohr Siebeck, 1994 (orig. ed. 1912).

Turchetti, Mario. "À la racine de toutes les libertés: la liberté de conscience." *Bibliothèque d'humanisme et renaissance*, vol. 56, pp. 625-39. Geneva: Droz, 1994.

————. "Calvin face aux tenants de la concorde (moyenneurs) et aux partisans de la tolérance (castellionistes)." In *Calvin et ses contemporains. Actes du colloque de Paris 1995,* ed. Olivier Millet, pp. 43-56. Cahiers d'humanisme et renaissance, vol. 53. Geneva: Droz, 1998.

————. "Droit de Résistance à quoi? Démasquer aujourd'hui le despotisme et la tyrannie." *Revue historique* 640 (2006): 831-77.

————. "La liberté de conscience." In *Encyclopédie du Protestantisme*, ed. Pierre Gisel and Lucie Kaennel, p. 798. Lausanne: Droz/Quadrige/PUF/Labor et Fides, 2006.

————. "La liberté de conscience et l'autorité du Magistrat au lendemain de la Révocation. Aperçu du débat touchant la théologie morale et la philosophie politique des Réformés: Pierre Bayle, Noël de Versé, Pierre Jurieu, Jacques Philipot et Elie Saurin." In *La liberté de conscience (XVIe-XVIIe siècle), Actes du Colloque de Mulhouse et Bâle (1989)*, ed. Hans Rudolf Guggisberg, Frank Lestringant, and Jean-Claude Margolin, pp. 289-367. Études de philologie et d'histoire, vol. 44. Geneva: Droz, 1991.

————. "Une question mal posée. Érasme et la tolérance. L'idée de synkatabasis." In *Bibliothèque d'humanisme et renaissance,* vol. 53, pp. 379-95. Geneva: Droz, 1991.

————. "Une question mal posée. La 'tolérance' dans les édits de Janvier (1562) et d'Amboise (1563). Les premiers commentaires et interprétations: Jean Bégat." In

La formazione storica della alterità, studi di storia della tolleranza nell'età moderna offerti a Antonio Rotondò, ed. Henry Méchoulan, Richard H. Popkin, Giuseppe Ricuperati, and Luisa Simonutti, vol. 1, pp. 245-94. Florence: L. S. Olschki, 2001.

Tylenda, Joseph N. "Calvin and Westphal: Two Eucharistic Theologies in Conflict." In *Calvin's Books: Festschrift Dedicated to Peter De Klerk on the Occasion of His Seventieth Birthday,* ed. Wilhelm H. Neuser, Herman J. Selderhuis, and Willelm van 't Spijker, pp. 9-21. Heerenveen: J. J. Groen, 1997.

———. "The Calvin-Westphal Exchange: The Genesis of Calvin's Treatise against Westphal." *Calvin Theological Journal* 9 (1974): 182-209.

Ulrich, Hans G. "Kapitalismus." In *Theologische Realenzyklopädie,* ed. Gerhard Müller, vol. 17, pp. 604-19. Berlin: de Gruyter, 1988.

Van Den Belt, Henk. *The Authority of Scripture in Reformed Theology: Truth and Trust.* Leiden/Boston: Brill, 2008.

Van Hoeven, James W., ed. *Piety and Patriotism: Bicentennial Studies of the Reformed Church in America, 1776-1976.* Historical Series of the Reformed Church in America, vol. 4. Grand Rapids: Eerdmans, 1976.

Van Stam, Frans Pieter. "Le livre de Pierre Caroli de 1545 et son conflit avec Calvin." In *Calvin et ses contemporains. Actes du colloque de Paris (1995),* ed. Olivier Millet, pp. 21-41. Cahiers d'humanisme et renaissance, vol. 53. Geneva: Droz, 1998.

———. "Das Verhältnis zwischen Bullinger und Calvin während Calvins erstem Aufenthalt in Genf." In *Calvin im Kontext der Schweizer Reformation. Historische und theologische Beiträge zur Calvinforschung,* ed. Peter Opitz, pp. 25-40. Zurich: Theologischer Verlag, 2003.

Venema, Cornelis P. *Heinrich Bullinger and the Doctrine of Predestination: Author of the "Other Reformed Tradition"?* Text and Studies in Reformation and Post-Reformation Thought. Grand Rapids: Baker, 2002.

Viallaneix, Paul, ed. *Réforme et Révolutions. Aux origines de la démocratie moderne.* Millau: Presses du Languedoc, 1990.

Vincent, Gilbert. *Exigence éthique et interprétation dans l'œuvre de Calvin.* Histoire et société, vol. 5. Geneva: Labor et Fides, 1984.

Vorster, J. M. "Calvin and Human Rights." *Ecumenical Review* 51, no. 2 (1999): 209-20.

Walker, Williston. *Jean Calvin — l'homme et l'oeuvre, aus dem Französischen.* Trans. E. and N. Weiss. Ed. Association du Monument international de la Réformation à Geneva. Geneva: A. Jullien, 1909.

———. *John Calvin: The Organiser of Reformed Protestantism (1509-1564).* New York/London: G. P. Putnam's Sons, 1906.

Walser, Peter. *Die Prädestination bei Heinrich Bullinger im Zusammenhang mit seiner Gotteslehre.* Studien zur Dogmengeschichte und systematischen Theologie, vol. 11. Zurich: Zwingli-Verlag, 1957.

Walzer, Michael. *The Revolution of the Saints: A Study in the Origins of Radical Politics.* Cambridge, Mass.: Weidenfeld & Nicolson, 1965.

Weber, Max. *L'éthique protestante et l'esprit du capitalisme.* Paris, [2]1967.

————. *L'éthique protestante et l'esprit du capitalisme.* Trans. Isabelle Kalinowski. Champs, vol. 424. Paris: Flammarion, 2001.

————. *The Protestant Ethic and the Spirit of Capitalism.* Trans. Talcott Parsons and Anthony Giddens. London: Allen & Unwin, 1976. Reprinted New York, 2003.

————. *Die protestantische Ethik.* 2 vols. Ed. J. Winkelmann. Gütersloh: Gütersloher Verlagshaus, ⁶1981.

Wells, David F., ed. *Reformed Theology in America: A History of Its Modern Development.* Grand Rapids: Baker, 1985; repr. 1997.

Wernle, Paul. *Calvin und Basel bis zum Tode des Myconius, 1535-1552.* Basel: F. Reinhardt Universitäts-Buchdruckerei, 1909.

White, Robert. "Castellio against Calvin: The Turk in the Toleration Controversy of the Sixteenth Century." *Bibliothèque d'humanisme et renaissance,* vol. 46, pp. 573-86. Geneva: Droz, 1984.

Witte, John, Jr. "Moderate Religionsfreiheit in der Theologie Johannes Calvins." In *Zeitschrift der Savigny-Stiftung für Rechtsgeschichte. Kanonistische Abteilung,* vol. 83, pp. 401-48. Vienna/Cologne/Graz: Böhlau, 1997.

Witte, John, and Robert M. Kingdon. *Sex, Marriage and Family in John Calvin's Geneva,* vol. 1: *Courtship, Engagement and Marriage.* Grand Rapids: Eerdmans, 2005.

Woolley, Paul. "Calvin and Toleration." In *The Heritage of John Calvin,* ed. John H. Bratt. Grand Rapids: Eerdmans, 1973.

Zuber, Valentine. *Les conflits de la tolérance. Michel Servet entre mémoire et histoire.* Vie des huguenots, vol. 36. Paris: Honoré Champion, 2004.

Zweig, Stefan. *Castellio gegen Calvin oder Ein Gewissen gegen die Gewalt.* Frankfurt a. M.: Fischer, 1936; repr. 1988.

————. *Conscience contre violence ou Castellion contre Calvin.* Trans. Alzir Hella. Bordeaux Cedex: Le Castor Astral, 1997 (orig. ed. Paris: Bernard Grasset, 1946).

————. *The Right to Heresy: Castellio against Calvin.* Trans. Eden and Cedar Paul. New York: Viking, 1936.

About the Authors and Editors

About the Authors

Philip Benedict has been professor ordinarius and director of the Institut d'Histoire de la Réformation of the University of Geneva since 2005; previously he was the William Prescott and Annie McClelland Smith Professor of History and Religion at Brown University in Providence, Rhode Island.

James D. Bratt is professor of American history at Calvin College in Grand Rapids, Michigan, and director of the Calvin Center for Christian Scholarship (CCCS).

Emidio Campi is professor of church history and director of the Institute of Swiss Reformation Studies, University of Zurich.

Wulfert De Greef is pastor emeritus of the Protestant Church in the Netherlands and administrator of the website Centrum voor Calvijnstudie/Center for Calvin Studies (www.calvijnstudie.nl), Leusden, Netherlands.

Christopher L. Elwood has been professor of historical theology at the Louisville Presbyterian Theological Seminary in Louisville, Kentucky, since 1996; he taught previously at the Harvard Divinity School in Cambridge, Massachusetts, and Davidson College in Davidson, North Carolina.

Eva-Maria Faber is professor of dogmatic and fundamental theology and rector of the Theologische Hochschule Chur.

Erich Fuchs is professor emeritus of theological ethics at the Theological Faculty of the University of Geneva.

Ulrich H. J. Körtner has been professor of systematic theology at the Evangelical-Theological Faculty of the University of Vienna since 1992; from 1990 to 1992 he was director of studies at the Evangelical Academy of Iserlohn.

Christian Link is professor emeritus of systematic theology at the Ruhr University, Bochum; from 1979 to 1993 he was professor of dogmatic theology at the Theological Faculty of the University of Bern.

Christian Moser is senior assistant at the Institute of Swiss Reformation Studies, University of Zurich.

Andrew Pettegree is professor of British and European history of the Reformation in Britain and Europe at the University of St. Andrews, Scotland, and founding director of the St. Andrews Reformation Studies Institute.

Christoph Strohm has been professor of the history of the Reformation and modern church history at the Theological Faculty of the University of Heidelberg and head of the Research Center for the Publication of Martin Bucer's German writings at the Heidelberg Academy of Sciences since 2006; from 1996 to 2006 he was professor of church history at the Ruhr University, Bochum.

Mario Turchetti is professor of modern history at the University of Fribourg (Switzerland); he was previously professor at the Universities of Messina (political philosophy), Tours (Renaissance philosophy), and Geneva (modern history).

About the Editors

Martin Ernst Hirzel has been the appointee for Ecumenism and Religious Communities for the Federation of Swiss Protestant Churches (FSPC) in Bern since 2006; previously he was professor of church history at the Theological Faculty of the Waldensian Church in Rome.

Martin Sallmann has been professor of modern church and theological history and confessional studies at the Theological Faculty of the University of Bern since 2007; previously he was the appointee for theology for the Federation of Swiss Protestant Churches (FSPC) in Bern.

241